Thomas M. Skrtic
*University of Kansas*

# Behind
# Special
# Education

*A Critical Analysis of*
*Professional Culture and*
*School Organization*

**LOVE PUBLISHING COMPANY**®
Denver, Colorado 80222

# Dedication

*For my father, Paul G. Skrtic*
*always critical, always pragmatic*

Copyright © 1991 Love Publishing Company
Printed in the U.S.A.
ISBN: 0-89108-217-4
Library of Congress Catalog Card Number 90-060831

# Contents

# Preface

Although special education is a central topic throughout the book, *Behind Special Education* is about the relationship among the institutional practices of special education, educational administration, and general education, and the structural and cultural implications of this relationship for achieving educational excellence and equity—the twin goals behind the idea of public education in a democracy. Some other title may have captured the book's scope more adequately, but I chose *Behind Special Education* because it best expresses my substantive premise, which is that a critical reading of special education—one that considers it from behind, in terms of its grounding assumptions—provides the insights necessary to deconstruct and reconstruct 20th-century public education for the emerging historical contingencies of the 21st century.

The deconstructive value of a critical analysis of special education stems from its role as the institutional practice that emerged in the 20th century to contain the inherent contradiction between the democratic ends and bureaucratic means of public education, a role that has become increasingly difficult for the field of special education to play since the 1960s. The reconstructive value of such an analysis is that, as the organizational mechanism for addressing diversity within the standardizing routines of bureaucratic schooling, special education emerged as the inverse of the bureaucratic form. This inversion of bureaucracy—what I refer to as adhocracy—is prototypical of the structural configuration and cultural sensibility that public education must assume if it is to prepare the citizens of the 21st century for full political, economic, and cultural participation in democracy.

The book's second premise is methodological. It is that the insights contained in philosophical pragmatism have to be recovered by the institution and profession of education, as both a method of inquiry and a mode of professional practice and discourse. The revival of interest in philosophical pragmatism, and particularly in the thought of John Dewey, has followed in the wake of the reemergence of antifoundationalism in the late 20th century. Drawing on the work of Dewey and other antifoundationalists such as Rorty, Weber, Foucault, and Derrida, I use philosophical pragmatism throughout the book as a method of inquiry for deconstructing public education. In the end, I recommend it as a mode of professional discourse for reconstructing public education for the next century, which is where the book's substantive and methodological premises come together. To be effective as a method for continuously constructing, deconstructing, and reconstructing educational practices and discourses, philosophical pragmatism requires the particular set of organizational conditions that the adhocratic form makes possible. Moreover, the emergence of postindustrialism in the late 20th century makes possible and begs for the methods and conditions of critical pragmatism and adhocracy as means for reconciling government, business, and education with the political, economic, and cultural relevancies of the 21st century and, more important, for reconciling government, business, and education with one another.

I am indebted to several individuals and institutions for their support and encouragement. I would like to thank the University of Kansas, which, under its Intra-University Visiting Professorship program, provided me with free time in 1985–1986 to pursue and expand my research interests in social and political philosophy. I owe a tremendous intellectual debt to Bob Antonio, Dwight Kiel, and Gary Shapiro, my mentors during and after the professorship, and to Egon Guba, who showed me that I needed something like the professorship and inspired me to pursue it. I also owe a debt to the University's Hall Center for the Humanities, which in 1987 supported my participation in its Seminar on Children and Youth, an experience that provided me with an opportunity to try my ideas about special education and school organization on an interdisciplinary audience. I also would like to thank the members of the Kansas Postpositivist Group whose intellectual companionship and generosity over the past several years helped shape my understanding of professional culture and end-of-philosophy philosophy.

As a teacher, I am of course indebted to my students for their patience and insights as I struggled through the work that led to this book. I am particularly indebted to Linda Ware and Rocky Hill, the two "students" who have been closest to me during this period, and who, together with my loving parents and sister, have had to bear the brunt of my frame of mind. Peter Leone and Dick Vitolo, close colleagues and friends, have always been invaluable sources of encouragement and helpful criticism. I also would like to thank Carolyn Acheson at Love Publishing for her editorial assistance and Thelma Simons at the University of Kansas for her competent and cheerful preparation of the original manuscript.

I am further indebted to Dwight Kiel for his insightful reading of the entire manuscript. He made this a better book than it would have been otherwise. Finally, Linda Ware has been a constant source of intellectual and emotional support. I will always be indebted to her for keeping me and the book on track.

# PART ONE
## Problems and Prospects

The Crisis in Modern Knowledge

Critical Pragmatism as a Method of Social Inquiry

# 1

# The Crisis in Modern Knowledge

The special education community is engulfed in its second round of self-criticism in 30 years. The first round began in the 1960s when the segregated special classroom, the traditional model for special education since the turn of the century, was called into question. Although criticism subsided in 1975 with enactment of Public Law 94–142, The Education for All Handicapped Children Act (EHA), and introduction of the mainstreaming model, both of which were presumed to be solutions to the problems associated with the special classroom, the second round of self-criticism began shortly after 1975 and has continued with increasing intensity until today. It rejects the EHA and mainstreaming and calls for yet another approach, the Regular Education Initiative (REI), which is presumed to be a solution to the problems associated with the EHA and mainstreaming. Whereas the first round of self-criticism ultimately increased the field's certainty in its professional practices, the current round has had just the opposite effect. After 15 years of the EHA and mainstreaming, the special education community is less certain about its practices than ever before.

Special education professionals are not alone in their uncertainty. The field of educational administration has been plagued by the same sort of self-criticism and uncertainty since at least the 1960s. And, of course, there is the unprecedented level of uncertainty in the field of general education and in public education itself, which has followed in the wake of publication of *A Nation at Risk* (National Commission on Excellence in Education, 1983)[1]. But there is more to this uncertainty in education than a waning of confidence in professional practices. Over the past 30 years, the level of certainty in all professional fields has been in a steady state of decline. In fact, since the 1960s the very legitimacy of the professions has been called into question by three overlapping waves of criticism: the *sociological* critique of professional practice, the *philosophical* critique of professional knowledge, and the *political* critique of professional power.

During their ascendancy from 1870 to 1930, the professions extended their influence and consolidated their authority in society on the basis of two claims: (a) that they had access to the scientific knowledge that society needed to achieve the good life, and (b) that they would release nature's potential in society in a disinterested way, in the interest of the common good, rather than for personal gain (Haskell, 1984a; Haber, 1964). On the basis of these claims, advocates of professionalization characterized professionals as the personification of the victory of science over traditional authority, and professionalization as the institutionalization of the ethic of service as a restraint on capitalistic self-interest. Moreover, they argued that combining scientific authority and moral obligation in a culture of professionalism would release in society a new class of citizens who, because they were mentally disciplined, fiercely autonomous, and socially committed, would serve as a liberating force and an example of democratic leadership (Bledstein, 1976).

The sociological critique of the professions questions these claims and characterizations by pointing to the inherent contradictions between the convergent and bureaucratic nature of the professions and the divergent and democratic character of society. As society has become more dynamic, new problems have been created that are so complex that no single profession can address them effectively. Although this trend has required professionals to think divergently and to work collaboratively across disciplinary boundaries, the professions have become increasingly convergent and specialized. This has worked against the type of thinking and interdisciplinary effort that is necessary, which has limited the utility of professional knowledge (Gilb, 1966). In addition, the fact that virtually all professionals work in organizations has circumscribed the application of professional knowledge to individual and social problems, as well as created serious ethical problems, particularly when the needs of the organization are in conflict with those of clients or of society (Marini, 1971; Schein, 1972). As a result of these and other contradictions, some of the most pressing problems faced by society are the direct result of professional intervention (Freidson, 1988; Schein, 1972).

Ultimately, however, the most troubling aspect of the sociological critique is that it calls into question the normative notion of the ethic of service to society. Whereas turn-of-the-century intellectuals characterized professionalization as "a grand cultural reform, capable of restoring sanity to a capitalist civilization intoxicated with self-aggrandizement" (Haskell, 1984a, p. 177), contemporary analysts characterize it as merely another form of self-aggrandizement (Collins, 1979), "a capitalist remedy for the defects of capitalism" (Haskell, 1984b, p. 219). Moreover, critics of professionalization have argued that the radical idea of professional as autonomous democrat has had only conservative consequences. The professionalization of social problems—that is, the dispassionate and disinterested isolation and control of phenomena such as poverty, crime, and disease—has meant that "every sphere of American life now [comes] within the power of the . . . professional to set apart, regulate, and contain" (Bledstein, 1976, p. 92).

Although the uncertainty caused by popular disclosures of ineffective and unethical practices in the professions makes the sociological critique seem all too obvious, the philosophical and political critiques are based on a less obvious but far greater uncertainty that is spreading throughout intellectual and cultural life. Behind this greater uncertainty lies the fact that Western civilization is experiencing a fundamental change in world view. Generally speaking, a world view—or a paradigm—is a shared pattern of basic beliefs and assumptions about the nature of the world and how it works. These beliefs and assumptions tell us what is real and what is not; they provide us with a sense of collective identity, and they guide and justify our actions. In this sense, paradigms are enabling. They unrandomize reality and permit us to act in the world. But paradigms are also normative because they conceal the very reasons for our actions in the unquestioned assumptions of the paradigm (Patton, 1975). We are rarely conscious of our paradigms because they and their underlying assumptions tend to surface only when they are changing. Western civilization is uncertain just now because it is in the midst of a paradigm shift—a fundamental change in world view.

Until the 17th century our world view was based on the Aristotelian paradigm of organic change, which collapsed under the weight of the scientific discoveries of the Enlightenment and was replaced by the Newtonian paradigm of mechanical change. As such, the mechanistic view became the foundation for the modern world: for our cultural, social, and political systems; for the natural and social sciences; and for the professions. And though we tend to think of a change of this magnitude as an extremely rare event, such a pattern of change is underway again in the 20th century.

> There is strong evidence that a number of the underpinnings of our basic beliefs are under challenge. . . . from a multifaceted revolution of the sort that we have experienced only a few times in the course of our civilization's history: the revolution that began more than a century ago and has gathered momentum ever since involves as great a change as the Copernical revolution or the emergence of the Enlightenment. (Schwartz & Ogilvy, 1979, 1980, p. 2)

As in the case of the Enlightenment, the dimensions of the emergent world view are manifested in the revolutionary developments in the sciences, humanities, and arts over the last 100 years. Based on these developments in virtually every substantive discipline—physics, chemistry, brain theory, ecology, evolution, mathematics, philosophy, politics, psychology, linguistics, religion, and the arts—the direction of the paradigm shift in Western civilization is away from the objectivism of science and mechanical change and toward the subjectivism of human consciousness and cultural change (see Bernstein, 1976; Rorty, 1979; Schwartz & Ogilvy, 1979, 1980).

As significant as a shift from objectivism to subjectivism might be, there is even more here to cause Western civilization to be uncertain. Although there have been previous paradigm shifts, the current one is more revolutionary because this time we recognize the existence of paradigms. The Newtonian paradigm is no longer adequate, and we know it. More significantly, however:

> We know that we know it. We know that we have accomplished a break from our previous paradigms. We know that there are such things as paradigms. Before our era, most people didn't think of themselves as being caught within a paradigm. . . . Now, however, not only do we appear to be on the edge of a new paradigm, but in addition, we know that there *are* paradigms. Precisely, *that* awareness is part of the new paradigm, that meta-leap to a self-reflective stance on all of one's thoughts, and how it is, finally, that thought thinks about itself. (Schwartz & Ogilvy, 1980, p. 6)

To assess the significance of the paradigm shift and meta-leap in Western civilization and their implications for the professions, it will be helpful at this point to introduce a conceptual framework for considering the notions of paradigm and paradigm shift in greater depth. Although I will return to these topics throughout the book, they are discussed here as background for understanding the philosophical and political critiques of the professions, presented next, as well as for discussions of my methodology and basic argument, presented in the next chapter.

## PARADIGMS AND PARADIGM SHIFTS[2]

For the past 30 years the concepts *paradigm* and *paradigm shift* have been associated most often with the work of Thomas Kuhn (1962, 1970). In his influential book, *The Structure of Scientific Revolutions*, Kuhn revolutionized the common understanding of science by using these concepts to distinguish between continuous and discontinuous scientific progress in the physical sciences. Continuous scientific progress, or what Kuhn called *normal science*, progresses by gradual additions to a knowledge base—a highly cumulative enterprise that refines, extends, and articulates a paradigm that already exists. An accepted paradigm is essential for scientific work because it unrandomizes nature enough to permit scientists to know what data are, what methods and instruments are necessary to retrieve them, and what concepts and theories are relevant to their interpretation (Kuhn, 1970).

Although this is the traditional image of science and scientific progress, the one that most of us have been taught, Kuhn argued that normal science is only a necessary prelude to *revolutionary science*—discontinuous breakthroughs that demand an entirely new paradigm for understanding data. Discoveries of this sort begin with the recognition and extended exploration of an anomaly, or a violation of the paradigm-induced expectations of normal science. When the anomaly comes to be seen as more than just another normal science problem, the scientific community enters a state of paradigm crisis in which the rules of normal science are blurred. Blurring of the paradigm's rules gives rise to extraordinary research and theoretical speculation, which further loosen the paradigm's stereotypes and begin to expose the parameters of a new paradigm. Although in some cases this foreshadows the shape of the new paradigm, more often the new paradigm emerges all at once, "sometimes in the middle of the night, in the mind of man deeply immersed in crisis" (Kuhn, 1970, p. 90). In any event, the shift to a new paradigm is revolutionary science. Whereas normal science requires the mutual acceptance of a given paradigm among a community of scientists, revolutionary science requires a paradigm shift. After the shift, the stage is set for the process to repeat itself. It is important to note that, although Kuhn's subjectivist image of science provided a fundamentally different way to understand scientific progress, his work is not a criticism of physical science; it is a critique of the *objectivist view of science* (Barnes, 1985), which, as we will see, has profound implications for the social sciences.

Although the concept of a paradigm was the central element in Kuhn's analysis, he was neither clear nor consistent about what he meant by it. Masterman (1970) noted more than 20 different uses of the term in Kuhn's original work, which she arranged into a hierarchy from most to least abstract. She called Kuhn's most abstract use of the term the *metaphysical paradigm.* It is the broadest unit of consensus within a given science, a total world view or gestalt that subsumes and defines all of the other levels of paradigms. Kuhn used paradigm in this sense to refer to a way of seeing, a perceptual organizer or mental map that defines for physical scientists which entities exist (and which do not) and how they behave. At the least abstract level she placed the *construct paradigm*, Kuhn's narrowest use of the term. According to Masterman, he used it to refer to the specific tools and instruments used in normal science to produce and collect data. Masterman's *sociological paradigm*, which falls between the extremes of the metaphysical and construct paradigms, is what Kuhn referred to in his 1962 edition as a concrete set of habits or a universally accepted scientific achievement, and in his 1970 edition as "the concrete puzzle solutions which, when employed as models or examples, can replace explicit rules as a basis for the solution of the remaining puzzles of normal science" (1970, p. 175).

Thus, a metaphysical paradigm is a set of presuppositions or basic beliefs that physical scientists use to provide coherence to their picture of the world and how it works. These presuppositions or *metatheoretical* assumptions yield a corresponding set of *theories*. Metatheories are more fundamental than theories because theories are grounded in observations (see Feigl, 1970) that are themselves shaped by a prior conceptual system of metatheoretical presuppositions (see Mulkay, 1979; Shimony, 1977). Below metatheories and theories in the hierarchy are implicit *assumptions*, derived from these higher levels of abstraction. Below the assumptions are *models* (or exemplars), which, in turn, define and subsume a set of *practices* and research *tools*. Thus, a scientific community engaged in normal science can be understood as operating on the basis of a hierarchy of implicit presuppositions, which, from most to least abstract, include metatheories, theories, assumptions, models, practices, and tools, each of which are defined and subsumed by the higher levels in the hierarchy of abstraction, and all of which, ultimately, are defined and subsumed by the metaphysical paradigm.

Although Kuhn reserved his conception of paradigms and paradigm shifts exclusively for the physical sciences, others have extended his insights to the social sciences. For example, Masterman (1970) used Kuhn's paradigm concept to differentiate among sciences on the basis of their paradigmatic status. A *paradigmatic science* is one in which there is broad consensus on a particular paradigm within the scientific community (e.g., experimental physics after Newton); whereas a *nonparadigmatic science* is one without such consensus (e.g., experimental physics before Newton). A *dual paradigmatic* state exists immediately before a Kuhnian scientific revolution, when an older, crisis-ridden paradigm and a new, emerging paradigm are vying for the dominance that only one of them will achieve (e.g., experimental physics when the Newtonian and Einsteinian paradigms were in competition). Finally, Masterman characterized *multiple paradigm* sciences as those in which several viable paradigms compete unsuccessfully for dominance within a scientific community.

The multiple paradigm state is particularly important for our purposes because it permits us to differentiate between the physical and social sciences on the basis of their paradigmatic status. The various physical sciences, more or less, are paradigmatic sciences. The birth of a particular physical science can be thought of as the point at which it emerged from a nonparadigmatic state and achieved its paradigmatic status. From there, its history is a series of discontinuous progressions in which normal science—now possible because of paradigmatic consensus—produces enough anomalies to create a crisis of sufficient scope and duration to yield a scientific revolution, and thus a new paradigm. The social and behavioral sciences and the humanities (hereafter, social sciences or social disciplines), on the other hand, are multiple paradigm sciences. Unlike the physical sciences, in which one paradigm dominates until crisis and revolution replace it with another one, multiple paradigms co-exist in the social sciences. Although one or more members of a social scientific community can shift paradigms, a paradigm shift in a multiple paradigm science has a fundamentally different meaning than a paradigm shift in a single paradigm science.

## Four Paradigms of Modern Social Scientific Thought

Burrell and Morgan (1979; also see Ritzer, 1980) conceptualized the multiple paradigms of the social sciences in terms of the relationship between two dimensions of metatheoretical assumptions: one about the nature of science, and one about the nature of society. Burrell and Morgan used four traditional strands of debate within philosophy of science to formulate the nature of science, or *subjective-objective* dimension of their analysis: ontology (the nature of reality), epistemology (the nature of knowledge), human nature (the nature of human action), and methodology (the nature of inquiry). Table 1.1 presents the extreme positions on each of the four strands.

**Table 1.1**
The Subjective-Objective Dimension of Social Scientific Thought

| Subjectivist | | Objectivist |
|---|---|---|
| Nominalism ---------------------------- ontology | --------------------------------- | Realism |
| Antipositivism ------------------------ epistemology | -------------------------- | Positivism |
| Voluntarism -------------------------- human nature | ----------------------- | Determinism |
| Idiographic -------------------------- methodology | ------------------------ | Nomothetic |

*Source:* Adapted from G. Burrell and G. Morgan, 1979, *Sociological Paradigms and Organizational Analysis,* p. 3, London: Heinemann Educational Books.

According to Burrell and Morgan (1979; also see Morgan & Smircich, 1980), the *realist* assumes that the social world exists "out there," independent of an individual's appreciation of it, and that it is virtually as hard and concrete as the physical world. The *nominalist,* on the other hand, assumes that social reality is made up of names, concepts, and labels that serve as tools for describing, understanding, and negotiating the social world. The *positivist* seeks to predict and control social events by searching for regularities and determinate causal relationships. Growth of knowledge is seen as a cumulative process in which new information is added to the existing knowledge base and false hypotheses are eliminated. Conversely, *antipositivists* assume that the social world is essentially relativistic—understandable, but only from the point of view of the individuals directly involved in it. Thus, they reject the notion of observer as a valid vantage point for understanding human thought and action.

In the Burrell and Morgan scheme *determinists* assume that humans respond mechanistically or even deterministically to the situations they encounter in the external world, whereas *voluntarists* ascribe a much more creative human role. Voluntarists assume that humans have free will and autonomy and thus that they are actively engaged in creating their environments rather than being controlled by them. Finally, Burrell and Morgan characterized *nomothetic* methodologies (systematic protocols, standardized instruments, quantitative analysis) as those adopted by social scientists who are realists, positivists, and determinists. Because they treat the social world as if it were a hard, objective reality, they use such methodologies to search for universal laws that can be used to predict and thus control the one, objective social reality that is presumed to exist. *Idiographic* methodologies (emergent protocols, nonstandardized instruments, qualitative analysis), on the other hand, are adopted by social scientists who are nominalists, antipositivists, and voluntarists. Because they assume that humans create or construct their social reality, the subjective experience of individuals in the act of reality construction is of central importance to these social scientists. They use idiographic methodologies to understand the ways individuals create and interpret their social world.

The extreme positions of Burrell and Morgan's subjective-objective dimension are reflected in two major intellectual traditions that have dominated social science for the past two centuries. Objectivist social science is logical positivism, the dominant position in the West during the modern period, which:

> . . . reflects the attempt to apply the models and methods of the natural sciences to the study of human affairs. It treats the social world as if it were the natural world, adopting a "realist" approach to ontology . . . backed up by a "positivist" epistemology, relatively "deterministic" views of human nature and the use of "nomothetic" methodologies. (Burrell & Morgan, 1979, p. 7)

The subjectivist position is German idealism, which stands in complete opposition to logical positivism in that:

It is based upon the premise that the ultimate reality of the universe lies in "spirit" or "idea" rather than in the data of sense perception. It is essentially "nominalist" in its approach to social reality . . . "antipositivist" in epistemology, "voluntarist" with regard to human nature and it favors idiographic methods as a foundation for social analysis. (Burrell & Morgan, 1979, p. 7)

The nature of society dimension can be considered in at least two ways: sociologically or analytically. Burrell and Morgan approached the problem sociologically by using "sociology of regulation" and "sociology of radical change" to describe the extreme positions on the nature of society, or *order-conflict*, dimension of their scheme. According to Burrell and Morgan, sociology of regulation is the dominant position in the West. It views modern society as orderly and integrated and is concerned with explaining its underlying unity and cohesion. Conversely, the sociology of radical change characterizes society in terms of conflict, modes of domination, and contradiction. It is concerned with emancipating people from existing social structures. Table 1.2 differentiates the two positions in terms of the issues with which each are concerned.

**Table 1.2**

The Order-Conflict Dimension of Social Scientific Thought

| The sociology of regulation (order) is concerned with: | The sociology of radical change (conflict) is concerned with: |
|---|---|
| the status quo | radical change |
| social order | structural conflict |
| consensus | modes of domination |
| social integration | contradiction |
| solidarity | emancipation |
| need satisfaction | deprivation |
| actuality | potentiality |

*Source:* Adapted from G. Burrell and G. Morgan, 1979, *Sociological Paradigms and Organizational Analysis*, p. 18, London: Heinemann Educational Books.

In his analytical treatment of the nature of society dimension, Ritzer (1980) used a "levels of social analysis," or *microscopic-macroscopic* distinction. Here, the magnitude of social phenomena is used to differentiate among metatheoretical positions, ranging from the microscopic level of individual thought and action, interaction, and groups, to the macroscopic level of organizations, whole societies, and total world systems. As used here, the microscopic and macroscopic levels of

Ritzer's interpretation correspond respectively to the order and conflict positions of the Burrell and Morgan scheme.[3] In either case, when the science and society dimensions are counterpoised, they produce four paradigms of modern social scientific thought, as depicted in Figure 1.1.

**Figure 1.1**

Four Paradigms of Modern Social Scientific Thought

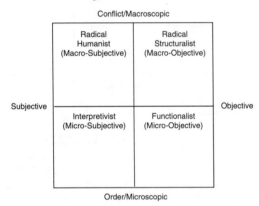

Conflict/Macroscopic

| Radical Humanist (Macro-Subjective) | Radical Structuralist (Macro-Objective) |

Subjective — Objective

| Interpretivist (Micro-Subjective) | Functionalist (Micro-Objective) |

Order/Microscopic

*Source:* Adapted from G. Burrell and G. Morgan, 1979, *Sociological Paradigms and Organizational Analysis,* p. 29, London: Heinemann Educational Books; and G. Ritzer, 1980, *Sociology: A Multiple Paradigm Science* (rev. ed.), p. 239, Boston: Allyn & Bacon.

Each of the four paradigms—*functionalist* (micro-objective), *interpretivist* (micro-subjective), *radical humanist* (macro-subjective), and *radical structuralist* (macro-objective)—is premised on a fundamentally different and mutually exclusive set of metatheoretical assumptions about the nature of science and of society, and thus a fundamentally different conceptualization of the nature of social science itself. In turn, each metatheoretical paradigm defines and subsumes a corresponding set of theories, assumptions, models, practices, and tools, as noted previously, and as shown in Figure 1.2 for the functionalist paradigm.

*Functionalist Paradigm*

According to Burrell and Morgan, and Ritzer, the functionalist paradigm is the dominant framework for social science in the Western world. It is firmly grounded in the sociology of regulation, takes a more or less microscopic view of social reality, and studies its subject

**Figure 1.2**

Hierarchy of Presuppositions

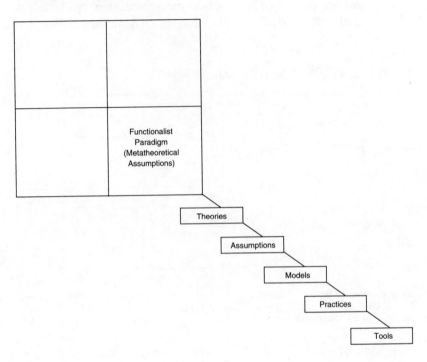

matter from an objectivist point of view. It seeks to provide rational explanations of social affairs for the purpose of prediction and control, using an approach to science premised in the tradition of logical positivism. As such, it:

> . . . reflects the attempt, *par excellence*, to apply the models and methods of the natural sciences to the study of human affairs. . . . The functionalist approach to social science tends to assume that the social world is composed of relatively concrete empirical artefacts and relationships which can be identified, studied and measured through approaches derived from the natural sciences. (Burrell & Morgan, 1979, p. 26)

The functionalist paradigm is equivalent to Ritzer's micro-objective approach to social science. Social scientists operating from this vantage point apply positivistic methodologies to microscopic social phenomena such as patterns of behavior, action, and interaction, in an attempt to predict and control social life. As Ritzer noted, the functionalist views society as a social system composed of interrelated parts, each of which contributes to the maintenance of the others. As such, the parts of society are:

> . . . believed to be in a kind of balance with a change in one part necessi-tating changes in the other parts. The equilibrium of the social system is not static, but a moving equilibrium. Parts of society are always chang-ing, and these changes lead to sympathetic changes in other parts of the system. Thus, change is basically orderly, rather than cataclysmic. (Ritzer, 1980, p. 48)

At the extreme, functionalists argue that all events and structures in society are functional because, if they were not, they would not exist. This, of course, leads to the conservative bias that all current aspects of society are indispensable to the system and that, as such, "all structures that exist should continue to exist . . . [which] holds out little possibility of meaningful change within a social system" (Ritzer, 1980, p. 49).

## Interpretivist Paradigm

Burrell and Morgan characterized interpretivist social scientists as being only implicitly committed to regulation and order. Although they assume that the social world is cohesive, orderly, and integrated, they (unlike the functionalists) are oriented toward understanding the ongo-ing processes through which humans subjectively construct their social world (see Berger & Luckmann, 1967). The interpretivist paradigm addresses the same social issues as the functionalist paradigm, but it is concerned with understanding the essence of the everyday world as an emergent social process. When a social world outside the conscious-ness of the individual is recognized, it is regarded as a network of assumptions and intersubjectively shared meanings. Burrell and Morgan's interpretivist paradigm corresponds to Ritzer's micro-sub-jective paradigm. Social scientists of this persuasion are concerned with understanding the social construction of reality—the way people create and share meaning.

## Radical Humanist Paradigm

Although radical humanists share a view of social science with the interpretivist paradigm, their frame of reference is the sociology of radical change. According to Burrell and Morgan, their view of society emphasizes the importance of transcending the limitations of existing social structures, which they view as distorting true human consciousness. Thus, society is viewed as being antihuman, as inhibiting human development and fulfillment. Humanist theorizing centers on a critique of the status quo, from Ritzer's macrosubjective paradigm. As such, radical humanists focus their analyses on ideological structures such as culture, norms, and values, and are concerned with the influence of these structures on human thought and action.

### Radical Structuralist Paradigm

Like radical humanism, the radical structuralist paradigm mounts a critique of the status quo and advocates change. But it takes this stance from the perspective of the objectivist, thus sharing a conceptualization of science with the functionalist paradigm. According to Burrell and Morgan, radical structuralists characterize contemporary society in terms of fundamental conflicts that generate change through political and economic crises. Whereas radical humanists are concerned with ideological structures and individual consciousness, radical structuralists focus their critique upon material structures and are concerned with the consciousness of entire categories of individuals, such as races, genders, and socioeconomic classes. They occupy Ritzer's macro-objective frame of reference and approach social science by concentrating on material structures such as law, bureaucracy, technology, and the economy.

Because each paradigm represents a unique combination of metatheoretical assumptions about the nature of the social world and how it may be investigated, as well as a corresponding set of theories, assumptions, models, practices, and research tools, the approach social scientists take depends on which of the four paradigms of modern social scientific thought serves as their metaphysical frame of reference. As such, each paradigm of metatheoretical assumptions explicitly or, as is most often the case, implicitly defines the frame of reference and thus the approach of the social scientists who work within it (Burrell & Morgan, 1979; Ritzer, 1980).

Each paradigm represents a mutually exclusive view of the social world and how it might be investigated because each one rests on an incommensurable set of metatheoretical assumptions about the nature of social science itself (Bernstein, 1983; Burrell & Morgan, 1979; Ritzer, 1980; Rorty, 1979). Each paradigm produces a unique form of knowledge; each is an historically situated way of seeing.

## Paradigm Shifts and the Meta-Leap in the Social Sciences

The multiple paradigm state in the social sciences means that Kuhnian paradigm shifts such as those in the physical sciences are conceptually impossible because there is simply no dominant paradigm of modern social scientific thought to be overthrown. Relative to the way physical science paradigms emerge, all four paradigms of social scientific thought emerged more or less together during the modern period. Each one is a conceptually viable and intellectually honest way to understand the social world, and each one has had its own followers. Although paradigm shifts occur in the social sciences, they have a different meaning than Kuhnian paradigm shifts in the single paradigm sciences. As we know, in the physical sciences a paradigm shift means the abandonment of an older, crisis-ridden paradigm and the adoption of a new one by, more or less, the entire scientific community. A paradigm shift in the social sciences, however, merely represents a change in paradigmatic commitment for someone or some portion of the scientific community. Such a paradigm shift affects only those who have shifted their allegiance; it does not overthrow the other paradigms or change the outlook of members of the scientific community who continue to remain loyal to them.

Although allegiances have shifted throughout history, as they are shifting today, and different paradigms have dominated particular regions of the globe, all four paradigms of social scientific thought continue to exist. Each one serves as the guiding framework for that portion of the social scientific community that subscribes to it (see Burrell & Morgan, 1979; Ritzer, 1980; Bernstein, 1976). Not only has the multiple paradigm status of the social sciences precluded revolutionary science in the Kuhnian sense, but it also has made normal science more difficult because, as Ritzer (1980) noted, the multiple paradigm state requires social scientists to spend an inordinate amount of energy on the politics of winning converts and defending their paradigms against attacks from competitors.

*Shifts in the 1960s, 1970s, and 1980s*

Because the functionalist paradigm has been the favored framework for social science in the West, most of the work in the social sciences has been done from the micro-objective perspective. Nevertheless, over the past 30 years three paradigm shifts occurred in the social sciences (see Bernstein, 1976; Burrell & Morgan, 1979; Rorty, 1979). First, during the 1960s there was a shift on the objectivist side of Figure 1.1, from the order or microscopic level to the conflict or macroscopic level. This shift from the functionalist paradigm to the radical structuralist paradigm was associated with a reemergence of interest in Marxism as a political philosophy (e.g., Marcuse, 1964; Althusser, 1969), as well as the emergence of structuralism as a methodological approach (e.g., Chomsky, 1959; Levi-Strauss, 1963).

Two parallel shifts during the 1970s and 1980s both reflect the general shift from objectivism to subjectivism. One shift was at the order or microscopic level of analysis, from the functionalist to the interpretivist paradigm, and was associated with the heightened critique of positivism in the social sciences and the reemergence of interest in various forms of idealism (see Bernstein, 1976; Geertz, 1983). The other was at the macroscopic level of analysis, from the macro-objective or radical structuralist paradigm to the macro-subjective or radical humanist paradigm, and was associated with the reemergence of interest in the work of the young (or Hegelian) Marx (see Habermas, 1973/1975; Held, 1980; Jay, 1973).

*The Meta-Leap to Postmodernism*

The first effect of these shifts has been the substantiative and methodological development of the other three paradigms, which, relative to functionalism, previously had been underdeveloped, particularly in the United States (Burrell & Morgan, 1979). The second, and far more revolutionary, development associated with these paradigm shifts in the social disciplines has been the meta-leap to *postmodernism,* which represents a frame of reference for social analysis that falls outside the four paradigms of modern social scientific knowledge altogether (see Bernstein, 1983; Lyotard, 1979/1984; Rorty, 1979). The broader significance of postmodernism is that it represents a reconceptualization of the nature of knowledge itself.

During the modern period, the general conceptualization of knowledge was *foundational*—the idea that there is a fixed set of foundational criteria against which all knowledge claims can be judged. Thus, the modern perspective is *monological*; it regards knowledge or truth as a monologue spoken by the voice of a single paradigm or frame of reference. But the postmodern conceptualization of knowledge is *antifoundational* and *dialogical*; it is based on the idea that there are no independent foundational criteria for judging knowledge claims, and thus that the "truth" about the social world is better understood as a conversation or a dialogue among many voices or perspectives (see Bernstein, 1983).

Social inquiry premised on the foundational view of knowledge has led to a monological quest for the single best methodology, theory, or paradigm for social analysis. But today, scholars in the social disciplines are calling for dialogical social analysis—an antifoundational, reflective discourse about, and appreciation of, the variety of possible methodologies, theories, and paradigms for interpreting social life (Bernstein, 1983; Rorty, 1979; Ricoeur, 1981).

Although at present postmodernism is a relatively vague conception in the social sciences, Antonio (1989) identified two predominant forms. The more *radical* or Continental form (e.g., Derrida, 1972/1982b; Foucault, 1980a) rejects modern social knowledge outright. It is incredulous toward paradigms per se, regarding them simply as historically situated meta-narratives about the social world written in the genre of philosophy (Lyotard, 1979/1984).

The second form of postmodernism is the *progressive liberal* or American version (e.g., Bernstein, 1983; Rorty, 1979), which is a reappropriation of American pragmatism. Grounded primarily in the thought of John Dewey,[4] the American postmoderns conditionally accept all four paradigms of modern social knowledge as a starting point for a critical and emancipatory form of social analysis (see Antonio, 1989; Kloppenberg, 1986). Like the original pragmatist philosophers, they propose that we use modern knowledge pragmatically by forging a *via media* between the order-conflict and subjective-objective dimensions, in the interest of a radically open and participatory form of social life, that is, in the interest of radical democracy (see Rorty, 1979; Kloppenberg, 1986).

Although there are other forms of emancipatory social analysis, such as Marxism and various types of neo-Marxism, most notably critical theory (e.g., Habermas, (1963/1973, 1968/1971), the difference is that Marxism and critical theory are grounded in the modern social knowledge of radical structuralism and radical humanism, respectively, whereas philosophical pragmatism is antifoundational and postmodern. It occupies a perspective outside the four paradigms of modern social knowledge.

## PHILOSOPHICAL AND POLITICAL CRITIQUES OF THE PROFESSIONS

I will return to the notion of antifoundationalism and the two forms of postmodernism in the next chapter, and to a more extended comparison of pragmatism and critical theory as alternative forms of emancipatory social analysis in chapter 6. For now, however, let us consider the philosophical and political critiques of the professions against the backdrop of the paradigm shift to subjectivism and the meta-leap to antifoundationalism in the social sciences.

### The Philosophical Critique

The philosophical critique of the professions is based on the epistemological implications of the paradigm shift and meta-leap in the social sciences. Inherent in the paradigm shift to subjectivism, of course, is a critique of logical positivism and the objectivist view of science. The *social* professions—that is, professional fields such as special education, educational administration, and general education which draw their knowledge claims from and thus ground their practices in one or more of the disciplines of the social sciences—are implicated in this critique.[5] This is so because, as we will see in chapter 4, they are premised on the positivist epistemology of knowledge and thus the assumption that, through the application of logical positivism, the social sciences produce objective knowledge about social reality (Schön, 1983; Shils, 1978). As such, the professional knowledge required for the performance of services to clients in these professions is presumed to be grounded in a foundation of objective social scientific knowledge (Schein, 1973).

But the subjectivist view of science rejects the traditional image of science as a purely technical undertaking that yields objective knowledge. As we have seen, the emergent view is that, rather than a neutral, technical activity, science is a form of engagement between an object of study and an observer who is conditioned to see it in a particular way by his or her paradigm. And, because what is observed in the object is a product of this interaction, the same object is capable of yielding many different kinds of knowledge, depending on the frame of reference employed. Thus, from the subjectivist perspective, science is a subjective act that produces "possible knowledges" (Morgan, 1983, p. 13). The idea that science produces possible knowledges rather than objective knowledge means that the knowledge that grounds thought and action in the social professions is not objective knowledge about social reality. It is subjective knowledge based on a particular frame of reference.

Antifoundationalism has two epistemological implications for the social professions, the first of which relates to the multiple paradigm status of their grounding disciplines. Given that these professions are grounded in the social sciences, each of which is a multiple paradigm science, the social professions can be thought of as *multiple paradigm professions*. As such, the antifoundational notion that each social discipline produces four incommensurable types of knowledge means that there are no independent or foundational criteria for these professions to adjudicate the question of which of the four paradigms of any given social science discipline is the correct paradigm for grounding their professional knowledge and practice.

The second implication is related to the fact that the emergence of antifoundationalism in the social sciences has blurred the distinctions among the disciplines themselves (Geertz, 1983). Thus, given the antifoundational conceptualization of knowledge as interpretation with no independent criteria for choosing among interpretations, there is no meaningful way to establish the cognitive authority of one social discipline over another (see Rorty, 1982). Figure 1.3 illustrates the antifoundational view of modern social knowledge and the philosophical implication that there is no set of independent cognitive criteria for a social profession to use in choosing a particular metatheoretical paradigm or disciplinary orientation as a grounding for professional knowledge and practice.

### The Political Critique

The political critique of the social professions is based on the political implications of antifoundationalism. Given a conceptualization of knowledge as interpretation—a distinctively human process in which no single paradigmatic or disciplinary interpretation ever has enough cognitive authority to privilege it over another—choosing an interpretation becomes a political and moral act with implications for social justice (e.g., Derrida, 1972/1982b; Feyerabend, 1975; Foucault, 1980a). A major outcome of this realization in the social sciences has

**Figure 1.3**

Antifoundational View of Modern Social Knowledge

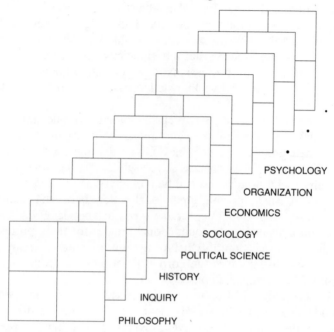

PSYCHOLOGY

ORGANIZATION

ECONOMICS

SOCIOLOGY

POLITICAL SCIENCE

HISTORY

INQUIRY

PHILOSOPHY

been a series of revisions in the metaphor for social life—from an organism to a game; from a game to a drama; and, finally, from a drama to a text (Geertz, 1983).

The text metaphor implies a mode of social analysis that views human and institutional practices as discursive formations that can be read or interpreted in many ways, none of which is correct in a foundational sense but each of which carries with it a particular set of political implications. Social analysis under the text metaphor is the study of that which conditions, limits, and institutionalizes discursive formations, or social practices, a form of analysis that asks how power comes to be concentrated in the hands of those who have the right to order, classify, exclude, and, generally, affirm or deny the truth of propositions—that is, how power comes to be concentrated in the hands of those who have the right to interpret reality (Dreyfus & Rabinow, 1983).

No aspect of social life has received more critical attention under the text analogy than the professions, for it is this group in modern society that has the authority to interpret normality, and thus the group that has accumulated the power to define and classify others as abnormal and to treat their bodies and their minds. And no one has devoted more energy or attracted more attention to the relations of power, knowledge, and the professions than the French political philosopher Michel Foucault (1980a). Foucault inverts social analysis and turns it on itself. That is, rather than search for some ultimate "truth" behind social practices, which, of course, is the customary approach, he studies the practices of the social sciences and social professions themselves and attempts to expose the unquestioned assumptions that guide thought and action in these fields (see Foucault, 1980b). His primary interest is the different modes by which, in our culture, human beings are turned into subjects. His analyses of the professions of psychiatry (1961/1973a), medicine (1963/1975), and criminology (1975/1979) are classic studies of the power of professionals to interpret normality.

Although in some ways Foucault's work is indistinguishable from that of an historian, the key difference is that he is far less interested in the events of history than in the modes of understanding that produced them. Ultimately, he wants to know what, in a particular time and place, led people to believe in what they were doing.

## BEHIND SPECIAL EDUCATION

This book asks Foucault's question *of special educators* and *about special education*. First, it asks what, in 20th-century America, led special educators to believe in their professional practices, recognizing that on two occasions, once in the 1960s and again in the 1980s, they suspended belief in these practices and proposed different ones. Second, it asks what, in 20th-century America, led educators to believe in the institutional practice of special education as a rational and just response to the problem of school failure. It attempts to answer these questions by considering them from two interrelated perspectives: *professional culture* and *school organization*.

Answering the first question is important for the field of special education in this time of uncertainty because, by providing insight into the grounds of past and current practices, it offers a more reflective way for the field to appraise and reconstruct its professional knowledge and practices. Although I believe that ultimately we must move *beyond* special education, my argument is that such a move must begin with, and constantly be informed by, the notion of looking *behind* special education. In this regard, I will argue that when we look behind special education practices, we will find the contradictions contained in the professional culture of special education. To understand what possibilities lie ahead for special education, special educators must understand and, more important, free themselves from that which has conditioned, limited, and institutionalized their professional thought and action.

Answering the second question is important for the field of education because, as an institutional practice of public education, special education, I will argue, prevents education from confronting its failures, and thus ultimately precludes meaningful reform. As such, looking behind special education as an institutional practice requires that we understand what conditioned, limited, and institutionalized professional thought and action in the field of education. I will argue in this regard that, when we look behind the institutional practice of special education, we will find the contradictions contained in the professional cultures of general education and educational administration. To understand what possibilities lie ahead for public education, general educators and educational administrators must understand and free themselves from that which has conditioned, limited, and institutionalized their professional thought and action. Ultimately, I will argue that when we look behind the professional cultures and practices of special education, general education, and educational administration, we will find the contradictions contained in the bureaucratic organization of schools, which not only has shaped and been shaped by all three professional cultures but also has distorted public education and the democratic ideals it is intended to promote and upon which it is based—a distortion that has reached crisis proportions.

Answering both questions is important for society because, in a Foucauldian sense, public education, acting through its institutional practice of special education, and under the legitimatizing effects of educational administration, is perhaps the most powerful profession in society. This is particularly true when we consider the pervasiveness and centrality of education in contemporary society and the fact that, as an institutional practice, it continues to classify more and more of its students as abnormal. As Foucault (1983) has argued, the most insightful way to understand society is to consider it from the perspective of the professions that have emerged to contain its failures. In this sense, special education can be understood as the profession that emerged in 20th-century America to contain the failure of public education to educate its youth for full political, economic, and cultural participation in democracy.

Finally, by refocusing our attention on the cultural aspects of the education professions and the structural conditions of school organizations—factors that are external to students themselves—I hope to hold out the possibility that, rather than seeing abnormal student behavior and special education simply as targets for professional and organizational manipulation, we may see them both as forms of strategic consciousness, as ways of resisting and coping with the failures of public education, and, ultimately, as texts which, if read critically, indicate a way out of the current crisis in education and democracy.

## NOTES

1. I use the term *educational administration* in both a narrow and a broad sense. In the narrow sense it refers to the professional field and institutional practice of educational administration. In the broad sense it refers to educational administration (narrow sense), special education administration, and, more important, to the professional fields and institutional practices of educational policy and educational change, school improvement, or educational reform (hereafter, simply educational change), inclusive of the role educational administrators play in these fields and practices. Except where noted, I tend to use the term narrowly in Parts One and Two and more broadly in Part Three. Here, however, I am using it in the broad sense because, as we will see in Part Three, both the field of educational administration and the field of educational change have been in a virtually constant state of self-criticism for at least the past 30 years (see chapter 2, note 5; chapter 7).

I use the term *general education* and, to a lesser extent, terms such as *regular education, regular classroom,* and *regular teacher* to refer to the professional field and institutional practice associated with the typical kindergarten through 12th-grade program within public education. Although I am sensitive to Lilly's (1989) argument that these terms often carry "decidedly neutral or even negative connotations" (p. 143) for professional educators outside the field of special education, clarity demands that I use them to distinguish between the professional fields and institutional practices of general education and special education, as well as between general education (narrow sense) and the entire professional field and institution of education (broad sense). I use phrases and terms such as "the field of education," "the institution of education," "public education," and, when clarity is not a problem, simply "education" to refer to education in the broad sense.

Although I use the term *special education* narrowly throughout the book to refer to the professional field (Part Two) and institutional practice (Part Three) of special education per se, the implications of my arguments in Parts One and Two for the other professional fields and institutional practices associated with special needs programming in public education (e.g., Chapter 1, and bilingual, migrant, remedial, and gifted education) should be amply clear. Moreover, these implications are made explicit in Part Three, relative to my discussion of school organization and adaptability, and they are extended to all professional and institutional practices that, in one way or another, group or track students within the general education program. Finally, although it plays a key role in special education classification practices under the EHA, I have not included the field of school psychology in the present analysis. For a separate treatment see Skrtic (1990b).

2. The conceptual framework developed in this section should be thought of as an "ideal type" (Weber, 1904/1949), which is one of several approaches to social analysis that I use throughout the book. The nature and purpose of the ideal-typical analytic is discussed in chapter 2. At this point it is sufficient to note that, as an ideal type, the conceptual framework is an exaggerated heuristic device for understanding the dominant value orientations that have shaped thought in the social disciplines during the modern era or, roughly, the last 200 years.

3. Ritzer most likely would not agree with equating the microscopic-macro-

scopic and order-conflict designations, because he made a point of using Gans's (1972) functionalist analysis of poverty to illustrate that functionalism *can be* used in an ideologically neutral manner. In this regard, one could also point to Farber (1968) as another example of a nonconservative functionalist analysis of, in this case, mental retardation. Nevertheless, the conservative bias in the way functionalism *has been* used historically is generally recognized (see Burrell & Morgan, 1979), even by Ritzer, as noted in text.

4. As an intellectual phenomenon, philosophical pragmatism emerged in the United States and Europe between 1870 and 1900 as a *via media* or road between both the extreme epistemological positions of objectivism and subjectivism and the extreme sociological positions of regulation and radical change which, by the middle of the 19th century, had dichotomized modern social theorizing. Although methodologically I draw from both the American and European pragmatist traditions (i.e., Dewey in the U.S., and Max Weber in Europe—see chapter 2), substantively I emphasize the American tradition because (a) like postmodernism today, philosophical pragmatism had different philosophical and political manifestations on either side of the Atlantic, giving rise to the political philosophy of progressivism in the U.S. and that of social democracy in Europe (see (Kloppenberg, 1986); and (b) I ultimately want to recover Dewey's notion of progressive education which, although grounded epistemologically and morally in philosophical pragmatism per se, is tied historically to the American cultural experience (see chapter 10). Although I will associate philosophical pragmatism with Dewey, it should be noted that it originated with C. S. Peirce (1878/1934) and was subsequently expanded upon and championed by Dewey and by William James (1909/1978a; 1907/1978b). Dewey's version of pragmatism, which he called instrumentalism, was first elaborated in *Studies in Logical Theory* (1903/1976b). Generally speaking, "pragmatism is primarily a means of settling otherwise interminable metaphysical disputes by asking, 'What difference would it practically make to anyone if this notion rather than that notion were true?'" (James, 1907/1978b, p. 28). As a method of social analysis, philosophical pragmatism raises this relatively straightforward idea to the level of metatheoretical presuppositions and paradigms of modern social thought. As the liberal progressive form of postmodernism, and in conjunction with the radical Continental form, I will expand the discussion of philosophical pragmatism in chapters 2 and 6, relative to its implications for social inquiry and professional discourse, respectively, and again in chapter 10, relative to Dewey's notion of progressive education and the idea of cultural transformation through education.

5. All references to the professions throughout the book will be to what I am calling the social professions, as defined in text, unless noted otherwise. My primary focus, of course, is on the social profession of education and, within it, the three professional fields of special education, educational administration, and general education.

I will treat special education as a social profession, even though, as we will see in subsequent chapters, it is grounded in the social science discipline of psychology and the physical science discipline of biology. I will treat educational administration as a social profession, even though, in a technical sense, one could argue that it is not a profession because it is grounded in the prescriptive knowledge of scientific management rather than in the disciplinary knowledge of a social science (see Spring, 1980; chapter 4; chapter 7).

# 2

# Critical Pragmatism as a Method of Social Inquiry

Professional practices (what professionals do) and professional discourses (what professionals think, say, write, and read about what they do) are shaped by anonymous, historically situated presuppositions that organize and give meaning to thought, language, and activity (Foucault, 1969/1972; Kuhn, 1970). These presuppositions are historically situated because they are specific to a particular time and place. They are anonymous because they are grounded in layers of largely unquestioned assumptions that are reflected in the values, interests, beliefs, norms, conventions, and interpretations contained in the knowledge tradition of the profession. I will refer to this totality—a profession's knowledge tradition and the associated metatheories, theories, assumptions, models, practices, and discourses of which it is constituted—as a *professional culture.*

Because the world is ambiguous and complex, a field of endeavor—be it a physical science, a social science, or a social profession—must have a way of unrandomizing complexity. Thus, like a scientific culture, to be productive a professional culture must have a paradigm, an accepted way of interpreting the world. Although a profession can never escape the need for a paradigm, it can be reflective about its paradigm and its implications for individuals and society. The problem, however, is that without a paradigm crisis, nothing compels a profession to question its paradigm of practice or the knowledge tradi-

**27**

tion and associated assumptions that stand behind it. A crisis in knowledge is a necessary prelude to growth of knowledge. Thus, although the crisis in modern knowledge can be viewed negatively, it is also a positive opportunity for growth, a stimulus for reflective introspection and critical renewal in society, the social disciplines, and the professions, including education.

Ultimately, however, whether the current crisis leads to positive growth and renewal depends upon the manner in which we make pragmatic choices and take pragmatic actions relative to our current situation. The manner in which we make these decisions can take one of two general forms: *naive pragmatism* or *critical pragmatism*. Naive pragmatism values functional efficiency—pure utility or expediency. It is premised on unreflective acceptance of the explicit and implicit assumptions that lie behind our practices and discourses. According to Cherryholmes (1988), naive pragmatism is "socially reproductive, instrumentally and functionally reproducing accepted meanings and conventional organizations, institutions, and ways of doing things for good or ill" (p. 151). Conversely, critical pragmatism approaches decision making in a way that treats such assumptions themselves as problematic; it "results when a sense of crisis is brought to our choices" (Cherryholmes, 1988, p. 151), when it is accepted that our assumptions themselves require evaluation and reappraisal.

I am using critical pragmatism in two ways: as a method of inquiry in this book, and as a recommendation for a mode of professional practice and discourse in the field of education.[1] As a method of inquiry, I use it as a way to look behind special education, as a way to question, and thus bring a sense of crisis to, the unquestioned assumptions that ground the professional practices and discourses of the field of special education, as well as the discourses and practices of the fields of general education and educational administration, relative to public education's institutional practice of special education.

In the discussion that follows in the next section, I describe the actual procedures and techniques I will use in my approach to critical pragmatism as a method of inquiry. In chapter 6 I describe critical pragmatism as a mode of professional practice and discourse in the field of public education. In Part Three, I address, among other things, the organizational conditions that I believe would be required for critical pragmatism to emerge and be sustained in public education. As such, I am suggesting that the various professions in the field of public education be reconceptualized, reorganized, and reactualized as modes of inquiry, and that the mode of inquiry should be critical pragmatism, an example of which is provided by the methods used in this book. Thus, following Cherryholmes, I am calling for *critical practice* in the field of public education, a mode of practice that is shaped and continually reshaped by a *critical discourse*. As such, critical practice is:

> ... continual movement between construction of a practice, which justifies why things are designed as they are, and deconstruction of that practice, which shows its incompleteness and contradictions. . . . Critical discourse is continual movement between the constitution of a methodology designed to [carry out the construction and deconstruction of practices] and subsequent criticism of that approach. (Cherryholmes, 1986, pp. 96–97)

Applied to the professions, critical pragmatism is both a way of continually evaluating and reappraising what a profession does (critical practice) and a way of continually evaluating and reappraising how it carries out such critical appraisals of its practice (critical discourse). Moreover, as a way for a profession to evaluate and reappraise what its members think, do, say, write, and read, the goal of critical pragmatism is not certainty; it does not seek objective knowledge or monological truth. Rather, the goal of critical pragmatism is *education*, or *self-formation*; it is a pedagogical process of remaking ourselves as we think, act, write, read, and talk more about ourselves and our practices and discourses (Gadamer, 1975). As such, critical pragmatism is premised on the notion of continually searching for "a new and more interesting way of expressing ourselves, and thus of coping with the world. From [this] educational . . . point of view, the way things are said is more important than the possession of truths" (Rorty, 1979, p. 359).

Rorty referred to this project of finding new and better ways of speaking as *edification,* a mode of inquiry that, by constantly forcing us to face the fact that what we think, do, say, write, and read as professionals is shaped by convention, helps us avoid deluding ourselves with the belief that we can know ourselves, our profession, our clients, "or anything else, except under optional descriptions" (1979, p. 379). More recently, Rorty (1989) elaborated upon his notion of edification by saying that it is:

> ... the same as the "method" of utopian politics or revolutionary science (as opposed to parliamentary politics, or normal science). The method is to redescribe lots and lots of things in new ways, until you . . . tempt the rising generation to . . . look for . . . new scientific equipment or new social institutions. This sort of philosophy . . . works holistically and pragmati-

cally. It says things like "try thinking of it this way"—or more specifically, "try to ignore the apparently futile traditional questions by substituting the following new and possibly interesting questions." (p. 9)

In the remaining chapters I redescribe the fields of special education, educational administration, and general education, as well as the school organizations in which these professions carry out their practices and discourses. My goal is to tempt the reader to look at these professions and organizations in new ways—mainly from behind, where their grounding assumptions are—and to try to think of them differently. I describe them separately but bring them together in the end to show how they maintain and reinforce one another. Above all, I want to be pragmatic; I want to use modern knowledge holistically and pragmatically, and I want to ask interesting questions: Why do we think, do, say, write, and read what we do? Are we living up to our ideals? How can we keep from deluding ourselves that we are when we are not? What methods and conditions will we need to do so?

## METHODOLOGY

To actualize critical pragmatism in public education, we need methods for producing optional descriptions of our practices and discourses and their implications for students and society, as well as conditions for initiating and sustaining the kind of critical dialogue that will permit us to question, or bring a sense of crisis to, the unquestioned models, assumptions, theories, and metatheories in which our professional practices and discourses are grounded. In subsequent chapters I will address critical pragmatism as a mode of professional discourse and the organizational conditions for implementing it. At this point, however, I want to address the methods that I will use in this book.

### Antifoundational Methodologies

As we saw in chapter 1, the paradigm shift from objectivism to subjectivism and the meta-leap from foundationalism to antifoundationalism have recast inquiry as a form of interaction between an object of study and an observer who is conditioned to see the object in a particular way by his or her paradigm, a distinctively human process through which potential knowledges, alternative interpretations, or optional descriptions are created (Bernstein, 1983; Derrida, 1972/ 1982b; Morgan, 1983; Rorty, 1979). As such, methodological debates in the social disciplines are moving beyond a foundational or monological quest for a single method of social analysis, and scholars are calling for a dialogical discourse on methodology—an antifoundational, reflective discourse about, and appreciation of, the variety of available and possible inquiry methodologies (Bernstein, 1976; Rorty, 1979; Ricoeur, 1981). This has produced new antifoundational methodologies, as well as reappropriated older ones. In my analysis of professional culture and school organization, I will use four of these methods: two of the older reappropriated methods, *immanent critique* and *ideal type*; and two of the newer methods, *deconstruction* and *genealogy*.

## Immanent Critique and Ideal Type

Immanent critique is more than a method of analysis. Historically, from Hegel and Marx to more contemporary emancipation theorists in the social disciplines (e.g., Habermas, 1968/1971; Horkheimer, 1947/1974) and in education (e.g., Giroux, 1981), it has been understood as the driving force behind social progress and cultural change. For example, Hegel (1807/1977) described the history of Western civilization as the progressive development of human consciousness and self-consciousness, a process driven by the affinity of humans for attempting to reconcile their claims about themselves (appearances) with their actual social conditions (reality) (see Kojeve, 1969; Taylor, 1977).

Although Marx criticized Hegel for the manner in which he applied the method of immanent critique, and neo-Marxists subsequently criticized Marxism on similar grounds (see Antonio, 1981), as a means to change through social analysis, it attempts to show how the ideals we claim to live by do not correspond to the reality of our life conditions. By exposing the contradictions between our claims and our conditions, the ideal and the real, an immanent critique seeks to transform the real into the ideal by confronting us with the fact that we are not living up to our own standards; that is, by first describing "what a social totality holds itself to be, and then confronting it with what it is in fact becoming" (Schroyer, 1973, pp. 30–31). As such, it is a particularly effective approach to change through social analysis, because, as Kiel (in press) noted:

It is the type of critique that self-conscious humans find most troubling . . .
it points out that they are not living up to their own standards. An immanent critique does not bring in outside standards, but instead demands that
actors reflect on the disjuncture between the standards and norms they
claim to live by and the existing social relations. . . . The immanent critique weighs in the minds of self-conscious actors, and can force, over
time, the actors to change their existing social relations or to change their
claims. (pp. 8–9)

Immanent critique is emancipatory, in that it is intended to promote change by freeing us from our unquestioned assumptions about
ourselves and our social practices, assumptions that prevent us from
doing what we believe is right (see Antonio, 1981; Benhabib, 1986;
Schroyer, 1973). As Antonio (1981, 1989) noted, however, historically,
immanent critique has been based on one of two types of emancipatory
theorizing: (a) an *evolutionary* form in which the emancipatory end-
point is assumed to be inevitable, and the normative standard of emancipation is a moral universal and, as such, is nonfalsifiable and closed
to empirical investigation and critical debate; and (b) an *historical* form
in which emancipation is contingent on historical struggles to reshape
institutional arrangements, and normative standards emerge out of historically situated critical discourses. The evolutionary form of immanent critique is dominant in the mature Marx (radical structuralism), as
well as in Hegel and critical theory (radical humanism), whereas the
historical form is the basis for emancipatory theorizing within philosophical pragmatism, particularly in the work of Dewey and other
American pragmatists such as George Herbert Mead (see Antonio,
1989). Although I will return to this important distinction in chapter 6,
in my discussion of critical pragmatism as a mode of professional discourse, at this point it is sufficient to know that I will use the historical
form of immanent critique throughout my analysis to expose the contradictions between the ideals and actual practices of the fields of special education, educational administration, and general education, and
ultimately between the ideals and practices of the institution of public
education. Finally, I should note that immanent critique involves a double burden: the burden placed on the readers to confront the contradictions between their ideals and practices; and the burden placed upon
the writer to present the ideals and practices in a way that the readers
can acknowledge.

Because ultimately I am proposing a change in the way educators
practice their profession, as well as in the organizational conditions

under which they do so, the historical immanent critique is particularly suited to my purposes. As a method, however, it does not on its own provide a way of identifying either the ideals or the actual conditions associated with a particular social phenomenon. For this I will use Max Weber's (1904/1949) notion of the ideal type, an analytic device that is both sensitive to and capable of relating cultural ideas and actual social phenomena. Weber argued that the meaning of social phenomena derives from the value orientation behind human and institutional action and historical events, and thus that the social sciences, properly construed, are cultural sciences—disciplines "which analyze the phenomena of life in terms of their cultural significance" (Dallmayr & McCarthy, 1977, p. 20). As such, he proposed the formulation of mental constructs, or ideal types, as a means for grasping the cultural significance of such phenomena. An ideal type is:

> . . . formed by the one-sided *accentuation* of one or more points of view and by the synthesis of a great many diffuse, discrete, more or less present and occasionally absent *concrete individual* phenomena, which are arranged according to those one-sidedly emphasized viewpoints into a unified *analytical* construct. . . . In its conceptual purity, this mental construct . . . cannot be found empirically anywhere in reality. It is a *utopia*. (Weber, 1904/1949, p. 90)

These mental constructions, Weber added, are always predicated on subjective presuppositions because "knowledge of cultural reality . . . is always knowledge from *particular points of view*" (Weber, 1904/ 1949, p. 81), which of course is a conceptualization of social science that is completely consistent with post-Kuhnian philosophy of science and the notion of paradigms; Rorty's (1989) notions of edification, optional descriptions, and utopian politics; and the method of philosophical pragmatism (see Huff, 1984; Kloppenberg, 1986).

An ideal-typical analysis entails developing an exaggerated mental construct as a heuristic for understanding a social phenomenon in terms of its cultural significance, using the construct to expose divergences between it and real cases, and attempting to explain the implications of the deviations in terms of the internal logic of the construct (see Dallmayr & McCarthy, 1977; Mommsen, 1974; Ritzer, 1983). Of course, an ideal type is not "true" in an objectivist sense; it is a mental construction, the value of which stems from its utility as an expository device, as a conceptual tool "for *comparison* with and the *measurement* of reality [or actual cases]" (Weber, 1904/1949, p. 97). Nor is a single ideal type ever sufficient. The more complex the phenomena of interest, and thus "the more many-sided their cultural *significance*" (p. 97), the less it is possible to operate on the basis of a single ideal type. "In such situations," Weber noted, "the frequently repeated attempts to discover ever *new* aspects of significance by the construction of new ideal-typical concepts is all the more natural and unavoidable" (p. 97).

Although he was writing at the turn of the century, before the subjectivist image of science held much sway in the social sciences, Weber anticipated the reactions of his objectivist critics by arguing that all social analyses, whether theory construction or empirical description, are ideal types. Even the ostensibly "presuppositionless" theoretical constructions of objectivists "*must* use concepts which are precisely and unambiguously definable only in the form of ideal types" (Weber 1904/1949, p. 92). Thus, all theoretical construction can be viewed as ideal types. The problem arises "in the belief that the 'true' content and the essence of historical reality is portrayed in such theoretical constructs" (Weber, 1904/1949, p. 94)—that is, when a theory is thought of as something more than an ideal type, something more than a utopia based on the accentuation of the presuppositions contained in a particular point of view.

The problem with empirical descriptions, Weber argued, is that consciously or, as is most often the case, unconsciously, they "contain what, from the point of view of the expositor, *should* be and what *to him* is 'essential' in [the phenomenon of interest] *because it is enduringly valuable* (p. 97). As such, the exposition no longer contains "ideas" or concepts with which the phenomenon is described, but, rather, "ideals" by which it is evaluatively or normatively judged, which means that "science has been left behind and we are confronted with a profession of faith, not [in the technical sense] an ideal-typical construct" (p. 98).

I will use ideal types in four ways throughout the book—in the three ways suggested by Weber, and the one way recommended by Rorty. That is, in Weber's sense, I will use: (a) ideal types that I or others have purposefully constructed to emphasize the cultural significance or value orientation of social phenomena; (b) the theoretical constructions of others which, although they were not intended as ideal types, can be used as such; and (c) the empirical descriptions of others that, in the same sense, were not intended to be, but nevertheless can be used as, ideal types. In Rorty's sense, I will use ideal types as (d) utopian characterizations or optional descriptions for the purpose of edification.

For example, I will use ideal types in Part Two to compare the traditional objectivist conceptualization of the professions with the newer subjectivist understanding that has followed in the wake of Kuhn, as well as in my reading of the REI debate, my characterization of the special education knowledge tradition, and my discussion of critical pragmatism as a mode of professional discourse. In Part Three I will use my own and others' ideal types extensively in my analysis of school organization and change, as well as in my characterization of educational administration's knowledge tradition, my organizational analysis of the EHA, REI, and the excellence movement, and my description of a new configuration for school organization. And, of course, I used the ideal-typical analytic in chapter 1 to highlight the value orientations that have shaped modern social knowledge, and I am using it in this chapter to expose the values behind my methodological aproach.

## Deconstruction and Genealogy

Because I am ultimately interested in deconstructing and reconstructing professional discourses and practices and school organizations by considering the metatheories, theories, assumptions, and models that lie behind them, certain aspects of Derrida's notion of deconstruction and of Foucault's method of genealogy are particularly suited to my purposes. Deconstruction and genealogy are antifoundational methodologies drawn from Continental or radical postmodernism, which, like the progressive liberal form of postmodernism, is a point of view that falls outside of the four paradigms of modern social knowledge. However, whereas the progressive liberal version of postmodernism proposes to use the four paradigms of modern social knowledge pragmatically, the radical version rejects the four paradigms; indeed, it is a critique of the very notion of metaphysical paradigms.

As such, both Derrida and Foucault reject modern knowledge, and thus the metatheoretical grounding of philosophy and, either explicitly (Foucault) or implicitly (Derrida), the social sciences and social professions. In this sense, they are both end-of-philosophy metaphilosophers; they argue that philosophy has come to an end and that philosophers must do something different, something beyond philosophy. As Hoy (1985) noted, however, the key difference between the two metaphilosophers is what they elect to do now that philosophy is over. Whereas Derrida has elected to "write metaphilosophical deconstructions of the history of philosophy" (p. 59), Foucault "writes concrete histories of practical attempts to gather social and psychological knowledge" (p. 59), that is, concrete histories of the practices and discourses of the social sciences and professions.

### Derrida and Deconstruction

In his reading of the history of philosophy, Derrida does not focus on the central ideas or arguments of philosophical texts. Rather, he emphasizes the margins of these texts—what is not said—and the various rhetorical and metaphorical devices that are used to gloss over their contradictions, inconsistencies, and silences. For Derrida, all texts are marked by their incompleteness. Whereas typical analyses of such texts purport to enable us to read them, Derrida's objective is to demonstrate that they are "unreadable." Rather than "assuming the text succeeds in establishing its message, Derrida's strategy is to get us to see that it does not work. In short, he does not reconstruct the text's meaning, but instead deconstructs it" (Hoy, 1985, p. 44). For Derrida, a philosophical work would succeed if it would recreate or represent a reality external to itself; deconstructing such texts "shows the failure of a work's attempt at representation and, by implication, the possibility of comparable failure by any such work, or by any text whatsoever" (Hoy, 1985, p. 44). This is an implication that refers to all of the texts of the social sciences and the social professions, *including this one*, because, metaphorically, it refers to "the 'general textuality' of the world" (Ryan, 1982, p. 22).

Epistemologically, deconstruction is more radical than the subjectivist notion of social analysis within modern knowledge because it means that there are no limits whatsoever on how a text can be read and thus that a text cannot refer beyond itself to an independent reality. This "leads deconstructionists to say that if a text seems to refer beyond itself, that reference can finally be only to another text . . . [which] can only refer to other texts, generating an intersecting and indefinitely expandable web called intertextuality" (Hoy, 1985, p. 53).

Derrida's work emphasizes the "undecidability" of philosophical texts because it is meant to be a criticism of metaphysics and foundationalism—that is, a criticism of "the assumption in philosophy that a set of formal logical axioms can be constructed which provides a complete account of the truth or meaning of the world, as well as of the related assumptions that a single foundation . . . could be posited . . . into which everything in the world ultimately resolves itself" (Ryan, 1982, p. 16). Given the intertextuality and undecidability of texts, and thus the futility of seeking true interpretations under conditions in which there is never enough authority to place one interpretation over another, Derrida (1972/1982a) argued that philosophers should abandon the project of interpretation and instead take up "dissemination"—the project of illustrating through example after example the fundamental illegibility of texts.

Given my claims about critical pragmatism as a method of social analysis and a mode of professional discourse, I want to distance myself somewhat from Derrida. Although, generally speaking, his insights are profound and his methods are useful, I believe that his radical attacks upon reading and understanding are overstated; that they assume a lack of communication which critical pragmatism makes possible. Indeed, this is a key distinction between the radical and progressive liberal versions of postmodernism. Nevertheless, with this caveat in mind, I will use deconstruction throughout the book to illustrate the inconsistencies, silences, and contradictions in the knowledge traditions of special education, general education, and in relation to school organization and change, the field of educational administration.

I will use deconstruction extensively in Part Two to deconstruct special education as a *professional* practice. In this regard, I will use it to reread the text of the REI debate, paying close attention to the implications of what is said, and left unsaid, for the metatheories, theories, and assumptions behind the models and practices contained in special education knowledge tradition. I will also use deconstruction in Part Two to reinterpret the dominant objectivist conceptualization of the professions, to reread the text of the special education knowledge tradition itself, and to present my case for critical pragmatism as a mode of professional discourse.

In Part Three I will use deconstruction to deconstruct special education as an *institutional* practice of public education. In this regard, I will use it to reread the traditional and emerging discourses on school organization and adaptability and, on the basis of this reading, to deconstruct the very notions of special education and disability. In the final chapter I will deconstruct the notions of "reflective teaching" (Schön, 1983, 1989) and the "thinking curriculum" (Resnick & Klopfer, 1989) to set the stage for my proposal for curriculum and instruction in the new school organization that I will recommend.

### Foucault and Genealogy

Although Foucault is also a metaphilosopher, his work emphasizes the political implications of antifoundationalism for the social sciences and social professions. In this regard, he has been critical of Derrida for not applying his metaphilosophical deconstructions in any practical way to the institutional practices of the social sciences and professions. Ultimately, Foucault argued that, to the degree that Derrida's approach precludes raising moral, social, and political questions, his notion of textual undecidability merely perpetuates the status quo (Foucault, 1983).

Philp (1985) summarized Foucault's primary objective as providing "a critique of the way modern societies control and discipline their populations by sanctioning the knowledge claims and practices of the human sciences: medicine, psychiatry, psychology, criminology, sociology and so on" (p. 67). In this regard, Foucault (1980b) argued that the classical notion of political rule based on sovereignty and rights has been subverted by the social sciences and, through them, the social professions. This new regime of power, this "non-sovereign power, which lies outside the form of sovereignty, is disciplinary power" (p. 105), a form of power in the modern world that is exercised through disciplinary practices that establish norms for human behavior.

> In workplaces, schoolrooms, hospitals and welfare offices; in the family and the community; and in prisons, mental institutions, courtrooms and tribunals, the human sciences have established their standards of "normality." The normal child, the healthy body, the stable mind . . . such concepts haunt our ideas about ourselves, and are reproduced and legitimated through the practices of teachers, social workers, doctors, judges, policemen and administrators. The human sciences attempt to define normality; and by establishing this normality as a rule of life for us all, they simultaneously manufacture—for investigation, surveillance and treatment—the vast area of our deviation from this standard. (Philp, 1985, p. 67)

In his earlier efforts Foucault's primary unit of analysis was the discourse, which "is best understood as a system of possibility for knowledge . . . a system . . . [that] allows us to produce statements which will be either true or false—[a system that] . . . makes possible a field of knowledge" (Philp, 1985, p. 69). Foucault favored discourse or, more accurately, discursive formations, over other units of analysis—texts, theories, paradigms—because he was interested in the rules that make discursive formations possible.[2] He was interested in discursive formations because he reasoned that, in modern societies, the multiplicity of relations of power that permeate, characterize, and constitute the social body "cannot themselves be established, consolidated nor implemented without the production, accumulation, circulation and functioning of a discourse" (Foucault, 1980b, p. 93). Thus, no exercise of power is possible without an *economy* of such discourses of truth. In a society such as ours:

> We are subjected to the production of truth through power and we cannot exercise power except through the production of truth. . . . Power never ceases its interrogation, its inquisition, its registration of truth: it institutionalizes, professionalizes and rewards its pursuit. . . . In the end, we are judged, condemned, classified, determined in our undertakings, destined to a certain mode of living or dying, as a function of the true discourses which are the bearers of the specific effects of power. (Foucault, 1980b, pp. 93–94)

In his later work, Foucault abandoned the attempt to develop a theory of discourse based on rules (Rabinow & Dreyfus, 1983). Although he had always been interested in the practices of the social sciences and social professions, he now began to focus on them directly. Discourse continued to be important to him, but now he focused on "norms, constraints, conditions, conventions, and so on" (Rabinow & Dreyfus, 1983, p. 108), more in the style of Kuhn's notion of a paradigm as an exemplar or model, which, of course, is the approach I am using in this book. In any event, what is of interest to me, given that I want to address practices and discourses in the profession of education, is Foucault's methodology for analyzing such practices—genealogy.

As opposed to traditional historical methods, genealogy "avoids the search for depth. Instead it seeks the surfaces of events, small details, minor shifts, subtle contours" (Rabinow & Dreyfus, 1983, p. 106). For the genealogist the goal and outcome of interpretation is not the uncovering of a hidden meaning or an ultimate truth. "If interpretation is a never-ending task," Foucault argued, "it is simply because there is nothing to interpret" (1964/1990, p. 189). In his genealogies, Foucault (1980b) looks for two kinds of knowledges. The first type is knowledge that has been "buried and disguised in a functionalist coherence or formal systemisation" (p. 81). This type of knowledge is the metatheoretical and theoretical knowledge that has been distorted and hidden from the social sciences and professions because of the dominance of functionalism—possible knowledges, alternative interpretations, and optional descriptions that have gone unrealized. The second type of knowledge is what Foucault has termed "disqualified knowledge (such as that of the psychiatric patient, of the ill person, of the nurse . . . of the delinquent etc.)" (p. 82); that is, the knowledge possessed by the practitioner, as well as by the "other" in our society—the marginalized, the subjugated, those who are the subjects of the normalizing practices and discourses of the social sciences and professions.

## Foucault and Power

In his analysis of power, Foucault provided several methodological precautions that illustrate his unique understanding of power. First, he is not interested in the centralized and juridical power of the State, with its various apparati and associated ideologies. Rather, he is "concerned with power at its extremities, in its ultimate destinations . . . that is, in its more regional and local forms and institutions . . . at the extreme points of its exercise, where it is always less legal in character" (Foucault, 1980b, pp. 96–97). Second, he is concerned to understand power as the domination that is associated with subjugation—not in the sense of an intentional desire of certain people to dominate others, but "at the level of those continuous and uninterrupted processes which subject our bodies, govern our gestures, dictate our behaviors etc. . . . In other words . . . how it is that subjects are gradually, progressively, really and materially constituted" (Foucault, 1980b, p. 97).

Foucault's third methodological precaution is that power is not to be taken as something that one person, group, or class exclusively possesses and retains against others that do not possess it. Rather, according to Foucault (1980b), "power must be analyzed as something which circulates. . . . It is never localized here or there" (p. 98). For him, "power is organized and exercised through a net-like organization . . . [in which] individuals circulate between its threads . . . always in the position of simultaneously undergoing and exercising this power" (p. 98). He is interested in the *economy* of power in which *all* participants are implicated, social scientists and professionals, as well as their subjects.

The fourth precaution begins with a caveat on the third: The notion that power circulates freely is true only to a certain point; although it circulates, it does not do so democratically or anarchically. Thus, Foucault cautions us not to analyze power deductively—that is, starting from a presumed center and tracing it down and out into the molecular elements of society. Rather, one must conduct "an *ascending* analysis of power, starting, that is, from its infinitesimal mechanisms, which each have their own history, their own trajectory, their own techniques and tactics, and then see how these mechanisms of power have been . . . invested, colonized, utilized, involuted, transformed, displaced, extended etc., by ever more general mechanisms . . . of domination" (Foucault, 1980b, p. 99). Here, Foucault targets the surface practices of the social sciences and the professions, and the various techniques, procedures, and apparati of surveillance, exclusion, confinement, and medicalization that they have developed and extended. For him, these are the micro-mechanisms of power that are deployed in modern societies to control and discipline their populations.

I use Foucault's method of genealogy at several points in the book to trace the development of professional knowledge, practices, and discourses in the field of education. I use it for this purpose with respect to the special education knowledge tradition in Part Two, and for that of educational administration of Part Three. I use it in a more general way to trace the development of the discourse on school failure within the institution of public education at the end of this chapter. Finally, in the last chapter of Part Three, I use Foucault's approach to develop a brief genealogy of the value orientation of the field of special education, which I use to illustrate and reinforce several important points that I make elsewhere in the book about the relationship between professional culture and school organization, as well as to argue for the importance of this particular value orientation for the future of public education. In all cases throughout the book, when I refer explicitly or implicitly to power or the power of the professions, I am using Foucault's notion of an economy of disciplinary power.

Ultimately, I am concerned with the nature and implications of professional and institutional practices and discourses in the field of public education. But, because these discourses and practices are grounded in unquestioned models, assumptions, theories, and metatheories, I am proposing critical pragmatism—a blending of immanent critique, ideal types, deconstruction, and genealogy—as a method of investigating the layers of presuppositions that have conditioned, limited, and institutionalized them. Considering these layers of presuppositions is important because it is the first step toward developing the critical reflective posture necessary to assess the sense of ethics and efficacy that they imply. Moreover, such an analysis can be used to demonstrate that it is possible and desirable to ground educational practices, discourses, and organizations in alternative metatheoretical assumptions, and, more important, that choosing a frame of reference is a political and moral act with implications for ethical practice and a just society.

In the following section I present my substantive and methodological arguments in condensed form, as a preview of where the book is heading. I must caution the reader, however, that my interpretation of the problem in public education today will sound offensive to persons in the fields of special education, general education, and educational administration who are operating under traditional assumptions. This is so because it presents these fields in a way that not only questions these assumptions but also forces professionals to confront the contradictions between their values and their practices. But that is the point of my analysis; it is intended to make us think about our practices, discourses, and organizational arrangements in alternative ways and to ask ourselves if they are consistent with what we believe is right.

## THE PROBLEM AND OPPORTUNITY IN PUBLIC EDUCATION

Functionalism, the dominant mode of social theorizing in the modern era, views social reality as objective, inherently orderly, and rational, and thus views social and human problems as pathologies (Foucault, 1954/1976; Ritzer, 1980). Given its dominance in society (Foucault, 1966/1973b), the social disciplines (Bernstein, 1976; Ritzer, 1980), and the professions (Glazer, 1974; Schön, 1983), including general education (Bowles & Gintis, 1976; Giroux, 1981), educational administration (Griffiths, 1983, 1988), and special education (Heshusius, 1982; Iano, 1986; Skrtic, 1986), functionalism, among other things, institutionalized the mutually reinforcing theories of *organizational rationality* and *human pathology* in society, the social sciences, and the profession and institution of education.

As such, when industrialization, immigration, and compulsory school attendance converged to produce large numbers of students who were difficult to teach and manage in traditional classrooms, the problem of school failure was reframed as two interrelated problems—inefficient school organizations and defective students. In effect, this distorted the problem of school failure by largely removing it from the general education discourse and compartmentalizing it into two separate but mutually reinforcing discourses: one in the developing field of educational administration, which, in the interest of maximizing organizational efficiency, was compelled to rationalize its orientation according to the precepts of scientific management (Callahan, 1962; Campbell, Fleming, Newell, & Bennion, 1987); and one in the new field of special education, which, in the interest of maintaining order in the rationalized school plant, emerged as a means to contain the most recalcitrant students (Lazerson, 1983; Sarason & Doris, 1979).

Given the highly specialized division of labor in the field of education (Spring, 1980), the three subfields developed as separate but mutually reinforcing discourses, each shaped by *explicit* presuppositions grounded in their respective foundations of professional knowledge and *implicit* presuppositions grounded in dominant social norms, all of which were shaped by the institutionalized theories of human pathology and organizational rationality.[3] The field of special education, which is grounded in the disciplinary knowledge of biology and psychology, presupposes explicitly that school failure is pathological (Mercer, 1973), and implicitly that school organizations are rational (Skrtic, 1987b, 1988b). Conversely, educational administration, which is grounded in the prescriptive knowledge of scientific management, presupposes explicitly that school organizations are rational (Clark, 1985; Griffiths, 1983), and implicitly that failure in such organizations is pathological (Skrtic, in press c).[4] Finally, general education is grounded in psychology *and* scientific management and thus presupposes explicitly and implicitly that school organizations are rational and that school failure is a pathological condition (psychological or sociological) that is exposed in them (Cherryholmes, 1988; Spring, 1980; Oakes, 1985). Taken together, these presuppositions yield corresponding sets of mutually reinforcing assumptions, models, practices, tools, and discourses in the three fields, which, in turn, shape the discourse on school failure in the profession and institution of education.

Because inquiry in these fields is dominated by functionalist research methodologies (Griffiths, 1983, 1988; Lincoln & Guba, 1985; Poplin, 1987; Skrtic, 1986, 1988a), which favor data over theory and assume, more or less, that data are objective and self-evident (Churchman, 1971; Mitroff & Pondy, 1974), the discourse on school failure is atheoretical and empirical. It is a form of naive pragmatism which, in effect, produces and interprets empirical data on student outcomes and school effects intuitively, according to the taken for granted and mutually reinforcing functionalist theories of organizational rationality and human pathology. The result is that the status quo is reproduced in all three fields, which reinforces the assumptions that school organizations are rational and school failure is pathological in the profession and institution of education.

Thus, the institutional practice of special education and the very notion of student disability are artifacts of the functionalist quest for rationality, order, and certainty in the field of education, a quest that is both intensified and legitimized by the institutional practice of educational administration. These artifacts distort the problem of school failure and, ultimately, prevent general education from entering into a productive confrontation with uncertainty. Because uncertainty is a necessary prelude to growth of knowledge in communal activities such as the physical sciences (Kuhn, 1970), the social sciences (Barnes, 1982; Bernstein, 1983), and the professions (Schön, 1983; Skrtic, 1986, 1988a), the objectification of school failure as student disability through the institutional practice of special education, and its rationalization and legitimization through the institutional practice of educational administration, prevents the field of general education from confronting the failures of its functionalist practices and, thus, acts to reproduce and extend these practices in the profession and institution of education.

The problem in special education and educational administration has been that, although these fields have experienced enough uncertainty to call their traditional practices into question,[5] they have lacked a critical discourse for addressing their problems in a reflective manner (see Bates, 1980, 1987; Skrtic, 1986; 1988a). The problem in the field of general education is more fundamental, however. Not only has it lacked a critical discourse (see Cherryholmes, 1988; Giroux, 1981), but it largely has been prevented from having to confront uncertainty altogether, precisely because of the existence of the fields of special education and educational administration. Even though school failure has been a persistent problem throughout the 20th century, it has been distorted and deflected from the field of general education by the separate but mutually reinforcing discourses on school failure in special education and educational administration.

The significance of the current round of self-criticism in special education is that, when read critically, the empirical arguments put forth in the REI debate provide the grounds to deconstruct special education as a *professional* practice, which, in conjunction with a critical reading of the discourse on school organization and adaptability,[6] provides the grounds to deconstruct special education as an *institutional* practice of public education. The broader significance of deconstructing the institutional practice of special education is that, together with a critical reading of the discourse on educational excellence in the field of general education,[7] it provides the grounds to deconstruct the discourse on school failure in the institution of public education. Ultimately, without the distorting and legitimizing effects of the discourse on school failure, the immanent contradiction between the institutional practices and democratic ideals of public education becomes apparent and thus prepares the way for the deconstruction and reconstruction of the institution of education.

The broader significance of the deconstruction and reconstruction of the institution of public education is twofold. First, with respect to special education, it raises the possibility of the type of professional renewal and organizational restructuring that will be required to actualize the value orientation of the special education community, as those values have been expressed in the *spirit* of the EHA and mainstreaming and, more recently, in the *spirit* of the reform proposals of the REI. Second, with respect to the institution of education per se, it raises the possibility of reconciling the institutional practice of public education with its democratic ideals, which, in turn, revives the possibility of cultural transformation through education—a vitally important possibility upon which the moral, political, and economic future of our democracy hinges.

Among other things, public education in a democracy must be both excellent and equitable (Greer, 1972). The problem with this ideal, however, is that its democratic ends are contradicted by the bureaucratic means that were used in this century to actualize a universal system of compulsory education. As such, the failure of public education to be either excellent or equitable in the 20th century can be understood in terms of the inherent contradiction between democracy and bureaucracy in the modern state (see Weber, 1922/1978). Special education, then, can be understood as the institutional practice that emerged in the 20th century to contain the failure of public education to realize its democratic ideals. And, because an insightful way to understand a social institution is to consider it from the perspective of the institutional practices that emerge to contain its failures (Foucault, 1983), special education is a particularly advantageous vantage point for deconstructing 20th-century public education. Moreover, the irony in all of this is that, when read critically, the professional and institutional practices of special education contain within them the cultural and structural insights necessary to begin the process of reconstructing public education for the historical conditions of the 21st century and, ultimately, for reconciling it with its democratic ideals.

## NOTES

1. I am indebted to Cherryholmes for the term *critical pragmatism*, as well as for a number of methodological insights. Although we are basically pursuing the same critical project, we differ in several respects, three of which are worth mentioning here. First, although we both draw insights from the American and Continental forms of postmodernism (which he calls "poststructuralism"), he leans more heavily toward the Continental form, whereas I favor the American form (see chapter 1, note 4). Second, whereas Cherryholmes applies his version of critical pragmatism directly to general education, I apply my version to special education and, to a somewhat lesser extent, educational administration, which I use as analytical perspectives for analyzing general education and public education per se (see notes 6 and 7). Finally, although we both use critical pragmatism as a method of inquiry and a mode of professional discourse, I am also interested in the organizational conditions that would support such a project in public education—thus Part Three of this book.

2. In his analysis of the rules of discourse that operate in the production of knowledge, Foucault focused on the "objects, statements, concepts, and theoretical options" (Foucault, 1969/1972, p. 72) contained within discursive formations. He was not concerned with the objects, statements, concepts, and theoretical options themselves but instead with the rules that produced them. Moreover, he did not consider these rules to be ones that were followed consciously. Rather, he understood them as merely preconditions for the formation of the objects, statements, concepts, and theoretical options contained within a discourse (see Rabinow & Dreyfus, 1983; Philp, 1985). As such, these discursive rules "operate 'behind the backs' of speakers of a discourse. Indeed, the place, function, and character of the 'knowers,' authors and audiences of a discourse are also a function of these discursive rules" (Philp, 1985, p. 69).

3. It is helpful to think of all three discourses as being grounded in *unquestioned* presuppositions. My use of the qualifiers "explicit" and "implicit" here is meant to convey the idea that certain presuppositions are an *explicit* part of the profession's knowl-

edge tradition, even though they are more or less unconscious or, at least, unquestioned, whereas others, although they are unconscious or taken-for-granted ideas that have taken on a rule-like status in society, are merely *implicit* social norms and, as such, are not an "explicit" part of the profession's knowledge tradition (see chapter 4). This problem will surface again (and be dealt with) in subsequent chapters because the implicitness or explicitness of the assumptions and presuppositions behind social and institutional practices is a central focus of this type of inquiry.

4. In chapter 7 I argue that the assumption that school failure is pathological is an explicit assumption within the knowledge tradition of educational administration.

5. Although in chapter 1 I dichotomized the recent history of the field of special education into a first and second round of self-criticism (and will do so again in chapter 3 relative to an earlier mainstreaming debate and a contemporary REI debate), we can think of the field as being in a more or less constant state of self-criticism since the early 1960s. As we will see in chapter 3, criticism subsided somewhat during the period shortly before and after enactment of the EHA, but it did not disappear. In chapter 7 we will see that the field of educational administration (narrow sense) went through three cycles of self-criticism and reform during the first half of this century and has been in a more or less constant state of self-criticism since the early 1950s. Moreover, we will see that the field of educational change has been characterized by the same sort of self-criticism since it emerged in the late 1950s.

6. By "the discourse on school organization and adaptability" I mean what educational administrators (broad sense) think, do, say, read, and write about managing and changing school organizations, as well as what organizational analysts in the multidisciplinary field of organization analysis (see chapter 7) think, do, say, read, and write about managing and changing organizations per se, including school organizations. The distinctions between these discourses and my approach for addressing them are presented in Part Three. Although my primary concern is with special education, the institutional practices of special education and educational administration cannot be separated in an analysis such as this, which should become apparent to the reader, particularly in chapter 3 and Part Three. As such, we will see that, although a deconstruction of special education as a *professional* practice can be carried out by focusing on its practices, discourses, and knowledge tradition per se (Part Two), a deconstruction of special education as an *institutional* practice of public education necessarily requires a deconstruction of educational administration (both senses) (Part Three). Moreover, a deconstruction of the professional practices, discourses, and knowledge tradition of educational administration requires a deconstruction of those of the field of organization analysis (chapter 7). Therefore, although I will not emphasize them as much as the deconstruction of special education, Part Three can be read as a deconstruction of educational administration, and chapter 7 as a deconstruction of educational administration and organization analysis. For a somewhat more comprehensive genealogical and deconstructive treatment of both fields, see Skrtic (1988b). Although they were not written as such, the insightful analyses of Bates (1980, 1987) and Foster (1986) can be read as genealogical and deconstructive treatments of the field of educational administration.

7. By "the discourse on educational excellence" in the field of general education, I mean what general educators think, do, say, read, and write about the nature of educational excellence and how to achieve it, a discourse that (over the past decade) can be understood in terms of two related debates, which I will refer to in Part Three as the "effective schools" debate and the "school restructuring" debate. As in the case of educational administration (note 6), although I will emphasize the deconstruction of special education throughout the book, my treatment of these two debates (chapter 9) can be read

as a deconstruction of the discourse on educational excellence in general education and, to the extent that these debates reflect its practices, discourses, and knowledge tradition, a deconstruction of the field and institutional practice of general education per se.

# PART TWO
# Professional Culture

# 3

## The Crisis in Special Education

When President Gerald Ford signed the EHA in 1975, special education professionals and advocates knew they had won a policy revolution. Although those who took part in the policy revolution were optimistic, they were not naive. They knew that if the EHA was to amount to anything more than "a comprehensive set of empty promises" (Abeson & Zettel, 1977, p. 115), an implementation revolution would also have to be mounted and won (Abeson & Zettel, 1977; National Advisory Committee on the Education of the Handicapped, 1976; Weintraub, 1977). Moreover, they knew that implementing the EHA "would only work if [they] and others made it work by using the procedures set forth in the law" (Weintraub, 1977, p. 114). What they didn't know, however, was that the procedures of the law would become the principal barrier to achieving the spirit of the law (see, e.g., Gartner & Lipsky, 1987; Reynolds, Wang, & Walberg, 1987; Stainback & Stainback, 1984b). Although special education professionals and advocates clearly won the policy revolution, their worst fear has been realized. After 15 years of trying to make the EHA and mainstreaming work, they have lost the implementation revolution.

Although no one in the special education community is questioning the spirit of the EHA, or the fact that some important implementation battles have been won, the sense of defeat is so pervasive that many of those who had been staunch supporters of the EHA and main-

**51**

streaming are now calling for a new revolution—the REI. Generally speaking, the new revolution represents a number of proposals for achieving the *spirit* of the EHA for *students with disabilities* by extending its rights and resources to *all* students. Although the REI has strong opposition, even its detractors agree that the EHA has serious problems that have to be addressed (Kauffman, Gerber, & Semmel, 1988; Keogh, 1988). They are concerned, however, that a new revolution could mean a loss of rights and resources and a full-circle return to the unacceptable conditions that existed before the EHA (e.g., Kauffman, 1988, 1989a, 1989b; Kauffman et al., 1988).

## COMPARISON OF THE MAINSTREAMING AND REI DEBATES

This section considers the similarities and differences between the mainstreaming debate of the 1960s (and early 1970s) and the REI debate of the 1980s. It begins with a discussion of the parallels between the two debates and then, because the ways in which the two debates are different concern the assumptions behind special education practices, moves to a discussion of these grounding assumptions. Beyond serving as background for considering the ways the mainstreaming and REI debates are different, the discussion of grounding assumptions is an extension of the preliminary discussion presented at the close of chapter 2 and a prelude to more in-depth treatments in chapter 5 and Part Three.

### Parallels Between the Mainstreaming and REI Debates

The REI debate parallels the mainstreaming debate in three ways. First, in both cases the ethics and efficacy of special education practices are criticized and a new approach is proposed. In the 1960s, the target of criticism was the segregated special classroom model, and mainstreaming emerged as the solution. Today, mainstreaming is under attack, and the REI is being advocated as the solution. In the 1960s, Lloyd Dunn (1968) argued that special education practices were unjustifiable because they were racially biased, instructionally ineffective, and psychologically and socially damaging. Although we will see that the EHA and mainstreaming have introduced new problems and intensified old ones, the basic problems identified in the REI debate are virtually identical to those identified in the 1960s—racial bias, instructional ineffectiveness, psychological and social harm (see Heller, Holtzman, & Messick, 1982; Wang, Reynolds, & Walberg, 1987a).

Second, in both cases the new approach draws opposition and the field is divided. Although mainstreaming had some opposition (e.g., Keogh & Levitt, 1976; MacMillan & Semmel, 1977), it was far less divisive than the REI because, though mainstreaming was radical for its time, it was a far less ambitious proposition than the REI. Moreover, there was little, if anything, to lose in the 1960s. As we will see, however, not only has the REI debate divided the field into two camps of REI proponents and opponents, but, more recently, it has divided the REI proponents themselves into two camps over the issue of which students should be included in the new revolution.

Finally, both debates take place during a period of apparent reform in general education. In the 1960s Dunn (1968) argued that mainstreaming was a real possibility because it was consistent with what he called the American Revolution in Education—that is, apparent reforms in (a) school organization (e.g., team teaching, ungraded primary and open classrooms, flexible grouping); (b) curriculum (e.g., more powerful instructional technologies); (c) personnel roles and practices (e.g., more ancillary staff and individualized instruction); and (d) instructional hardware (e.g., computers, teaching machines, educational television). He believed that these reforms were consistent with mainstreaming because they held the promise of making the general education system "better able to deal with individual differences in pupils" (p. 10). Although he recognized that the revolution was "still more an ideal than a reality," Dunn argued that the field of special education "should begin moving now to fit into a changing general education program and to assist in achieving the program's goals" (p. 10).

In the current debate, the REI proponents are making the same argument. Although they recognized that the push for higher standardized text scores associated with the initial phase of the excellence movement had negative implications for the REI and mainstreaming (Pugach & Sapon-Shevin, 1987; Sapon-Shevin, 1987; Shepard, 1987), they believe that the recent call for school restructuring within the excellence movement is consistent with the REI concept (e.g., Pugach & Lilly, 1984; Wang, Reynolds, & Walberg, 1985, 1986; Lipsky & Gartner, 1989a). Moreover, like Dunn, they are arguing that more powerful instructional technologies (e.g., cooperative learning, peer-mediated instruction, adaptive learning) and professional practices (e.g., curriculum-based assessment, collaborative consultation, prereferral assessment) make the REI a real possibility (e.g., Pugach & Lilly, 1984; Stainback, Stainback, & Forest, 1989; Wang, 1989a, 1989b).

## Special Education's Grounding Assumptions

Although these parallels are interesting and instructive, there are two important differences between the situation today and the one in the 1960s, both of which concern the assumptions that ground the field of special education. Drawing from Bogdan and Knoll (1988), Bogdan and Kugelmass (1984), Mercer (1973), Skrtic (1986, 1988a), and Tomlinson (1982), these assumptions are that:

1. Disabilities are pathological conditions that students have.
2. Differential diagnosis is objective and useful.
3. Special education is a rationally conceived and coordinated system of services that benefits diagnosed students.
4. Progress results from incremental technological improvements in diagnosis and instructional interventions.[1]

Given the discussion in Part One of the book, we can understand assumptions such as these as falling midway in the hierarchy of presuppositions that guides communal activities like the physical and social sciences and the social professions, including general education, educational administration, and special education. That is, we can understand these four assumptions as falling midway in the hierarchy of grounding metatheories, theories, assumptions, models, practices, and tools that guide thought and action in the field of special education. As such, special education's four grounding assumptions are defined and subsumed by the theories of human pathology (assumptions 1 and 2) and organizational rationality (assumptions 3 and 4), which are themselves defined and subsumed by the metatheoretical assumptions of the functionalist paradigm of social scientific thought (see Skrtic, 1986, 1988a), as illustrated in Figure 3.1.

Moving down the hierarchy, the four grounding assumptions define and subsume the models, practices, and tools that special educators use to perform services to clients. As noted in Part One, and as we will see below in the critical analysis of the REI debate, discourse in the field of special education historically has centered on the ethics and

**Figure 3.1**

Special Education Hierarchy of Presuppositions

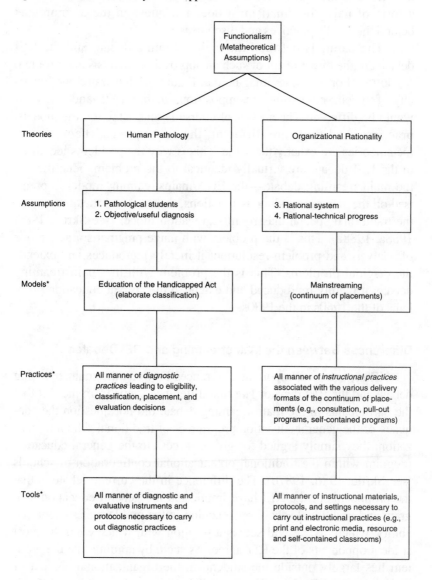

*The models, practices, and tools illustrated here are those that emerged *after* 1975. If the figure depicted the hierarchy of presuppositions *before* 1975, the models, practices, and tools would be (more or less) different, but the assumptions, theories, and metatheories would be the same.

efficacy of its models, practices, and tools but *not* on its assumptions, theories, and metatheories. As such, the special education discourse is a form of naive pragmatism; it does not question the assumptions behind the field's practices and discourses.

The parallels between the mainstreaming debate and the REI debate are the direct result of such an approach to analysis and problem resolution. For example, imagine that Figure 3.1 illustrated the hierarchy of special education presuppositions *before* 1975 and ask what would be different. The answer of course is that, although the models, practices, and tools are different, the assumptions, theories, and metatheories are exactly the same. This is why the problems identified in the REI debate are virtually identical to the problems identified in the mainstreaming debate—the EHA/mainstreaming model is premised on the same grounding assumptions, theories, and metatheories as the traditional special classroom/segregation model (see Skrtic, 1986, 1988a, 1988b). This is the problem with naive pragmatism as a mode of analysis and problem resolution; it merely reproduces and extends the original problems. This is the problem with the mainstreaming debate; it merely reproduced and extended the special education problems of the 1960s in the 1980s.

### Differences Between the Mainstreaming and REI Debates

There are two important differences between the mainstreaming debate and the REI debate. The first difference stems from the fact that the participants in the mainstreaming debate did not question the adequacy of the general education program or of traditional school organization; they simply argued for greater access to the general education program within the traditional organizational configuration of schools (see Skrtic, 1986, 1987b). The difference in the current debate is that the proponents of the REI have implicated the general education program and traditional school organization in the problem of student disability, which, as we will see, is a position with which even the most strident opponents of the REI agree. As such, by arguing that the problem lies largely outside the student, in the organizational context of schooling, the REI debate is an *implicit* critique of special education's grounding assumptions. Nevertheless, the participants in the REI debate do not explicitly recognize the connection between practices and assumptions. Thus, in the final analysis the REI debate also is a form of naive pragmatism, and, as a result, neither the proposals of the REI proponents nor the counterproposals of the opponents solve the problems they identify. As such, we will see in Part Three that, if the REI debate continues on its acritical trajectory, it will reproduce and extend the special education problems of the 1980s in the 1990s and beyond.

The second difference between the mainstreaming and REI debates is that in the 1960s the field of special education had no meaningful way to interpret the negative empirical evidence on the ethics and efficacy of its practices, and thus no way to conceptualize the sources of the problems associated with the special classroom model or how to address them, other than by defaulting implicitly to its traditional assumptions. In the end, the mainstreaming/EHA model (and its associated practices and tools) emerged as the solution to these problems, not because it was conceptually sound but because, morally and politically, it was the right thing to do (Ballard-Campbell & Semmel, 1981; Biklen, 1985; Skrtic, 1986).

Today, however, an array of conceptual resources is available for interpreting the ethics and efficacy of special education practices in a variety of ways. This is so because an alternative, *theoretical discourse* has emerged within the field, one that appropriates theoretical insights from the social sciences and applies them to the problem of special education (e.g., Bogdan & Knoll, 1988; Carrier, 1983; Ferguson, 1987; Heshusius, 1982, 1986; Iano, 1986, 1987; Poplin, 1984, 1987; Sigmon, 1987; Skrtic, 1986, 1988b, in press a; Sleeter, 1986; Tomlinson, 1982, in press). Whereas the REI debate is an *empirical* critique of the field's current *practices*, the alternative discourse is a *theoretical* critique of its grounding *assumptions*.

### The Theoretical Discourse and the REI Debate

Although theoretical criticism of special education from outside the field has been available for some time (e.g., Gould, 1982; Farber, 1968; Goffman, 1961; Scott, 1969; Szasz, 1961), it has had virtually no effect on the field's practices (Bogdan & Kugelmass, 1984) or on its assumptions (Skrtic, 1986, 1988a). The advantage of a theoretical discourse *within* the field is that it is more difficult for the special education community to ignore and thus, in principle, more likely to have an impact on its practices and assumptions. But, even though the internal theoretical discourse has begun to capture the imagination of some members of the special education community (Skrtic, in press a), others in the field have attacked it as ill informed, misleading, and unscientific, at best (e.g., Lloyd, 1987; Simpson & Eaves, 1985; Ulman & Rosenberg, 1986), and rude, ideological, and dangerous, at worst (Carnine, 1987; Forness & Kavale, 1987; Kavale & Forness, 1987). As we will see in chapters 4 and 5, such reactions are completely understandable; they are typical of professionals who are confronted with theoretical criticism of their practices. What I would like to stress here, however, is the significance of the fact that the REI debate and the alternative discourse have emerged together.

The REI debate is important in this regard because it is empirical. As such, it questions special education practices in the language of the field and in terms of its own standards, which makes it comprehensible to members of the special education community, and thus difficult for them to ignore. But, because empirical data can be interpreted in a variety of ways, depending on the explicit or implicit assumptions, theories, and metatheories of the interpreter (see Lincoln & Guba, 1985), the atheoretical nature of the field means that it must default conceptually to its grounding assumptions to interpret the meaning of the empirical evidence put forth in the REI debate. Without an explicit theory, the proponents of the REI, like the proponents of mainstreaming before them, ultimately must base their reform proposals on the same unquestioned assumptions that have grounded the field historically. Thus, as we will see in chapter 9, the REI reform proposals reproduce and extend the same problems they propose to solve, in the same way that the EHA and mainstreaming reproduced and extended the problems associated with the special classroom approach.

The significance of the theoretical discourse is that it is critical. It is critical in that it explicitly questions the field's unquestioned assumptions and proposes a number of explicit alternative theories for grounding the field's practices. The advantage of such an approach is that it recognizes that the field's practices are grounded in its unquestioned assumptions, and that altering practices in ways that do not reproduce and extend current problems will require altering the assumptions upon which current practices are based. A major problem with the alternative discourse, however, is that its alternative theoretical languages are not immediately comprehensible to the members of the special education community, which minimizes the potential impact of its theoretical insights on the field. As we have seen, such insights tend to be ignored, if they come from outsiders, or condemned, if they come from insiders.

Thus, whereas the REI debate is *comprehensible* but acritical, the theoretical discourse is *critical* but largely incomprehensible to the field. Nevertheless, by combining the empirical evidence of the REI debate and the critical insights of the theoretical discourse, the potential exists for an expanded discourse in special education that is both *critical* and *comprehensible* to the field. The significance of such an expanded discourse is that it would make available for theoretical and critical analysis the empirical evidence produced by the field itself, according to its traditional assumptions and standards and in its traditional language.

An expanded discourse of this sort is necessary, but it is not sufficient. Although the theoretical discourse is *critical* (because it questions the field's grounding assumptions and provides a number of alternative theories for interpreting data and conceptualizing solutions), it is not *pragmatic* because it does not solve the problem of choosing among the various theories that it puts forth. I will return to this discussion in chapters 5 and 6. At this point it is sufficient to say that, to be critical *and* pragmatic, the expanded discourse not only must look behind practices to expose the assumptions and theories in which they are grounded but also must look behind the theories themselves. It must question the metatheoretical assumptions in which the various theories are grounded; it must be critical and pragmatic at the *metatheoretical* level, which, of course, is precisely what critical pragmatism is meant to do.

In the next section I look behind the REI debate by considering the REI proponents' and opponents' empirical arguments about special education practices and models in terms of their implications for the unquestioned assumptions, theories, and metatheories in which these practices and models are grounded. The section begins with some background information on the REI debate and then proceeds to a critical analysis of the arguments put forth by both sides in the debate relative to the two points of controversy: the ethics and efficacy of current special education practices, and the feasibility of the REI reform proposals.

## THE REGULAR EDUCATION INITIATIVE DEBATE

Hallahan, Kauffman, Lloyd, and McKinney (1988), key opponents of the REI, argue that the concept first appeared in a paper by Reynolds and Wang (1981), which, in revised form (Wang, Reynolds, & Walberg, 1985, 1986) subsequently received formal recognition from Madeleine Will (1986a; cf. 1985, 1986b), Assistant Secretary for the Office of Special Education and Rehabilitative Services (OSERS) in the Reagan Administration. This is an important connection because, in subsequent criticism of the REI, a major argument has been that it is "entirely consistent with Reagan-Bush policies aimed at decreasing federal support for education, including the education of vulnerable children and youth" (Kauffman, 1989a, p. 7; Kauffman, 1989b). Although Wang (Wang & Walberg, 1988), a key proponent of the REI, agreed that Will (1986a) provided the OSERS policy statement for the REI, she argued that the REI itself is grounded in empirical evidence on the inadequacies of the current system contained in three major studies of contemporary practices (i.e., Heller et al., 1982; Hobbs, 1975, 1980; Wang et al., 1987a).

Thus, opponents of the REI tend to characterize it as a political phenomenon grounded in conservative ideology, whereas proponents characterize it as a rational phenomenon grounded in empirical research. Nevertheless, as we will see below, it is more accurate to think of it as being grounded in the liberal ideology of progressive inclusion—that is, in the conviction of Maynard Reynolds, another key proponent of the REI, that the entire history of special education is (and should continue to be) one of incremental progress toward more socially inclusive instructional placements for students with disabilities (see Reynolds & Rosen, 1976; Reynolds & Birch, 1977).

Even though the REI is generally thought of as a 1980s phenomenon, Reynolds provided the first criticism of the EHA and mainstreaming, in the language of what was to become the REI, in November, 1976 (Reynolds, 1976; cf. Reynolds & Birch, 1977), barely a year after the EHA had been signed into law, and nearly 2 years before it was to become fully effective. In his 1976 paper, Reynolds rejected his own notion of the "continuum of placements," the source of the pull-out logic that underwrites mainstreaming (Reynolds, 1962; see also Deno, 1970), in favor of making "regular classrooms . . . more diverse educational environments, [thus reducing] the need to . . . use separate . . . educational environments" (1976, p. 8). He proposed that such an approach was possible "through the redistribution of resources and energies, through training, and, finally, through the redistribution of students" (1976, p. 18). Thus, although there most likely is a moment of truth in both the opponents' and proponents' characterizations of the motivation behind the REI, Reynolds actually formulated the concept before either the empirical data were available or the conservative ideology held much sway in Washington.

### Literature and Participants

Besides Will's (1984, 1985, 1986a, 1986b) statements on or related to the REI, and several papers that attempt to place the REI in perspective (e.g., Davis, 1989; Davis & McCaul, 1988; Lieberman, 1984, 1988; Sapon-Shevin, 1988; Skrtic, 1987b, 1988b), the vast majority of literature promoting the REI has been produced by four teams of writers whose names have become synonymous with the concept. These include: (a) Maynard Reynolds and Margaret Wang (Reynolds, 1988; Reynolds & Wang, 1981, 1983; Reynolds, Wang, & Walberg, 1987; Wang, 1981, 1988, 1989a, 1989b; Wang & Reynolds, 1985, 1986; Wang, Reynolds, & Walberg, 1985, 1986, 1987a, 1987b, 1988, 1989; Wang & Walberg, 1988); (b) M. Stephen Lilly and Marleen Pugach (Lilly, 1986, 1987, 1989; Pugach & Lilly, 1984); (c) Susan Stainback and William Stainback (Stainback & Stainback, 1984b, 1985a, 1985b, 1987a, 1987b, 1989; Stainback, Stainback, Courtnage, & Jaben, 1985; Stainback, Stainback, & Forest, 1989); and (d) Alan Gartner and Dorothy Kerzner Lipsky (Gartner, 1986; Gartner & Lipsky, 1987, 1989a, 1989b; Lipsky & Gartner, 1987, 1989a, 1989b).

In this literature the proponents of the REI present two lines of argument: one against the current special education system, and one for certain reforms in general education and special education that are intended to correct the situation. The arguments against the current system address problems related to the practices and tools associated with the elaborate classification process required by the EHA model, which I will refer to as *diagnostic practices,* as well as problems related to the practices and tools associated with the pull-out approach implied by the mainstreaming model, which I will refer to as *instructional practices.* In this criticism, all four teams of REI proponents refer, more or less, to a common body of EHA implementation research, virtually all of which is reviewed, synthesized, or cited in Wang et al. (1987a), Gartner and Lipsky (1987), and Lipsky and Gartner (1989a). Although each of the REI reform proposals is somewhat unique, all of the REI proponents agree that the diagnostic and instructional practices associated with the EHA and mainstreaming models are fundamentally flawed, particularly for students who are classified as mildly handicapped who, depending on which categories of disability are included in the calculation, represent from 68% to 90% of the 4.5 million students currently served under the law.

The 68% figure includes students classified as mentally retarded, emotionally disturbed, and learning disabled (USDE, 1988). When students with mild forms of speech and language problems and students with physical and sensory impairments (which are not accompanied by other severely disabling conditions) are included in the calculation (see Reynolds & Lakin, 1987), estimates of the proportion of students who are considered mildly handicapped range from 75% to 90% of those students classified as handicapped in school (Algozzine & Korinek, 1985; Shepard, 1987; Wang et al., 1989). Overall, the 4.5 million figure represents an increase of about 20% in the total number of students identified as handicapped since 1976–77. Much of this increase has resulted from increases in the number of students identified as learning disabled, a classification which currently represents more than 43% of all students identified as handicapped, and which, despite attempts to tighten eligibility criteria, has increased more than 140% since 1977 (Gerber & Levine-Donnerstein, 1989).

The first published reactions to the REI (Lieberman, 1985; Mesinger, 1985) were decidedly negative but focused exclusively on one REI position paper (i.e., Stainback & Stainback, 1984). These reactions were followed by others from three formal or informal subgroups within the field that, although sensitive to current problems and generally supportive of reform, merely called for more information (Teacher Education Division, Council for Exceptional Children, 1986, 1987), proposed a mechanism for interpreting information and building a consensus (Skrtic, 1987a), and specified several preconditions of reform (Heller & Schilit, 1987). Neither these reactions nor those of other individuals who have criticized the REI in part (e.g., Davis, 1989; Davis & McCaul, 1988; Lieberman, 1984, 1988; Sapon-Shevin, 1988; Skrtic, 1987b, 1988b) or in whole (e.g., Vergason & Anderegg, 1989) have had much of an impact on the course of events.

A full-blown controversy developed in 1988 when the *Journal of Learning Disabilities (JLD)* published a *tour de force* response to the REI by several leading figures in the three mild disability subfields of mental retardation, emotional disturbance, and learning disabilities.

Since then, the controversy over the REI has been fueled largely by a series of articles and rebuttals written by the four teams of REI proponents and some of the authors of the *JLD* reaction papers. The major articles opposing (to one degree or another) the REI include: (a) Braaten, Kauffman, Braaten, Polsgrove, and Nelson (1988); (b) Bryan, Bay, and Donahue (1988); (c) Council for Children with Behavioral Disorders (CCBD) (1989); (d) Gerber (1988a, 1988b); (e) Hallahan, Kauffman, Lloyd, and McKinney (1988); (f) Hallahan, Keller, McKinney, Lloyd, and Bryan (1988); (g) Kauffman (1988, 1989a, 1989b); (h) Kauffman, Gerber, and Semmel (1988); (i) Keogh (1988); (j) Lloyd, Crowley, Kohler, and Strain (1988); (k) McKinney and Hocutt (1988); and (l) Schumaker and Deshler (1988). The controversial nature of the REI debate and the degree to which it has divided the field is clear in some of the more recent encounters in the literature.

In these encounters the REI advocates have characterized the opponents as segregationists (Wang & Walberg, 1988) and compared the current system of special education to slavery (Stainback & Stainback, 1987b) and apartheid (Lipsky & Gartner, 1987). The REI opponents have responded by characterizing the proponents as politically naive liberals and the REI as the Reagan-Bush "trickle-down theory of education of the hard-to-teach" (Kauffman, 1989b, p. 256). When one cuts through this rhetoric, however, the REI debate centers on two sets of issues: the ethics and efficacy of the diagnostic and instructional practices associated with the EHA and mainstreaming, on one hand, and the wisdom and feasibility of the REI reform proposals, on the other. The next section addresses the issue of the adequacy of the current system; the following one addresses the issue of the feasibility of the REI reform proposals.

## Adequacy of the Current System

In this section the arguments on both sides of the REI debate relative to the adequacy of current models and practices are considered in terms of special education's four unquestioned assumptions, which are recast below in the form of questions. By looking behind the surface arguments over the meaning of empirical evidence, the REI debate becomes an *implicit* debate over special education's four grounding assumptions, the theories of human pathology and organizational rationality, and ultimately the metatheoretical perspective of functionalism, all of which underwrite and legitimize special education as a professional practice.[2]

As noted in chapter 2, my approach to analysis is deconstruction. On one level, I want to deconstruct the text of the REI *debate* by exposing its internal contradictions, inconsistencies, and silences. The point of such an analysis, however, and thus the broader significance of the current controversy in special education, is that, given a critical reading, the REI debate deconstructs the *professional practice* of special education by exposing its contradictions, inconsistencies, silences, and general incompleteness relative to the assumptions, theories, and metatheories in which it is grounded. The purpose of deconstructing special education as a professional practice is to show that the field's grounding assumptions are inadequate and in need of reappraisal (chapter 3), that alternative assumptions are desirable and possible (chapters 4–6), and, most important, that choosing grounding assumptions is a political and moral act with implications for ethical practice and a just society.

### Are Mild Disabilities Pathological?

Although at times the REI debate has been quite heated, there is virtually no disagreement on this point.[3] The REI proponents and opponents agree that, for some students, the mildly handicapped designation is an objective distinction based on a pathology, but that, because of a number of definitional and measurement problems, as well as problems related to the will or capacity of teachers and schools to accommodate student diversity, many students identified as mildly handicapped are not truly disabled in the pathological sense—a situation that is particularly true for students identified as learning disabled. Moreover, both sides in the debate agree that additional students in school remain unidentified and thus unserved, some who have mild pathological disabilities and others who do not but nonetheless require assistance.[4] On the related matter of the attribution of student failure, the REI opponents and proponents agree that an exclusively "student-deficit" orientation is inappropriate. Although some of the REI opponents argue that the proponents lean too far toward an exclusively "teacher-deficit" orientation (Kauffman et al., 1988; Keogh, 1988), most of the REI proponents clearly recognize the student's responsibility in the learning process (e.g., see Gartner, 1986; Wang & Peverly, 1987).

Although the REI proponents recognize that many students, including those who have or are thought to have mild disabilities, present difficult problems for classroom teachers, their point is simply that neither the general education system nor the special education system is sufficiently adaptable to accommodate the individual needs of these students (e.g., Wang et al., 1986, 1987a; Stainback & Stainback, 1984b, Stainback et al., 1989; Gartner & Lipsky, 1987; Lipsky & Gartner, 1989a, 1989b), a point with which most REI opponents agree, implicitly or explicitly (see Bryan et al., 1988; Kauffman, 1988; Kauffman et al., 1988; Keogh, 1988). A further argument of the REI proponents relative to the nonadaptability of the general education system is that the existence of the special education system is a barrier to developing a responsive capacity within general education, both in public schools and in teacher education (see Lilly, 1986, 1989; Pugach, 1988; Pugach & Lilly, 1984; Reynolds, 1988).[5]

## Is Diagnosis Objective and Useful?

The REI proponents argue that differential diagnosis does not result in objective distinctions, either between disabled and nondisabled students or among the three mild disability categories (e.g., Wang et al., 1986, 1987a; Stainback & Stainback, 1984b; Gartner & Lipsky, 1987). As noted above, the REI opponents generally agree that distinctions between disabled and nondisabled students are not objective. Moreover, they agree that distinctions among the three mild disability categories are not objective because, in addition to measurement and definitional problems, the decision-making process in schools is "embedded in a powerful economic, political, and philosophical network" (Keogh, 1988, p. 20; see also CCBD, 1989; Gerber & Semmel, 1984; Hallahan & Kauffman, 1977; Kauffman, 1988).

On the matter of the utility of differential diagnosis, the REI proponents argue that there are no instructionally relevant reasons for distinguishing between disabled and nondisabled students, or among the three mild disability classifications. Their point is that all students have unique learning needs and, moreover, that students in the three mild disability classifications, as well as those in the other special needs classifications (e.g., Chapter 1, bilingual education, migrant education, remedial education), often can be taught using similar instructional methods (Lipsky & Gartner, 1989a; Reynolds et al., 1987; Stainback &

Stainback, 1984b, 1989; Wang et al., 1986, 1987a; Wang, 1989a, 1989b). Here, too, most of the REI opponents agree, admitting that "effective instructional and management procedures will be substantially the same for nonhandicapped and most mildly handicapped students" (Kauffman et al., 1988, p. 8; Gerber, 1987; cf. Hallahan & Kauffman, 1977).

The only REI opponent who makes a case for the potential instructional relevance of differential diagnosis considers it to be an empirical question which, if answered in the negative, should signal discontinuance of the practice of differential diagnosis and the categorical approach to special education (Keogh, 1988). Although Bryan et al. (1988, p. 25) do not make an explicit argument for the instructional relevance of differential diagnosis, by arguing that "one cannot assume that any two learning disabled children would be any more similar than a learning disabled child and a normally achieving child, or a normally achieving child and an underachieving child," they actually make an implicit argument against the instructional utility of differential diagnosis and thus implicitly agree with the REI proponents' position that all students have unique learning needs and interests, even those within the traditional mild disability categories.

## Is Special Education a Rational System?

The REI proponents argue that the only rational justification for the existence of the special education system is that it confers *instructional* benefit on students who are designated handicapped (Lilly, 1986; Lipsky & Gartner, 1987; Reynolds, 1988; Reynold et al., 1987; Stainback & Stainback, 1984b; Wang et al., 1987a), a position with which the REI opponents agree (e.g., Kauffman et al., 1988; Keogh, 1988). On the basis of this justification, the REI proponents argue that special education is not a rational system. They believe that, given the weak effects of special education instructional interventions and the social costs of labeling, special education is, at best, no better than simply permitting most students to remain unidentified in regular classrooms and, at worst, far less effective than regular classroom placement in conjunction with appropriate in-class support services (e.g., Lipsky & Gartner, 1987, 1989a; Pugach & Lilly, 1984; Stainback & Stainback, 1984b; Wang et al., 1987a).

None of the REI opponents argue that the handicapped designation has been shown to lead to direct *instructional* benefit. In fact, there is general agreement among them that the instructional effectiveness of special eduction interventions has not been demonstrated (see Hallahan, Keller, McKinney, Lloyd, & Bryan, 1988; Keogh, 1988).[6] Nevertheless, some of the REI opponents argue that the handicapped designation is beneficial in a *political* sense. That is, they justify the current system of special education on the political grounds that it targets resources and personnel to designated students. Such targeting, they argue, is essential if these students are to receive instructional assistance in the context of the resource allocation process in schools (CCBD, 1989; Kauffman, 1988; Kauffman et al., 1988). Of course, these same authors agree that to be justifiable, the special education system must confer instructional benefit on designated students. Moreover, they agree with their fellow REI opponents that special education interventions do not confer such benefits. Therefore, in effect they are saying that, although special education is not an instructionally rational system in its current form, it is a politically rational system because the nonadaptability and political inequity of the general education system make the pull-out logic of mainstreaming and the targeting strategy of the EHA absolute necessities if designated students are to receive instructional assistance in school, even though the assistance they receive does not appear to be effective.

As we will see below, in response to the question of the nature of progress, the REI opponents argue that the diagnostic and instructional practices of the current system can be improved incrementally through additional research and development. Thus, the opponents' response to the question of the rationality of the special education system cannot be separated from their response to the question of the nature of progress in the field. In effect, by linking the two responses they are saying that, although special education is not an instructionally rational system *at present*, it is politically rational, and, moreover, that it can be rendered instructionally rational *in the future*, given the assumption of the possibility of rational-technical progress. Thus, on the weight of the political argument, let us say that the REI opponents are arguing that special education *is* an instructionally rational system, given the caveat that, to be rational in an instructional sense, rational-technical progress *must* be possible.[7]

As for the question of whether special education is a rationally coordinated system of services, the REI proponents argue that it is neither coordinated with the general education system nor with the other special needs programs. Rather than a rationally coordinated system, they characterize the entire special needs enterprise, including the special education system, in terms of disjointed incrementalism—a collection of disjointed programs, each with its own clients, personnel, administrators, budget, and regulations, which have been added to schools incrementally over time (Reynolds & Birch, 1977; Reynolds & Wang, 1983; Reynolds et al., 1987; Wang et al., 1985, 1986). Although the REI opponents who address the coordination issue agree that coordination is lacking, they consider the lack of coordination to be an unavoidable outcome of the *politically* essential targeting strategy that is fundamental to the very notion of categorical programs (Kauffman et al., 1988).

### Is Progress Rational and Technical?

This question asks whether progress can be made *under the current system* through incremental improvements in the diagnostic practices required by the EHA and in the instructional practices implied by mainstreaming. The REI proponents argue that both types of practices within the current system are fundamentally flawed and thus cannot and should not be salvaged; the entire system must be replaced through a fundamental restructuring of the special education and general education systems, which is an argument against the possibility of rational-technical change (see Lilly, 1986; Lipsky & Gartner, 1987, 1989a; Pugach & Lilly, 1984; Reynolds et al., 1987; Stainback & Stainback, 1984b; Stainback et al., 1989).

Although the REI opponents recognize that the current system has serious problems, they believe that incremental progress is possible through additional research and development on special education diagnostic and instructional practices while maintaining the current system, including the pull-out approach of mainstreaming (see Braaten et al., 1988; Bryan et al., 1988; CCBD, 1989; Hallahan, Keller, McKinney, Lloyd, & Bryan, 1988; Kauffman et al., 1988; Kauffman, 1988; Keogh, 1988; Lloyd et al., 1988). This, of course, is an argument for the possibility of rational-technical change.

### Summary: Adequacy of Current System

The REI proponents and opponents agree that most mild disabilities are not pathological and that the mildly handicapped designation is neither objective nor useful. However, their disagreement over the rationality of the special education system and the nature of progress has resulted in total disagreement about an appropriate course of ameliorative action. Given the negative evidence on the ethics and efficacy of special education practices *and* the nonadaptability of the general education system, the REI proponents believe that the special education diagnostic and instructional practices associated with the EHA and mainstreaming models should be eliminated. As a replacement, they propose a new system in which all or most students (see below) are eligible for in-class assistance, which is to be created by restructuring the current general education and special education systems into a single adaptable system. Given the same negative evidence on the ethics and efficacy of special education practices, however, the REI opponents believe that the diagnostic and instructional practices of the EHA and mainstreaming models should be retained for political purposes, *given* the nonadaptability and political inequity of the general education system. And, because they recognize the inadequacies of the current system, they propose to improve it incrementally through additional research and development. Thus, because the proponents and opponents agree that the current system has serious problems that must be resolved, the REI debate turns on the question of the nature of school organizations and how best to go about changing them.

Table 3.1 summarizes my critical reading of the REI debate to this point. When the arguments put forth in the REI debate are read critically—from the perspective of their implications for special education's grounding assumptions, theories, and metatheories—both sides in the debate reject the first two grounding assumptions and thus reject the theory of human pathology as an explanation for school failure. With regard to the third assumption, both sides agree that special education is neither rationally conceived nor rationally coordinated in an instructional sense. Nevertheless, whereas on the basis of this assessment the REI proponents reject the current system, the REI opponents retain it on the grounds that it is a politically rational system that can be rendered instructionally rational in the future.

Finally, there is no doubt where the REI proponents and opponents stand on the question of whether progress in special education is rational and technical—that is, whether the current system can be improved incrementally through research and development or whether it must be replaced fundamentally through restructuring. The REI proponents argue that the current special education system must be

**Table 3.1**

Summary of the Critical Reading of the REI Debate on the Adequacy of the Current System

| Grounding Assumptions | Proponents Reject | Proponents Retain | Opponents Reject | Opponents Retain | Guiding Theories | Proponents Reject | Proponents Retain | Opponents Reject | Opponents Retain | Metatheoretical Perspective | Proponents Reject | Proponents Retain | Opponents Reject | Opponents Retain |
|---|---|---|---|---|---|---|---|---|---|---|---|---|---|---|
| 1. Pathological students | X | | X | | 1. Human Pathology | X | | X | | Functionalism | | | | |
| 2. Objective/useful diagnosis | X | | X | | | | | | | | | | | |
| 3. Rational system | X | | | X* | 2. Organizational Rationality | X | | | X | | | | | |
| 4. Rational-technical progress | X | | | X | | | | | | | | | | |

*The REI opponents agree that, *at present*, special education is not an *instructionally* rational system, but they argue that (a) it is a *politically* rational system at present, and (b) it can be rendered instructionally rational *in the future* through rational-technical improvements.

replaced and thus implicitly reject the fourth grounding assumption, whereas the opponents argue that the current system can be improved incrementally and thus retain it.

For the REI proponents, the rejection of the third and fourth grounding assumptions, of course, means that they reject the theory of organizational rationality. And, given that they reject the first two grounding assumptions, and thus the theory of human pathology, the REI proponents reject the metatheoretical perspective of functionalism. As such, given their rejection of the EHA and mainstreaming models and their associated diagnostic and instructional practices, the REI proponents reject the entire hierarchy of presuppositions that guides and shapes special education practices and discourses. Thus, on the basis of my critical reading of their empirical analysis of the current system of special education, the REI proponents call into question the very functionalist conceptualization of special education and student disability that underwrites the field.

Although the REI opponents reject special education's first two grounding assumptions and thus the theory of human pathology, they retain the third and fourth assumptions and thus retain the theory of organizational rationality. This, of course, means that, in the final analysis, they retain the metatheoretical perspective of functionalism. True to the functionalist outlook, the REI opponents, in effect, are saying that, although the diagnostic and instructional practices of the EHA and mainstreaming may not be effective, the best course of action, given the political inevitabilities of schooling, is to maintain the EHA and mainstreaming models and work toward improving special education practices incrementally through research and development. The fact that this is a functionalist argument, however, does not mean that it should be discredited. On the contrary, given the assumptions of functionalism, it is a politically astute argument and, as such, cannot and should not be ignored, which is a matter I will return to in Part Three of the book. For now, let us continue the discussion of the implications of the REI debate for special education's four grounding assumptions by considering the actual REI proposals and the opponents' reactions to them.

## The Feasibility of the REI Proposals

The REI proposals and the opponents' reactions are presented separately below, followed by a summary of my critical reading of the

REI debate and its implications for special education as a professional practice. At this point in the book, I am interested in analyzing the *arguments* for and against the REI proposals relative to their implications for special education's grounding assumptions and presuppositions, and not in analyzing the REI *proposals* themselves. I will reserve my analysis of the REI proposals for Part Three, in which I provide a critical reading of the EHA and the REI proposals from an organizational perspective.

## The REI Proposals

The reform proposals of the four teams of REI proponents are considered here in terms of (a) the students who are to be integrated into the new system and (b) the nature of this system and the manner in which it is to be created.

*Who all is to be integrated?* Although each of the reform proposals put forth by the four teams of REI proponents is unique, they all call for eliminating the special education classification system required by the EHA and the pull-out approach implied by mainstreaming, and restructuring the separate general and special education systems into a new system in which "all students" are eligible for in-class assistance.[8] Although the four teams generally agree that the restructured system should be "flexible, supple and responsive" (Lipsky & Gartner, 1987, p. 72), a "totally adaptive system" (Reynolds & Wang, 1983, p. 199) in which professionals personalize instruction through "group problem solving . . . shared responsibility, and . . . negotiation" (Pugach & Lilly, 1984, p. 52), they disagree on the definition of "all students." In fact, this is the issue that separates the four teams of REI advocates into two camps.

The Gartner and Lipsky and the Stainback and Stainback teams have distanced themselves from the REI concept, noting that, although it has resulted in some positive momentum for reform, ultimately it is lacking. For Gartner and Lipsky (1989a), it is merely "blending at the margin" (p. 271), because ultimately it maintains two separate systems. For Stainback and Stainback (1989), it is too restrictive because it "does not address the need to include in regular classrooms and regular education those students labeled severely and profoundly handicapped" (p. 43).

Although all of the REI proponents believe that the restructured system should provide in-class assistance for all students currently served in compensatory and remedial education programs, as well as every other student who needs help in school but is not targeted for it, they differ with respect to which students currently classified as handicapped under the EHA should be served in this manner. The Lilly and Pugach proposal is the least inclusive; in addition to the students noted above, it includes only "the vast majority of students [currently] served as 'mildly handicapped'" (Pugach & Lilly, 1984, p. 53). Their approach not only excludes students with moderate, severe, and profound disabilities, who, according to the proposal, would be taught by special educators in separate settings within regular school buildings, but also excludes students classified as mildly handicapped who have "developmental learning disabilities" (cf. Kirk & Chalfant, 1983). The Reynolds and Wang proposal is somewhat more inclusive in that it includes "most students with special learning needs" (Wang et al., 1985, p. 13; Reynolds & Wang, 1983). It reserves the option of separate settings for some students, presumably those with severe and profound disabilities, because Reynolds and Wang believe that "surely there will be occasions to remove some students for instruction in special settings" (1985, p. 13).

The Gartner and Lipsky proposal includes all students currently served under each EHA classification except students with the most severely and profoundly handicapping conditions, who would receive their primary instruction in separate classrooms in regular, age-appropriate school buildings, and would be provided with "structured opportunities for regular and sustained interactions [with] nondisabled students . . . [and] participation . . . in all nonacademic activities of the school" (Gartner & Lipsky, 1987, p. 386; cf. Sailor, 1989; Sailor et al., 1986). Finally, in what is the most inclusive proposal, Stainback and Stainback argue for the integration of all students, including those with the most severely and profoundly disabling conditions, while recognizing the need to group students "in some instances, into specific courses and classes according to their instructional needs" (Stainback & Stainback, 1984b, p. 108; Stainback et al., 1989).

*What all is to be merged?* Although the strategy for creating the adaptable classrooms necessary to implement the REI proposals is most often characterized as a merger of the general education and special education systems, only the Stainback and Stainback and the Gartner and Lipsky proposals actually call for a merger of the two systems at the classroom level.[9] The Reynolds and Wang and the Lilly and

Pugach proposals call for a merger of instructional support personnel above the classroom level.

Reynolds and Wang (1983) propose a two-step merger: first, among the three traditional mild disability categories, forming "a 'generic' or noncategorical base," and then between the merged special education programs and the "other compensatory services that are provided for disadvantaged, bilingual, migrant, low-English proficiency, or other children with special needs" (p. 206). Supported by paraprofessionals, these generic specialists form a "school-based, instructional and administrative support [team]" that works "mostly in the regular classrooms . . . to supply technical and administrative support to regular classroom teachers" (p. 206). Above the regular classroom teachers and generic specialists, they propose a merger of district-level consultants who would provide the classroom teachers and generic specialists with consultation and training on generic topics (see also Wang et al., 1985). Although they do not provide a great deal of detail on the matter, it appears that Reynolds and Wang also are proposing two additional mergers: one among teacher education faculty members who would prepare personnel for the generic specialist and consultant roles (but not for the regular classroom teacher role), and one among general education and special education applied researchers at universities and research and development centers.

In the Lilly and Pugach proposal, merger represents the "'blending' of special and general education support service programs *under the rubric of general education*" (Lilly, 1986, p. 10). By "blending" they mean an actual "divestiture in special education," a *"return to regular education* of the responsibility for provision of many [support] services heretofore considered to be firmly within the boundaries of special education" (Lilly, in press, p. 14; cited in Pugach & Lilly, 1984, p. 50). Under this plan, special education personnel who currently provide resource and support services "for the mildly handicapped, and primarily for the learning disabled" (Pugach & Lilly, 1984, p. 54) would be merged into the ranks of the traditional general education support service of remedial education. Although they recognize the need for supportive services for children with learning and behavior problems, Lilly and Pugach argue for a single, coordinated system of support services based in general education, rather than the current array of special programs, on the grounds that such an arrangement will be quicker to respond to the needs of students and teachers, less stigmatizing, and more efficient (Lilly, 1986; Pugach & Lilly, 1984).

The merger of remedial education and special education at the school site requires, at the level of teacher education, the "meshing of what is now special education for the mildly handicapped [in departments of special education] with what are currently departments of elementary and secondary education or curriculum and instruction" (Pugach & Lilly, 1984, p. 53). And "this is not simply a matter of renegotiating an existing relationship, but means enacting fundamental change in which former special [education teacher] educators and general [education] teacher educators share responsibility for providing instruction of the highest quality . . . for advanced preparation of support services specialists at the graduate level" (p. 54), as well as undergraduate instruction for persons in preparation for the role of classroom teacher.

Although these proposals modify the current notion of instructional support services by replacing the categorical pull-out approach with either a noncategorical or a remedial model of in-class support services, both of them retain the traditional notion of a classroom, in the sense of one teacher with primary responsibility for a group of students. The primary difference at the classroom level, in addition to the recommended use of what are characterized as more powerful instructional technologies, such as cooperative learning, curriculum-based assessment, peer tutoring, and adaptive learning,[10] is that students who would have been removed under the current system remain in the classroom on a full-time basis where they, their classroom teacher, and any other students who need assistance are provided with in-class support services.

Stainback and Stainback (1984b) argue for a merger of general and special education as a means of forming a "unified system" to replace the current "dual system" (p. 102), which they characterize as inefficient and, in any case, unnecessary. Although their proposal calls for merger at the classroom level, it actually merges general education and special education subject areas, not general and special education instructional programs or personnel. It calls for disbanding special education programs and integrating the residual personnel into the general education system according to instructional specializations. Each teacher in this system would have "a strong base in the teaching/learning process" (Stainback & Stainback, 1984b, p. 107) and a particular specialization in a traditional general education subject (e.g., science, reading, history) or special education subject (e.g., adaptive learning approaches, supported employment, or alternative communication systems), and each would work individually in a separate classroom (see also Stainback & Stainback, 1987a; Stainback et al., 1989).

As with the Reynolds and Wang and the Lilly and Pugach proposals, the merged or unified system proposed by Stainback and Stainback also requires a merger above the classroom level, at the support services and teacher education levels. It calls for disbanding special education programs at these levels as well, and integrating the residual personnel into the corresponding level of the general education system according to instructional specialization. Thus, current special education faculty members in teacher education would join elementary and secondary education faculties to prepare classroom teachers who have a particular specialization in a traditional general or special education subject area (Stainback & Stainback, 1987a).

At the support services level, resource personnel and consultants also would be organized according to traditional general and special education subject area specializations, which modifies the current categorical pull-out approach by replacing it with in-class subject area support services (Stainback & Stainback, 1984b, 1987a). As in the case of the other two support services models, this one also retains the traditional notion of a classroom, that is, one teacher and a group of students.

The Gartner and Lipsky proposal calls for a merged or unitary system in which education is "both one and special for all students" (Lipsky & Gartner, 1987, p. 73), which means completely abandoning a separate special education system for all students except those with the most severely and profoundly handicapping conditions, as noted above. Although originally they had characterized their merged system simply as one in which "curricular adaptations and individualized educational strategies" are augmented by "appropriate supports" (Gartner & Lipsky, 1987, p. 388), recently they revised their proposal by linking it explicitly with the excellence movement in general education, which, for them, is the effective schools movement. As such, their basic assertion is that, through broad adoption of the principles and practices identified in the effective schools research, "the education of students labeled as handicapped can be made effective" (Lipsky & Gartner, 1989a, p. 281), an assertion based on several interrelated arguments.

First, drawing on the work of Allington and McGill-Franzen (1989), which compares the students and practices of remedial and special education and finds little that is different, they argue that all students with special needs can learn effectively from the same pedagogy. Second, drawing on the findings of the effective schools research (Edmonds, 1979), as well as Lezotte's (1989) attempt to relate its findings to students labeled handicapped, they broaden their assertion about a common pedagogy to all students per se, and argue that this generic pedagogy is known and codified in the principles and practices contained in the research literature of the effective schools movement. Third, referring once more to Edmonds (1979) and Lezotte (1989), they argue that the principles and practices of effective schools pedagogy are replicable through school improvement programs. Next, by combining Edmonds' (1979) assertion that if some schools are effective, all schools can be effective, with Gilhool's (1976) parallel assertion relative to effective integration of students with disabilities, they argue that effective schools, and thus effective education for students labeled handicapped, is a matter of will and commitment on the part of schools and teachers. Finally, and somewhat ironically, given their assertion about will and commitment, they call for reshaping the EHA into a new mandate "that requires a unitary system [which] is 'special' for all students" (Lipsky & Gartner, 1989a, p. 282). That is, they call for transforming the EHA into "an effective schools act for all students" (1989a, p. 282).

## Reactions to the REI Proposals

The REI opponents argue against the possibility of the type of adaptable system proposed by the REI proponents on historical, practical, and political grounds. On the basis of these arguments, they conclude that students with special needs have not, are not, and simply cannot be accommodated in regular classrooms.

Kauffman (1988) argued that, historically, the creation of a separate system of special education was necessary to serve students who were forced out of a single general education system "in which most mildly handicapped students were not identified as such, one in which nearly all general educators were expected to teach nearly all students regardless of their characteristics" (p. 493). For him, nothing has changed in these general education classrooms and, thus, recreating a single general education system most likely will result in rediscovering the need for a separate special education system in the future (see also

CCBD, 1989). Keogh (1988) argued that, practically, it is a strange logic indeed that calls for the current general education system, which inadequately serves "regular" students, "to take over the educational responsibility for pupils it has already demonstrated it has failed" (p. 20). For her, something must change in the regular classroom; major reforms in general education would be required if it is to serve a broader range of students (see also Bryan et al., 1988).

Of the three arguments against the proposition of accommodating students with special needs in regular classrooms, the political argument of Kauffman et al. (1988; cf. Gerber, 1988b; Gerber & Semmel, 1985) is the most interesting and compelling. They argue that "teachers, whether in regular or special class environments, cannot escape the necessary choice between higher means [i.e., maximizing mean performance of the group by concentrating resources on the most able learners] and narrower variances [i.e., minimizing the variance in performance of the group by concentrating resources on the least able learners] as long as resources are scarce and students differ" (Gerber & Semmel, 1985, p. 19, cited in Kauffman et al., 1988, p. 10). This is true, they argue, "whenever a teacher instructs a group of students," except "when new resources are made available or more powerful instructional technologies are employed" (Kauffman et al., 1988, p. 10).

Although all three of these arguments are valid and important, they are not arguments against the REI proposals; they are implicit arguments against the 20th-century notion of a classroom. Kauffman's historical argument ignores the fact that the REI proponents are calling for a restructured general education system, one in which the classrooms are adaptable, and not a return to the traditional system. And, although Keogh's practical argument at least recognizes that accommodating students with special needs in regular classrooms will require a major reform of the general education system, it ignores the fact that this is precisely what the REI advocates are proposing.

Finally, although the political argument of Kauffman et al. is compelling, it ignores the fact that the availability of new resources and more powerful instructional technologies—the exact conditions that can narrow variances without negatively effecting class means, according to the argument itself—is precisely what the REI advocates are proposing. Thus, the political argument, like the historical and practical arguments, is not an argument against the REI proposals; implicitly, it is a very compelling argument against the traditional notion of a classroom. As such, by arguing that no teacher, whether in a general education or a special education setting, can escape the microeconomic implications of the resource allocation process inherent in a classroom, Kaufman et al. make a stronger case against the instructional rationality of the current system of special education than the REI proponents have made. Moreover, by arguing that the regular classroom has not changed historically, and that neither it nor the special classroom can change practically or politically, the REI opponents contradict their position on the possibility of rational-technical change, and thus their support for the fourth grounding assumption of special education.[11] Furthermore, given the inseparability of their arguments relative to the third and fourth assumptions, by reversing their position on the possibility of rational-technical change, they also reverse their position on the rationality of the special education system.

## THE REI DEBATE AND SPECIAL EDUCATION AS A PROFESSIONAL PRACTICE

In their arguments relative to the adequacy of the current special education system, the REI proponents reject all four of the field's grounding assumptions outright, and thus reject the theories of human pathology and organizational rationality and, ultimately, the metatheoretical perspective of functionalism. In their assessment of the current system, the REI opponents reject the first two assumptions but retain the last two, which means that they reject the theory of human pathology but retain the theory of organizational rationality and, ultimately, the metatheoretical perspective of functionalism. In their reaction to the REI reform proposals, however, the REI opponents reverse their position on the third and fourth assumptions and thus, in the end, reject them and the theory of organizational rationality. Given their rejection of the theory of human pathology, in the final analysis they, too, reject the metatheoretical perspective of functionalism (see Table 3.2).

Given that both sides in the REI debate explicitly recognize the inadequacy of current special education diagnostic and instructional tools, practices, and models, and the fact that, read critically, their arguments about an appropriate course of ameliorative action reject the field's grounding assumptions, guiding theories, and metatheoretical perspective, the empirical evidence and interpretive dialogue contained

# Table 3.2

Summary of the Critical Reading of the REI Debate on the Feasibility of the REI Reform Proposals

| Grounding Assumptions | Proponents | | Opponents | | Guiding Theories | Proponents | | Opponents | | Metatheoretical Perspective | Proponents | | Opponents | |
|---|---|---|---|---|---|---|---|---|---|---|---|---|---|---|
| | Reject | Retain | Reject | Retain | | Reject | Retain | Reject | Retain | | Reject | Retain | Reject | Retain |
| 1. Pathological students | X | | | X | Human Pathology | X | | X | | Functionalism | X | | X | |
| 2. Objective/useful diagnosis | X | | | X | | | | | | | | | | |
| 3. Rational system | X | | | X | Organizational Rationality | X | | X | | | | | | |
| 4. Rational-technical progress | X | | | X | | | | | | | | | | |

within the REI debate deconstruct special education as a professional practice. In turn, by deconstructing special education as a *professional* practice, the REI debate calls into question public education's *institutional* practice of special education and thus the 20th-century discourse on school failure, which ultimately provides the grounds for an immanent critique of public education itself.

Although a critical analysis of the REI debate provides grounds for a deconstruction of the institutional practice of special education and an immanent critique of public education, I will not rely on it alone for such purposes. In fact, among other things, Part Three of the book is devoted to a deconstruction of the institutional practice of special education and an immanent critique of public education from the perspective of school organization. What I want to do here, however, is to make one final point about the REI debate, both as a way to conclude this chapter and to foreshadow the remaining chapters in Part Two.

Although at this point in my analysis of the REI debate, the proponents and the opponents both appear to reject special education's guiding functionalist theories of human pathology and organizational rationality, we will see in Part Three that the restructuring proposals of the REI advocates, though they call for a new system, actually retain and elaborate the traditional organization of schools and employ a rational-technical approach to change. As such, they reverse their position on the third and fourth assumptions and thus retain the theory of organizational rationality.

Both sides in the REI debate reject the assumptions that mild disabilities are pathological and that diagnosis is objective and useful and thus reject the theory of human pathology. As we have seen, however, there is a great deal of confusion about the third and fourth assumptions. On one hand, opponents of the REI recognize that the current system is not instructionally rational and propose a rational-technical change strategy to improve it. But then they argue against the possibility of rational-technical change on the grounds that the system is nonadaptable. On the other hand, proponents of the REI recognize that the current system is not rational and propose to replace it with a different system on the grounds that it cannot be improved incrementally. But, in the end, they propose the same type of system and a rational-technical change strategy for implementing it. What is so troubling about this confusion surrounding the third and fourth assumptions, of course, is that the REI debate, and thus the legitimacy of special education as a professional practice in the 1990s and beyond, hangs on the question of the nature of school organization and adaptability, the very question about which there is so much uncertainty.

The arguments in the REI debate reject the theory of human pathology but are contradictory and inconsistent about the theory of organizational rationality because, as we know from chapter 2, human pathology is an *explicit* presupposition grounded in the field's disciplinary knowledge, whereas organizational rationality is an *implicit* presupposition grounded in a social norm. I will return to the question of organizational rationality in Part Three of the book. At this point, however, I want to focus my attention on the question of what led 20th-century special educators to believe in the theory of human pathology, an idea that seems so wrong today.

## NOTES

1. The assumptions listed in text are presented in the language of the special education discourse. The corresponding assumptions in the language of general education and educational administration (in an ideal-typical sense) are that: (a) school failure is a (psychologically or sociologically) pathological condition that students have, (b) differential diagnosis (identification by ability, need, interest, or some combination of these) is objective and useful, (c) special programming (homogeneous grouping in general education tracks and segregated and pull-out classrooms in special, compensatory, gifted, and remedial education) is a rationally conceived and coordinated system of practices and programs that benefits diagnosed students, and (d) progress in education (increases in academic achievement and efficiency) results from incremental technological improvements in differential diagnosis and intervention practices and programs (see, e.g., Bridges, 1982; Cherryholmes, 1988; Erickson, 1979; McNeil, 1986; Oakes, 1985; Sirotnik & Oakes, 1986; Spring, 1980).

2. Participants in the REI debate clearly are not speaking *explicitly* to the four assumptions, two theories, or the metatheory of functionalism. Indeed, that is the problem with the REI debate, as noted in text. Thus, from this point on in the book (including notes), I will at times omit the qualifiers "implicit" and "explicit" when discussing the implications of REI proponents' and opponents' arguments *for the assumptions, theories, and metatheory*, particularly when including it is cumbersome, as it is in this section because the discussion includes two other levels of implicitness. First, there is the nature of agreement (implicit or explicit) between the REI proponents' and opponents' assessments of current practices, *a level I will retain in text*. Second, there is the nature of the unquestioned presuppositions that ground the field (*explicit* in its professional knowledge tradition or *implicit* in a social norm) (see chapter 2, note 3), which, generally speaking, *I will not retain in text*. So, when I say that the REI proponents or opponents "reject" or "retain" an assumption or presupposition, it should be understood that they (or, more accurately, their arguments) do so *implicitly*. The same will hold true (relative to the four assumptions, two theories, and one metatheory) for the arguments of the participants in what I will call the "effective schools" and "school restructuring" debates in general education, which will be addressed in Part Three. In all cases where it seems necessary for clarity, however, I

will use the qualifiers in text, parenthetically, or in a note.

3. There is no argument over the fact that many disabilities in the moderate range and virtually all disabilities in the severe to profound range are associated with observable patterns of biological symptoms (syndromes) and thus are comprehensible under the pathological model (see Mercer, 1973). The issue here is the degree to which a pathology is actually the presenting problem among students who have difficulties in school and, as a result, are classified under the EHA as having so-called mild to moderate disabilities (simply "mild disabilities" in text). This is particularly an issue relative to students in the mild disability severity range who are classified as learning disabled, emotionally disturbed, and mildly mentally retarded, most of whom do not show biological signs and thus are not comprehensible under the pathological model (see chapter 5 and Algozzine, 1976, 1977; Apter, 1982; Hobbs, 1975; Mercer, 1973; Rhodes, 1970; Rist & Harrell, 1982; Ross, 1980; Schrag & Divorky, 1975; Skrtic, 1988b; Swap, 1978).

4. On these points, compare the arguments of Gartner and Lipsky (1987), Pugach and Lilly (1984), Stainback and Stainback (1984b), and Wang et al. (1986, 1987b) with those of Bryan et al. (1988), Braaten et al. (1988), CCBD (1989), Kauffman et al. (1988), and Keogh (1988).

5. My position on the assertion that special education is a barrier to development of a responsive (or reflective) capacity in general education in the public schools is addressed extensively from an organizational perspective in Part Three (also see Skrtic & Ware, in press). Although less explicit than my position relative to public schools, my position on this assertion relative to teacher education should be apparent throughout the book, particularly in chapters 1, 4, 6, and 10. For an explicit statement on the implications of my analysis relative to teacher edcuation, particularly on the organizational implications for schools of education, see Thousand (1990).

6. The REI opponents make two *practical* arguments in favor of instruction delivered in special education settings, neither of which is based on the claim that current special education instructional interventions have been shown to be effective. The first argues in favor of instruction in special education settings on the basis of the inability of general education teachers to meet the diverse needs of students with learning disabilities in regular classrooms (Bryan et al., 1988); the second rests on the speculation that more powerful instructional techniques might be more easily implemented in special education settings than in regular classrooms (Hallahan, Keller, McKinney, Lloyd, & Bryan, 1988; cf. Hallahan & Keller, 1986).

7. The argument that the current system is politically rational cannot be divorced from the argument that progress is rational-technical because, given that the REI opponents reject the assumption that differential diagnosis is objective and useful, their argument for the political rationality of special education as a targeting mechanism loses its force if rational-technical progress in the area of special education diagnostic practices is not possible. Furthermore, if rational-technical progress is not possible in the area of instructional practices, the argument that special education is a politically rational system is meaningless because, although targeting students for services that are ineffective at present but will be rendered effective (or at least more effective) in the future is a politically rational argument, targeting them for ineffective services that will not be rendered more effective in the future is neither politically nor ethically rational.

8. Although she has been a major figure in the REI debate, Madeleine Will has not offered a specific proposal as such. Relative to the question of integration, Will's (1986a) position in this regard is similar to those of Lilly and Pugach and of Reynolds and Wang, in that her version of a restructured system continues to rely on separate

instructional settings for some students, a position that has been criticized by Stainback and Stainback (1987b) and Gartner and Lipsky (1987, p. 385) as perpetuating "a dual system approach for a smaller (more severely impaired) population."

9. Each of the four teams of REI proponents, as well as Madeleine Will (1986a), takes a unique stance on this point, both in terms of the degree to which education and special education should be merged, and the level or levels of the eduation establishment at which merger should take place. Although neither Will nor any of the four teams of proponents speaks to each of the following levels, taken together they implicitly or explicitly recommend changes at or have implications for: (a) the U.S. Department of Education (b) research and development centers, (c) teacher education programs, (d) local education agencies, (e) school buildings, and (f) classrooms. Reynolds and Wang (1983) address levels (b), (c), (d), (e), and (f), and call for some degree of merger at all of these levels except (f); Pugach and Lilly (1984) address levels, (c), (e), and (f), and call for merger at (c) and (e), but not (f); Stainback and Stainback (1984b, 1987a) address levels (c), (e), (f), and call for merger at (c) and (e) but, as we will see, given their approach to merger, not at (f); Lipsky and Gartner address (e) and (f) primarily, and call for merger at both of these levels. Although she is somewhat contradictory on the matter (see Stainback & Stainback, 1987b; Gartner & Lipsky, 1987), Will calls for "enhanced component parts," better cooperation, and shared responsibility between the two systems at all levels, particularly at levels (a) and (e), but not for outright merger of the two systems at any level (Will, 1986a, p. 415).

10. For reviews of these and other emerging technologies for heterogeneous instruction relative to their suitability for the REI proposals, see Lloyd et al. (1988) and Thousand and Villa (1988, 1989).

11. Both the historical and the practical arguments presented in CCBD (1989), Kauffman (1988), and Kauffman et al. (1988) contradict the arguments for the possibility of incremental change through research and development presented in Braaten et al. (1988), Bryan et al. (1988), CCBD (1989), Hallahan, Keller, McKinney, Lloyd, and Bryan (1988), Kauffman (1988), Kauffman et al. (1988), Keogh (1988), and Lloyd et al. (1988).

# 4

# The Crisis in
# the Professions

In chapter 3 we saw that the empirical arguments of the REI debate participants reject special education's professional models and practices. Moreover, we saw that, when these same arguments are read critically, they ultimately reject the field's explicit presupposition of human pathology, which is associated with its disciplinary grounding and has shaped its practices and discourses throughout this century. In the remaining chapters of Part Two, I want to focus on two questions about this relationship between a profession's disciplinary grounding and its practices and discourses.

First, I want to ask Foucault's question of special educators. That is, I want to ask what led 20th-century special educators to believe in their practices, discourses, and disciplinary grounding. In this chapter I address the question broadly by considering the nature of the professions and the process of professionalization, which will set the stage for a more focused treatment of the special education knowledge tradition itself in chapter 5. Ultimately, in the present chapter I will argue that the very nature of professionalization makes professionals susceptible to the delusion that their knowledge tradition and its associated practices and discourses are objective and inherently correct.

The second question I want to ask is how professional educators can guard against this delusion of certainty. In chapter 6 I address the problem of professional delusion by drawing on the arguments presented to that point, and by reconsidering critical pragmatism *as a mode of professional practice and discourse*. In the sections to follow I present two ideal-typical characterizations of professionalization: the traditional objectivist version and the emerging subjectivist view.

## PROFESSIONALIZATION: THE OBJECTIVIST VIEW

Perhaps the most straightforward way to begin a discussion of the objectivist understanding of professionalization is by considering the nature of professional work. I should note at the outset, however, that one cannot divorce professional work from the organizational context in which it is performed. I do so here only for expository purposes. In Part Three I will return to the important question of the organizational context of professional work.

### Professional Work

*Simple work* is work that can be *rationalized*, or task-analyzed, into a series of routine jobs, each of which can be done by a separate worker. The classic example, of course, is the automobile assembly line. Although automobile assembly can be a complex undertaking, reduction of the process to a sequence of thousands of routine subtasks makes it simple work. By design, this type of work does not require that the people who do it have extensive knowledge or skills. It is done by unskilled workers who are trained for their jobs in a matter of days, or even hours (Braverman, 1974).

Conversely, *complex work* is work that is too ambiguous, and thus too uncertain, to be reduced to a sequence of routine subtasks. Thus, rather than rationalization as a means to comprehend the work, complex work ordinarily requires *specialization*, a situation in which the entire job is done by a single worker who has the specialized knowledge and skills to contain all of the uncertainty of the work. As such, complex work requires that the people who do it have an extensive knowledge base and an associated repertoire of skills that take a prolonged period of time to learn (Mintzberg, 1979).

Complex work can be further differentiated on the basis of whether the knowledge and skills necessary for doing it have been codified—that is, systematically identified, arranged, and recorded. *Craft work* is complex work for which the required knowledge and skills have not been codified. People learn to do it over extended time on the job, in the role of an apprentice under the guidance of a master, an experienced practitioner who previously learned the job in the same way. Thus, the knowledge and skills required to do craft work exist as the conventions and customs of a craft culture, conveyed from person to person as a tradition of experienced practice (Mintzberg, 1979).

Professional work is complex work for which the required knowledge and skills have been codified. Like all complex work, professional work requires that the people who do it have an extensive knowledge base and an associated set of skills that take an extended period of time to learn. Unlike craft knowledge, however, professional knowledge exists as a codified body of specialized knowledge and skills (Mintzberg, 1979; Schein, 1972). Whereas people gain access to craft knowledge on the job as apprentices, people gain access to professional knowledge in universities and professional schools, which are the repositories for the codified knowledge and skills necessary to do professional work (Schön, 1983).

Although considering the nature of work provides some insight into the professions and professionalization, it does not provide a complete picture because the nature of work has not remained constant. As new technologies have become available and as new knowledge has been developed, much craft work has been transformed into simple work through rationalization, or into professional work through specialization (Braverman, 1974). Thus, in a knowledge-based, technological society such as ours, understanding the professions and professionalization requires consideration of the concept of professionalism.

## Professionalism

Professionalism is a key concept in the social disciplines because the professions have a special relationship with society, the essence of which is that the professions are given greater autonomy than other social groups (see, e.g., Hughes, 1963; Parsons, 1939; Wilensky, 1964). The professions set their own standards, regulate entry into their ranks, discipline their members, and, in general, operate with fewer restraints than the arts, trades, or business. In return, the professions are expected to serve the public good and to set and enforce higher standards of conduct and discipline than these other groups.

The argument for allowing the professions to govern themselves is based on the two claims noted in the first chapter. In more practical terms, the first claim is that (De George, 1982):

> The knowledge that members of the professions control is specialized, useful to society, and not easily mastered by the layman. The second is that the members of the professions set higher standards for themselves than society requires for its citizens, workers, and business men and women. (p. 226)

Thus, professionalism is premised on a logic of confidence. Society assumes that the professions' specialized knowledge is useful and adequate, and it has faith that the professions will set and enforce high standards in the application of their professional knowledge to the solution of problems on behalf of the public good.

Given this logic of confidence, and the fact that in a complex, specialized society such as ours it is advantageous to be considered a professional, it is, of course, important for society to know which occupations are professions and, as such, can be trusted to govern themselves. Thus, it has become necessary to specify criteria for identifying the professions. Although social scientists who study the professions do not agree completely on these criteria, most agree on the necessity of a multiple criterion definition. Schein (1972) provided such a definition, which he formulated on the basis of a synthesis of the work of a number of social scientists:

1. The professional, as distinct from the amateur, is engaged in a *full-time occupation* that comprises his principal source of income.
2. The professional is assumed to have a *strong motivation* or calling as a basis for his choice of a professional career and is assumed to have a stable lifetime commitment to that career.
3. The professional possesses a *specialized body of knowledge and skills* that are acquired during a prolonged period of education and training.
4. The professional makes his decisions on behalf of a client in terms of *general principles, theories, or propositions*, which he applies to the particular case under consideration. . . .
5. At the same time, the professional is assumed to have a *service orientation*, which means that he uses his expertise on behalf of the particular needs of his client. . . .
6. The professional's service to the client is assumed to be based on the *objective needs of the client* and independent of the particular sentiments that the professional may have about the client. . . . The professional relationship rests on a kind of *mutual trust between the professional and client.*
7. The professional is assumed to know better what is good for the client than the client himself. In other words, the professional demands *autonomy of judgment of his own performance.* Even if the client is

not satisfied, the professional will, in principle, permit only his colleagues to judge his performance. . . . The profession deals with this potential [client] vulnerability by developing strong ethical and professional standards [of conduct] for its members . . . usually enforced by colleagues through professional associations. . . .

8. Professionals form *professional associations which define criteria of admission, educational standards, licensing or other formal entry examinations, career lines within the profession, and areas of jurisdiction* for the profession. Ultimately, the professional association's function is to protect the autonomy of the profession. . . .

9. Professionals have great power and status in the area of their expertise, but *their knowledge is assumed to be specific.* A professional does not have a license to be a "wise man" outside the area defined by his training.

10. Professionals make their service available but ordinarily are *not allowed to advertise or to seek out clients.* Clients are expected to initiate the contact and then accept the advice and service recommended, without appeal to outside authority. (pp. 8–9)

According to Schein, then, professionals are highly motivated and committed to a lifelong career of full-time employment in a professional occupation. They are prepared for service during a prolonged period of education in which they are given access to professional knowledge in the form of theories and propositions, which yield general principles that are applied to particular cases. Professionals adopt a posture in which a particular set of expert services is made available to clients, who initiate the contact and accept the services on trust.

Here again, confidence plays a key role in the concept of professionalism. In this case, it emerges in the special relationship between the client and the professional. On the basis of access to specialized professional knowledge, the professional is assumed to know best what is good for the client. Although client vulnerability is recognized and accounted for by the profession through enforcement of codes of ethics, the standards of ethical conduct, as we have seen, are developed and enforced by the professionals themselves, through the collective action of professional associations.

The circularity in this proposition stems from the argument that only the professions can judge the adequacy of their performance because they alone have access to the specialized knowledge upon which professional performance is based (De George, 1982). Thus, when we consider the concept of professionalism, understanding the professions and professionalization turns on understanding the relationship between professional autonomy and professional knowledge.

## Professional Autonomy

Most social scientists consider professional autonomy to be the ultimate criterion of professionalism. As we have seen, professional autonomy implies that professionals know best what is good for their clients because they have access to the profession's specialized knowledge and skills. On this basis, all decisions as to the adequacy of professional knowledge (as well as professional skills, standards, performance, and jurisdiction) can be made only by the professionals themselves, through peer-group association. Given these implications, a profession is a community of members characterized by "a common sense of identity, self-regulation, lifetime membership, shared values, a common language, clear social boundaries, and strong socialization of new members" (Schein, 1972, p. 10).

The relationship between professional autonomy and professional knowledge turns on the fact that society allows the professions greater autonomy than other groups because the professions have access to and control of specialized knowledge that society needs. And, as we know, professional autonomy leaves the question of the adequacy of professional knowledge to the professionals themselves. In effect, a profession is an insulated, self-regulating community of members who share an image of the world, their work and their clients, and their profession and themselves—an image which, as we will see, is based on strong socialization and common exposure to a body of specialized knowledge. The special relationship between the professions and society yields professional autonomy. The special relationship between professional autonomy and professional knowledge creates a situation in which a profession is the sole judge of the adequacy of its professional knowledge, a matter that I will return to. For now, let us consider the nature of professional knowledge itself.

## Professional Knowledge

The objectivist conceptualization of professional knowledge is premised on the positivist epistemology of knowledge (Schein, 1972) and the logical positivist approach to social inquiry (Schön, 1983). As we know, logical positivism represents an attempt to apply the methods of the physical sciences to the study of society and human affairs (Bernstein, 1976; Hesse, 1980). As an epistemology, positivism represents the belief that "the growth of knowledge is essentially a cumulative process in which new insights are added to the existing stock of knowledge and false hypotheses are eliminated" (Burrell & Morgan, 1979, p. 5). Thus, among other things, positivist knowledge is assumed to be cumulative, convergent, and objective (Wolf, 1981), the end product of a rational-technical process in which it is possible to separate the observer from the observed and thus the knowledge produced from the influence of any value system (Harre, 1981; Lincoln & Guba, 1985).

Although positivism is a particular epistemology of knowledge, the objectivist view is that it is the *only* epistemology of knowledge. And even though it has and continues to be discredited (see Hesse, 1980; Wolf, 1981; Bernstein, 1976; Rorty, 1979), positivism is the model of knowledge upon which the modern university is premised (Shils, 1978). As such, it permeates the very structure of the university and its professional schools, where it serves as the epistemological foundation for professional knowledge as well (Schön, 1983; Schein, 1972; Glazer, 1974). As such, positivism yields a threefold division of professional knowledge, described by Schein (1972) as:

1. An underlying discipline or basic science component upon which the practice rests or from which it is developed.
2. An applied science or "engineering" component from which many of the day-to-day diagnostic procedures and problem solutions are derived.
3. A skills and attitudinal component that concerns the actual performance of services to the client, using the underlying basic and applied knowledge. (p. 43)

Thus, the positivist model of professional knowledge assumes an interdependent, hierarchical relationship among three sub-types of knowledge: *theoretical* knowledge, *applied* knowledge, and *practical* knowledge. As such, the assumption is that the actual performance of professional services to clients is grounded in applied knowledge, which itself rests on a foundation of disciplinary or theoretical knowledge (see also Greenwood, 1981).

Applying the positivist model of professional knowledge to the social professions, the social sciences are assumed to produce theoretical knowledge, which is cumulative, convergent, and objective (Schön, 1983). Applied scientists in professional schools *receive* this theoretical knowledge from the social sciences and subsequently engineer it into diagnostic procedures and problem solutions for use in everyday practice. The professional practitioner receives this applied knowledge during a formal program of professional education and subsequently uses it in the performance of services to clients.

The distinction between *received* and *objective* knowledge is an important one that I will return to. At this point, however, I want to stress that both the applied researcher and the practitioner are assumed to operate on the basis of received knowledge, which they accept on faith from the next higher level in the hierarchy of professional knowledge (Schön, 1983). The assumption for social scientists, however, is that, rather than receiving knowledge, they discover it through application of the positivist approach to social inquiry and, moreover, that it is cumulative, convergent, and objective, according to the positivist theory of knowledge (Popper, 1970).

Thus, rigorous practice in the social professions is assumed to be the end product of a rational-technical process of knowledge production in which the cumulative, convergent, and objective theoretical knowledge of the social sciences is engineered by applied scientists to produce the diagnostic procedures and problem solutions used by professional practitioners in the performance of services to clients (Glazer, 1974; Schön, 1983). Ultimately, the objectivist view of the social professions, grounded as it is in the positivist epistemology of professional knowledge and the positivist approach to social inquiry, is one of *technical rationality* (Schön, 1983), an orientation that is the antithesis of traditionalism and conventionalism (see Parsons, 1939).

### Professional Induction

Individuals are inducted into a profession—given access to professional knowledge and skills—through a formal program of professional education and socialization. The professional education curriculum follows the hierarchy of professional knowledge presented above. Students are exposed first to the theoretical knowledge of the relevant discipline(s) in colleges of liberal arts and sciences, then to the applied knowledge of the profession in the relevant professional school, and finally to a practicum or internship in which they apply the theoretical and applied knowledge to the problems of professional practice (Schein, 1972; Schön, 1983). For example, persons preparing for professional roles in education ordinarily are exposed to the theoretical knowledge of the discipline of psychology (among others); then to the applied knowledge of educational psychology (diagnostic procedures) and curriculum and instruction (problem solutions) in professional schools of education; and finally to a practicum in which they apply this theoretical and applied knowledge in actual classroom situations under the guidance of an experienced teacher.

After their coursework in the academic disciplines, students preparing for professional roles matriculate through an extended program of education and socialization, carried out in a professional school and sanctioned by a professional association. Students are on their way to becoming full-fledged professionals when they can demonstrate that they have internalized the profession's theoretical and applied knowledge, as well as its practical knowledge and skills. But there is more to becoming a professional than internalizing knowledge and skills; the would-be professional also must be socialized.

Socialization is the process by which a new member internalizes the value system, norms, and established behavior patterns of the group he or she is entering (Etzioni, 1961). Professional socialization inculcates the standards for how members of the profession ought to act (Schein, 1968). It is a vital part of professional education because it is the mechanism by which the professions regulate and discipline the professional behavior of their members, according to their special relationship with society (De George, 1982; Mintzberg, 1979). When students can demonstrate that they have internalized the profession's knowledge, skills, norms, and values—how to think and act as a professional—they are duly certified as professionally competent by the professional school, admitted to the professional community by the relevant professional association, and licensed by the state to practice the profession.

## PROFESSIONALIZATION: THE SUBJECTIVIST VIEW

Whereas the objectivist view of professionalization dominates the literature on the professions, the actual processes and events associated with professionalization have not received a great deal of attention. This is true in education (see Champion, 1984; Haberman, 1983; Koehler, 1985; Zeichner & Tabachnick, 1981), as it is in virtually all professional fields (Barnes, 1982; Schön, 1983), largely because professional induction has been taken for granted, according to the objectivist perspective. The general assumption has been that professional education and socialization are different means for accomplishing different ends. Professional education is assumed to be a rational-technical process for conveying an objective body of knowledge and its associated skills, according to the positivist model of professional knowledge (Schön, 1983). Professional socialization is assumed to be a nonrational or social process for inculcating a subjective value system and its associated behavior norms, according to the self-regulatory responsibility of the professions (De George, 1982; Greenwood, 1981; Schein, 1968).

Although the objectivist view of professionalization has dominated most writing and thinking about professionalization, it has been called into question by Kuhn's (1970) analysis of the induction of physical scientists into scientific communities. Kuhn's analysis is relevant to the induction process in the professions because, as we will see, another important outcome of this work has been the demystification of scientific education, which, in all of its essential dimensions, is virtually identical to that of professional education (see Cherryholmes, 1988; Kuhn, 1977; Popper, 1970).

A key element in Kuhn's original work was that the process by which one paradigm replaces another one is a subjective phenomenon, a process of persuasion and conversion in which the victorious paradigm is the one that wins the most converts (Ritzer, 1980). In this sense, his work was important for what it had to say about the role of culture and tradition in the production of knowledge. His analysis of the conventional nature of knowledge, and the nature of convention itself, contradicted the objectivist view that science and knowledge are objective, and it advanced the subjectivist position that both depend on their cultural context for meaning and interpretation. The importance of culture, convention, and communal activity in science cannot be overemphasized (see Bloor, 1976; Law, 1975; Phillips, 1973; Knorr, Krohn, & Whitley, 1981). For example, drawing on Kuhn's analysis, Barnes (1982) noted that "culture is far more than the setting for scientific research; it is the research itself" (p. 10). The objectivist image of the scientist as an objective observer who *discovers* knowledge has given way to the subjectivist image of the scientist as craftsperson who, bound by the culture of a particular time and place, *creates* knowledge that is of temporary utility and validity (Ravetz, 1971).

At this point we can begin to see the parallels between the work of the basic scientist and that of the applied scientist and professional practitioner. As we know, according to the objectivist view the latter groups are presumed to operate on the basis of received knowledge—knowledge that each accepts on faith from higher levels in the hierarchy of professional knowledge. Although it is generally understood that this is the case for applied scientists and professional practitioners, the assumption had been that the theoretical knowledge of the basic or social scientist is objective knowledge about reality. From the subjectivist point of view, however, the basic or social scientist, like the applied scientist and professional practitioner, operates on the basis of received knowledge—the knowledge received by looking at the world through a particular paradigm of metatheoretical presuppositions. What is missing from the threefold positivist model of professional knowledge, then, is this additional level of metatheoretical knowledge, which, as we know, defines and subsumes the other three levels (see Kuhn, 1970; Masterman, 1970).

Thus, all three groups—basic or social scientists, applied scientists, and professional practitioners—are inducted into a culture of conventional knowledge, which they receive on faith and assume is the only way to unrandomize the complexity of their particular worlds of practice. Like the craftsperson, each is bound by the culture of a particular time and place. Like the image of science and the legacy of knowledge, the subjectivist view brings the roles of basic and social scientist down to earth.

Of the two objectivist assumptions about professional induction—internalization of objective knowledge through education, and inculcation of subjective norms through socialization—there is no argument about the subjectivity of values and norms, or of socialization itself. But Kuhn's conceptualization of the relationship between scientific knowledge and scientific culture characterizes the internalization of knowledge and skills as a subjective process of socialization as well (Barnes, 1982; Popper, 1970). According to this interpretation, professional education, like scientific education, is a process whereby a student is inducted into a culture of customs and conventions, not unlike the induction of an apprentice into a craft culture.

The implication, of course, is that professional knowledge is not objective, in the sense that it represents an objective reality that exists apart from and prior to its definition by the profession. Instead, a profession's knowledge tradition and associated skills are the time-honored, mutually agreed-upon conventions of its members. In this sense, a profession's knowledge and skills are as subjective as its values and norms. Rather than being a rational-technical process that is the antithesis of traditionalism and conventionalism, professionalization *is* a matter of being inducted into a culture of traditions and conventions. At this point, let us reconsider the process of professional induction, using the Kuhnian conceptualization as a frame of reference.

### Professional Induction

The process of professional induction requires the inductee to submit to the authority of the teacher (who ordinarily is also an applied scientist) and the institutional legitimacy of the profession. The information the teacher conveys is taken on trust by the student because of the institutional context in which it appears. As such, professional education tends to be dogmatic and authoritarian, as well it might be, given its institutional context and the fact that the inductee initially lacks enough of the profession's specialized knowledge and skills to be able to evaluate it on its own terms (Barnes, 1982). And this applies to the professional education of both the applied scientist and the practitioner of the profession. Although the applied scientist learns to apply theories and methodologies, and the practitioner learns to apply techniques and procedures, both are taught in a dogmatic spirit. Each receives knowledge from a higher authority in the status hierarchy of professional knowledge, and each accepts it on faith (Popper, 1970). Each is regarded as a novice whose very perception must be guided and shaped to conform to the profession's conventional knowledge, to its established way of structuring the world and seeing itself, its clients, and its work (Barnes, 1982; Greenwood, 1981). The process is identical to Kuhn's (1970) characterization of the induction of physical scientists:

> Looking at a contour map, the student sees lines on paper, the cartographer a picture of a terrain. Looking at a bubble-chamber photograph, the student sees confused and broken lines, the physicist a record of familiar subnuclear events. Only after a number of such transformations of vision does the student become an inhabitant of the scientist's world, seeing what the scientist sees and responding as the scientist does. (p. 111)

Teaching textbooks play a particularly important role in the transformations of vision necessary for an inductee to become an inhabitant of the world of a professional culture. They convey the profession's mutually agreed-upon substantive domain—its theories, assumptions, models, and practices, and, by implication, its metatheoretical paradigm. In the hands of the teacher, who personifies for the student the authority and legitimacy of the profession, the teaching textbook becomes the principal vehicle for maximizing the authority and credibility of the profession's knowledge (see Barnes, 1982; Kuhn, 1977). The authority implied by the teaching textbook is essential because professional induction demands complete acceptance of the profession's received knowledge on faith. Anything that might question or offer an alternative to the profession's established knowledge tradition is avoided. Past and current unorthodox perspectives tend to be overlooked in training and rarely find their way into teaching textbooks (Kuhn, 1970). This sort of textbook education demands complete concentration on one knowledge tradition to the exclusion of all others. Its goal is to inculcate in the would-be professional a deep commitment to a particular way of viewing the world and operating in it.

Although Kuhn's description of induction can be read as critical commentary, he offered it as an account of an effective system of education (see Kuhn, 1970; 1977). If we can conceive of a field of endeavor—whether in the physical sciences, social sciences, or professions—as a collective enterprise premised upon conventionally based, communal judgment, then an authoritarian textbook-based education is a productive preparation for it. As Barnes (1982) noted with regard to the induction of physical scientists into scientific communities:

> Standardization of perception and cognition facilitates communication, organization, interdependence and division of labor: the more dogmatic their training, the more scientists are bound together into a communal enterprise with all the familiar gains in efficiency which that entails. . . . The consequence of the commitment encouraged by dogmatic training is that investigation is narrowed and focused, and is thus made more productive. (p. 19)

Like scientific work, professional work is too complex to be approached in a random, unsystematic manner. As in the case of scientific knowledge and skills, professional knowledge and skills are premised on a commitment to view the world in a particular way, which unrandomizes complexity and thus narrows and focuses activity, making it more productive. Thus, the same benefits that Kuhn and Barnes noted for the physical sciences accrue for the social sciences and the social professions. But what begins as an advantage for all three groups, and remains so for the physical sciences, can turn into a severe disadvantage for the social sciences and social professions. Ultimately, the degree to which a narrow, dogmatic focus remains an advantage, rather than becoming a disadvantage, is related to the *paradigmatic status* of the communal enterprise and the *organizational conditions* of its work activities. The issue of the organizational conditions of professional educators is the topic of Part Three of the book. For now, let us turn our attention to the issue of paradigmatic status.

Paradigmatic status is a key factor because it relates to the degree to which the members of a scientific or professional culture are prepared to recognize anomalies. As Barnes (1985) noted, in the physical or *single* paradigm sciences:

> A group of scientists engaged in normal science is a very sensitive detector of anomaly. Precisely because the group is so committed to its paradigm and so convinced of its correctness, any . . . residue of recalcitrant anomalies . . . may eventually prompt the suspicion that something is amiss with the currently accepted paradigm, and set the stage for its demise. (pp. 90–91)

Given the *multiple* paradigm status of the social sciences and professions, however, the inherent dogmatism associated with the induction process has been a disadvantage because, in a sense, it is not dogmatic enough.

As we know, in the multiple paradigm sciences and professions, the kind of revolutionary paradigm shifts characteristic of the physical sciences are conceptually impossible because there is no single paradigm to be overthrown. This has retarded the advances made by the social sciences and professions (relative to the physical sciences) because, as Kuhn (1977) noted, although "one can practice science—as one does philosophy or art or political science—without a firm consensus, this more flexible practice will not produce the pattern of rapid consequential scientific advance [in which] . . . development occurs from one consensus to another" (p. 232). This is why the meta-leap to antifoundationalism in the social sciences is so revolutionary. If we ignore the fact that there are four paradigms of modern social knowledge and think of the four-paradigm arrangement as a single paradigm, the meta-leap can be understood as a revolutionary shift from the paradigm of foundational, monological, or modern social knowledge to that of antifoundational, dialogical, or postmodern knowledge. As such, the meta-leap to antifoundationalism is equivalent in magnitude, if not in form, to an episode of Kuhnian revolutionary science.

As we have seen, the professions' special relationship with society yields professional autonomy, which leaves determination of the adequacy of professional knowledge to the professionals themselves. Moreover, by design, professional education, like scientific education, produces professionals with a deep commitment to a particular knowledge tradition. The problem is that, whereas the focused vision of physical scientists periodically uncovers anomalies that force them to question the adequacy of their scientific knowledge tradition, professional communities, including the professional community of education, are less sensitive to anomalies because of the multiple paradigm status of the professional culture. Thus, professionals ordinarily do not question the adequacy of their professional knowledge. They tend to remain confident in the adequacy of their knowledge tradition because, lacking a sufficient "residue of recalcitrant anomalies," they implicitly assume that it is valid, credible, and, above all, objective.

Like all professionals, educators believe in their professional and institutional practices and discourses because professionalization inculcates in them a deep commitment to a particular way of viewing the world and operating in it. Without such a focus, an educator would not be a professional; without such a focus, education would not be a profession. On its own, of course, a focused outlook is not the problem. To be productive, all communal activities must have one. The problem is that, like the multiple paradigm sciences in which they are grounded, multiple paradigm professions such as special education, general education, and educational administration ordinarily have a diminished capacity for detecting sufficient anomalies to call their paradigm into question, and thus lack the "essential tension" between certainty and uncertainty that drives progress (Kuhn, 1977). What is worse is that in the field of education the problem of the convergent nature of professional culture is compounded by the traditional organization of schools. As we will see in Part Three, this particular organizational configuration not only reinforces conventional thinking but also acts to distort anomalies so that they are consistent with the prevailing paradigm of practice, which in effect eliminates them as a source of uncertainty and thus as an occasion for innovation.

On the positive side, of course, the meta-leap to antifoundationalism provides an opportunity to address these problems in fundamentally new and critical ways. As I noted in Part One, the crisis in modern knowledge is an opportunity for critical introspection and renewal. To take advantage of this opportunity, we need adequate methods and conditions of discourse. Chapter 6, the last chapter of Part Two, addresses the question of methods of discourse, and Part Three is devoted to the important problem of conditions of discourse. At this point, however, let us return to looking behind special education as a professional practice, given what we have learned in this chapter about professionalization and professional culture.

# 5

# The Special Education
# Knowledge Tradition

By considering the nature of professionalization and professional culture chapter 4 provided some of the background needed to address
the question of why 20th-century special educators have been so
committed to the presuppositions of their knowledge tradition. As we
have seen, the essence of being a professional means making and
operating under a commitment to a particular knowledge tradition.
This chapter attempts to address the question more fully by considering the nature of the special education knowledge tradition itself, an
undertaking that is complicated by several factors.

First, the field of special education is a conglomeration of several
sub-fields, each of which has a somewhat unique knowledge base and
associated set of skills that reflect the presumed differences among various categories of disability. Nevertheless, behind these surface differences is a basic foundation of communal knowledge to which each sub-
field subscribes. What is of interest here is this underlying knowledge
tradition, which I will refer to simply as special education knowledge.

Second, given the arguments put forth in the last chapter, discussing special education knowledge is complicated by the fact that
special educators cannot be expected to provide an adequate exposition
of it; it is so basic to them that they take it for granted. Thus, it will be
helpful to bring a number of perspectives to bear upon the subject,
which I will do by considering some of the criticisms of the field.

The third and most significant factor is special education's historical and structural relationship to general education and educational administration. As I noted in my opening argument, and as I hope to demonstrate in this chapter, and particularly in Part Three of the book, special education is an artifact of the functionalist world view that has dominated education historically. Thus, to consider the question of special education knowledge, it will be helpful at the outset to consider the manifestation of the functionalist world view in the discourses and practices of public education itself. I begin with a brief ideal typical analysis of functionalist education, in which I attempt to show how the very notion of special education emerges out of the functionalist value orientation that dominates public education. Following that, I consider special education knowledge genealogically, by reviewing various forms of criticism of the field and its discourses and practices.

## FUNCTIONALIST EDUCATION

As we know, the functionalist paradigm is grounded in the sociology of regulation, takes a more or less microscopic view of social reality, and studies its subject matter from an objectivist point of view. Because functionalists are realists and determinists, they believe that there is a single reality "out there," independent of human appreciation of it, to which humans react in a mechanistic or even deterministic fashion. Because they are positivists, they believe that we can discover objective truth about this single reality, and about the way humans react to it, by using the nomothetic methods of the physical sciences to state generalized principles or laws that permit us to predict and control social action and interaction. And because they subscribe to the sociology of regulation and approach inquiry from a micro-objective perspective, they tend to view the current arrangement of society as functional and indispensable, if not inherently correct, and thus they view social and human problems as pathologies that exist within people or groups.

As the dominant framework for social science, functionalism has different manifestations in the various social science disciplines, two of which are particularly important for our purposes: sociology and psychology. Functionalist sociology is important because it best illustrates the functionalist outlook applied to society and social functions such as education. To the sociological functionalist, society is composed of interrelated parts, each of which contributes toward maintaining the others. The parts of society are always changing; these changes lead to sympathetic changes in other parts of the system, and thus change is essentially orderly, balanced, and integrated. At the extreme, functionalists argue that all events and structures in society are functional and thus indispensable to the system. This leads to the conservative bias that all current aspects of society should continue to exist, which limits the possibility of fundamental change (Ritzer, 1980).

Functionalist psychology is important because of its central place in educational discourses and practices. Two branches of functionalist psychology are particularly important in this regard: *psychological behaviorism,* which shapes the conceptualization of curriculum and instruction (Kohlberg & Mayer, 1972); and *experimental psychology,* which grounds the psychometric approach to assessment and evaluation (Cherryholmes, 1988; Spring, 1980).

The manifestation of functionalism in education is, in part, a product of both psychological and sociological functionalism, which, of course, are themselves shaped by the metatheoretical assumptions of the functionalist paradigm. These assumptions shape virtually every aspect of public education, including the view of knowledge itself, the nature of curriculum and instruction, the nature of learning and thus the roles of teacher and learner, the means of evaluation, the function of schooling, the organization and mangement of schools, the approach to change, and the mode of accountability (see, e.g., Cherryholmes, 1988; Feinberg & Soltis, 1985; Giroux, 1981; Skrtic, 1988b; Spring, 1980).

Given the paradigm's objectivist ontology and epistemology, knowledge is viewed as certain, objective, and monological—a body of objective facts about a single reality that exists apart from and prior to human appreciation of it. Curriculum, then, is the codification of this knowledge in the form of a rationalized (task-analyzed) hierarchy of higher- and lower-order facts and skills; and instruction is the application of a systematic hierarchy of behavioral procedures for knowledge and skill acquisition (see Cherryholmes, 1988).

Combining this view of knowledge with the functionalist conceptualization of human nature, the teacher's role is that of a technician who organizes the factual material for efficient presentation and arranges the environmental contingencies to reward and punish desirable and undesirable responses. The learner's role is that of a passive receiver of the factual material and skill training under the conditions imposed by the environmental contingencies. Learning, as such, is understood as "an accumulation of pieces of knowledge and bits of skill . . . placed in learners' heads through practice and appropriate rewards" (Resnick & Klopfer, 1989, p. 2).

The positivist orientation of functionalist educational psychology yields a quantitative approach to evaluation in the form of psychometrics, which serves two functions. First, through the use of standardized ability testing, students are grouped into tracks for efficient delivery of instruction. Second, standardized achievement tests are used to evaluate student acquisition of the knowledge and skills contained in the rationalized, hierarchical curriculum. Ability testing serves the interest of school organization efficiency by reducing student variability within tracks (see Oakes, 1985), achievement testing serves the interest of economic efficiency by providing a means of credentialing graduates for efficient assignment to occupational slots in business and industry (Meyer & Rowan, 1978). Thus, the function of schooling from the functionalist outlook is one of industrial psychology—the efficient slotting of workers into occupational roles in the political economy (Spring, 1980).

The organization of such a system takes on the configuration of the machine bureaucracy—the pyramid-shaped, top-down structure of control relations common to the mass production firm. In Part Three I will have much more to say about the implications of this organizational configuration. For now, we can understand it as a centralized hierarchy of authority relations through which the codification of knowledge, the efficient implementation of behavioral technology, and the awarding of credentials is administered. This is accomplished through scientific management, an approach to administration designed for use in the factory and, as we will see in Part Three, premised on the notion of the separation of theory and practice. Applied to schooling, the goal of scientific management is to assure teacher-proof and learner-proof instruction through standardization of personnel roles, student classifications, curricular content, and instructional procedures, as well as the enforcement of these standards through supervision and competency testing (see Cherryholmes, 1988; Skrtic, 1988b; Spring, 1980).

Managing planned change in such a system follows the procedures for planned change used in the industrial machine bureaucracy. The assumption is that the organization is a machine that can be fine-tuned in a rational-technical manner, through further role specification, increased standardization of work processes and outcomes, elaboration of existing rules, and closer supervision (see House, 1979). As we will see in Part Three, change is viewed as building a better machine bureaucracy (see also Cuban, 1989; Skrtic, 1988b).

Accountability from the functionalist outlook is a matter of legal/bureaucratic control of personnel, work processes, and outcomes. Such a mode of accountability is based on detailed specification of roles and standardization of services, and aimed at efficiency of operation and equal treatment of clients (Romzek & Dubnick, 1987). Standardization of services and equality of treatment, however, produce a routinized system in which inevitable client variability means that the needs of some students cannot be accommodated by the standard routines. This creates the need for various organizational responses which, in the interest of protecting the legitimacy and thus the very survival of the system, distort the problem of system failure by deflecting it onto society, parents, or the students themselves (see Oakes, 1985; Rist, 1973; Skrtic, 1988b; chapters 8 and 9). This is accomplished administratively by designating recalcitrant students as gifted, disadvantaged, handicapped, or, more recently, at risk; and subsequently removing them, to the extent possible, from the system (Skrtic, 1988b; Sleeter, 1986; Tomlinson, 1982; chapters 8 and 9).

## FUNCTIONALIST SPECIAL EDUCATION

Given the assumptions and value orientation of functionalist education, we can understand special education as a more extreme version of functionalist education, more extreme in both an objectivist and a microscopic sense. As such, the field's guiding theories of human pathology and organizational rationality yield an approach to diagnosis and instruction premised on diagnostic-prescriptive teaching and behavioristic theory (Bogdan & Knoll, 1988; Skrtic, 1986). Diagnostic-prescriptive teaching is the attempt to design instructional programs on the basis of test performance, using one of two approaches: ability training or task analysis. Given the lack of psychometric technology necessary for actualizing the ability training model, however, the preference in special education has been for the task analysis approach (Salvia & Ysseldyke, 1981), which is based on the application of behavioristic theory to instruction in specific knowledge and skills. Relatively complex instructional goals are selected from the hierarchical general education curriculum and are task-analyzed further into subskills, which are taught using an even more systematic application of behavioral procedures for skill acquisition (see, e.g., White & Haring, 1976). The special education teacher, even more so than the general education teacher, is conceptualized as a technician.

This more advanced application of behavioral technology, commonly referred to as systematic instruction, is premised on the experimental analysis of behavior. According to special education applied scientists, systematic instruction:

> . . . has grown out of the experimental analysis of behavior, which, as a scientific discipline, sought to find a systematic interpretation of human behavior based on generalized principles, or laws, of behavior. The goal of this search for laws of behavior was much the same as in any other branch of science—to make reliable predictions (Skinner, 1953). The development of behavior analysis has been rigorously scientific, beginning with basic laboratory research and slowly generalizing the results to social situations. (Haring, 1978, p. 21)

Metatheoretically, psychological behaviorism is located in the extreme objectivist region of the functionalist paradigm.

> Skinner's perspective is a highly coherent and consistent one in terms of the four strands of the subjective-objective dimension of our analytical scheme. Ontologically, his view is firmly realist; epistemologically, his work is the archetype of positivism; his view of human nature reflects a determinism of an extreme form; [and] the highly nomothetic methodology reflected in his experimental approach is congruent with these other assumptions. (Burrell & Morgan, 1979, p. 103)

Thus, special education's grounding in the psychometrics and behavioral technology of functionalist psychology locates its knowledge tradition in the most extreme objectivist region of the functionalist paradigm (see Heshusius, 1982; Iano, 1987; Skrtic, 1986), as illustrated in Figure 5.1.

Given special education's extreme objectivist outlook, progress is conceptualized as the application of positivistic methodologies to the improvement of diagnosis, intervention, and technology. As we will see in Part Three, the EHA is the actualization of this notion of progress. The law itself is perceived as a new technology for improving the ethics and efficacy of diagnosis (nondiscriminatory evaluation and multidisciplinary assessment) and instructional intervention (parent participation, least restrictive environment, individualized educational plans, and comprehensive system of personnel development) (see Gilhool, 1989; Turnbull, 1986).

Special education's sense of justice is grounded in the functionalist world view and the liberal ideology of benevolent humanitarianism.

**Figure 5.1**

Paradigmatic Status of Special Education Knowledge

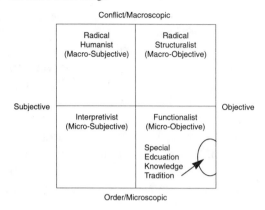

Conflict/Macroscopic

|  |  |
|---|---|
| Radical Humanist (Macro-Subjective) | Radical Structuralist (Macro-Objective) |
| Interpretivist (Micro-Subjective) | Functionalist (Micro-Objective) |

Subjective — Objective

Special Edcuation Knowledge Tradition

Order/Microscopic

## As Sally Tomlinson (1982) noted:

The way in which children are categorized out of . . . mainstream education and into special education is generally regarded as enlightened and advanced, and an instance of the obligation placed upon civilized society to care for its weaker members. Special education is permeated by an ideology of benevolent humanitarianism, which provides [the] moral framework within which professionals . . . work. (p. 5)

True to both the functionalist and liberal ideologies, justice for the special education community historically has been based on accepting the inevitability of the status quo in public education, while at the same time seeking rational-technical progress in the form of quantitative and bureaucratic solutions to educational inequities (see chapter 3; Part Three). Thus, for the special education community, progress toward a just educational system is calculated in terms of identifying more students as disabled and securing for them more rights, resources, and participation within the general education system—outcomes that are to be achieved bureaucratically through procedural compliance with the rules and regulations of the EHA, and administratively through adherence to the logic of mainstreaming. Moreover, in the face of criticism that such an approach does not achieve its goals, special education's response is completely consistent with the functionalist outlook.

For example, in response to the REI proponents' assertion that most of the students identified as handicapped are not actually disabled (e.g., Reynolds et al., 1987; Stainback & Stainback, 1984b), the REI opponents have argued that, even if students are overidentified, the problem lies in the technological inadequacies of our diagnostic procedures and categorical definitions, not in the validity of our basic orientation (Kauffman et al., 1988; Keogh, 1988). As we saw in chapter 3, when the REI proponents asserted that students are ill served in special education programs, the REI opponents argued that, although these programs may not be effective, progress is possible through additional scientific research on specific interventions (e.g., Hallahan, Keller, McKinney, Lloyd, & Bryan, 1988). And, when the REI advocates argued for the introduction of a new integrated technology of services (e.g., Reynolds et al., 1987; Stainback & Stainback, 1984b), the REI opponents insisted that the current organization of schooling is inevitable and, thus, mainstreaming, with all its recognized inadequacies, is the best we can hope for because it at least targets rights and resources to handicapped students (e.g., Kauffman, 1988; Kauffman et al., 1988).

## CRITICISM OF THE SPECIAL EDUCATION KNOWLEDGE TRADITION

Although I used special education's response to criticism above to illustrate its functionalist orientation, in this section I want to consider criticism of special education's practices, models, assumptions, theories, and metatheories in more depth, as a way of developing a genealogy of special education professional knowledge. The genealogy is admittedly incomplete, but it is sufficient for present purposes, which are, first, to identify some of the sources of confusion, contradiction, and incompleteness in special education's knowledge tradition; and, second, to illustrate further some of my earlier arguments about the conditioning, limiting, and institutionalizing effects of professional knowledge.

Like all professional knowledge, special education knowledge is assumed to follow the threefold objectivist model of professional knowledge described in chapter 4—that is, it is assumed that special education knowledge is grounded in the theoretical knowledge of an underlying discipline(s) and engineered at an applied science level into the diagnostic procedures and problem solutions for application to the day-to-day problems of practice. Thus, according to the model, special education's theoretically grounded applied knowledge is assumed to yield practical knowledge, which is transmitted to special education practitioners through an extended program of professional education and socialization. Ultimately, the performance of special education professional services to clients is assumed to be based on practical knowledge, which is the end product of a rational system of knowledge production that engineers theoretical knowledge into solutions for the problems of special education practice.

Although the discussion to follow is organized in terms of this model, because of its hierarchical nature, clear distinctions among the levels of the model are difficult to make. Criticism of one level of the hierarchy necessarily spills over onto one or more of the other levels. Therefore, what I will call *practical criticism* refers to special education practices (instructional and diagnostic) and models (the EHA and mainstreaming), which correspond to the practical knowledge and applied knowledge levels of the objectivist model of professional knowledge. What I will call *theoretical criticism* refers to criticism of special education's four grounding assumptions and two theories (human pathology and organizational rationality), which correspond to the applied and theoretical levels of the objectivist model. Finally, I will use *metatheoretical criticism* to refer to criticism of special education's theoretical grounding in the disciplines of psychology and biology, which corresponds to the theoretical level of the objectivist model, as well as its metatheoretical grounding in functionalism, which of course is not represented in the model of professional knowledge.

Although the hierarchical and interdependent nature of the objectivist model of professional knowledge means that metatheoretical and theoretical criticism is also criticism of applied and practical knowledge, the reverse is not true. As we will see, the problem with practical criticism is that it tends to be just that: criticism of practical and applied knowledge (practices and models) and not of the theoretical or metatheoretical knowledge in which both are grounded. That is, the problem with practical criticism is that it is a form of naive pragmatism.

### Practical Criticism

Of the three general types of criticism, practical criticism has been the most abundant and visible and, relatively speaking, has had the greatest impact on the nature of special education diagnostic and instructional practices. Such criticism has been mounted by parents and advocates, as well as by special educators themselves, first in the 1960s (e.g., Dunn, 1968; Blatt & Kaplan, 1966), and again in the 1980s relative to the REI, as we saw in chapter 3.

Capitalizing on the increased sensitivity to human and civil rights in the 1960s, parents, advocates, and special educators mounted a case against the ethics and efficacy of the segregated special classroom model of special education and its associated diagnostic and instructional practices (see chapter 3). This particular round of practical criticism led to victories in courtrooms and statehouses across the country and eventually in the U.S. Congress, which ultimately redefined special education diagnostic and instructional practices in terms of the EHA and mainstreaming models.

Among other things, the EHA mandated that all students with disabilities be provided with appropriate, or individually tailored, instruction in the least restrictive environment possible, which for most students was to be the regular classroom. The EHA sought to overcome the weakness of traditional diagnostic practices by specifying an elaborate set of procedures and timelines for referral, assessment, classification, and placement of students, and by extending to students and their parents certain constitutional rights and procedural safeguards, including due process of law (Abeson & Zettel, 1977; Turnbull, 1986).

Although the instructional practice of mainstreaming was not required by the law, it was the new instructional model developed at the applied science level of the field during the 1960s and 1970s (Reynolds, 1962; Deno, 1970) to overcome the problems associated with the special classroom model. As such, it and its associated instructional practices emerged as the preferred model during the mainstreaming debate. And, although critical commentary and legal action over the precise meaning of key EHA concepts such as appropriate education and least restrictive environment have continued over the years since enactment of the law (Turnbull, 1986), there is no doubt that the EHA and mainstreaming did bring about changes in special education diagnostic and instructional practices, even though, as we saw in chapter 3, these changes reproduced and extended the problems associated with the special classroom model.

It is important to recognize that the EHA and mainstreaming resulted from practical criticism—moral, political, and legal arguments against the special classroom model and its associated practices (Ballard-Campbell & Semmel, 1981; Biklen, 1985)—and not from theoretical or metatheoretical criticism of the assumptions in which the model and its practices were grounded. Moreover, as we know, the current criticism of special education practices within the REI debate follows the same pattern: It criticizes the ethics and efficacy of special education diagnostic and instructional practices without explicitly recognizing and questioning their grounding assumptions.

There are two important differences, however. First, of course, the target of criticism has shifted from the special classroom model to the EHA and mainstreaming models. Second, the REI debate expands the target of criticism to include general education practices and organization. As we have seen, whereas both rounds of criticism question the relationship between general and special education, the 1960s critics were interested merely in greater access to the general education system for students with disabilities (see Dunn, 1968). As we saw in chapter 3, however, the REI critics are calling for a restructured general education system and, depending on which proposal one refers to, the integration of most or all students identified as handicapped into regular classrooms on a full-time basis. Nevertheless, the fact that the REI criticism of current special education practices is virtually identical to the criticism of the special classroom model illustrates my point about practical criticism. It is a form of naive pragmatism; it leaves intact the assumptions that ground the practices in question—a situation in which the new practices reproduce and extend the original problems because they are based on the same assumptions.

**Theoretical Criticism of Special Education Knowledge**

Theoretical criticism focuses on special education's assumptions and theories and the manner in which they are used (or not used) at the applied science level of the profession to develop diagnostic and instructional models and practices. Whereas practical criticism was mounted primarily by parents, advocates, and special educators, prior to emergence of the alternative theoretical discourse within the field of special education, theoretical criticism came primarily from social scientists who, generally speaking, made three claims: that special education is *atheoretical,* that it *confounds theories,* and that it uses the *wrong theory.*

*The Atheoretical Claim*

The first type of theoretical criticism is based on the claim that the field of special education operates in the absence of any guiding theory (e.g., Bogdan & Kugelmass, 1984; Rist & Harrell, 1982). Instead of being grounded in the theories of an underlying discipline or basic science, the argument is that special education applied science and professional practice are guided by unconscious assumptions. Although it is true that the special education community is guided by unquestioned assumptions, it is more accurate to think of the special education community as being *acritical* rather than atheoretical.

This is a more accurate characterization because, as we have seen, ultimately these assumptions are grounded in the theories of human pathology and organizational rationality contained in the functionalist conceptualization of society. Moreover, as we will see in the following paragraphs, the assumptions that disabilities are pathological and that diagnosis is objective and useful derive directly from a confounding of theories of deviance drawn from the disciplines of psychology and biology. And, as we will see in Part Three, the assumptions that special education is a rational system and that progress in the field is rational and technical derive from various theories of organization which, until recently, have dominated thinking and writing about all organizations, including schools. Thus, although special education practices, like those of all professional fields, are shaped by a largely unquestioned commitment to a hierarchy of assumptions contained in a particular knowledge tradition, the real problem is the field's unquestioned, and thus acritical, posture toward these assumptions, and not whether they are grounded in theory.

### The Confounded Theory Claim

The second type of theoretical criticism rests on the claim that special education diagnostic practices are based on a confounding of theories. The best example of this type of criticism is Mercer's (1973) explanation of the way biological and psychological theories of deviance are confounded within the clinical model of mental retardation (also see Foucault, 1954/1976). The clinical model derives from medicine and psychology and is the frame of reference that guides research and practice in most social professions, including special education.

According to Mercer, the clinical model contains two contrasting theories of normal/abnormal: the *pathological theory* from medicine (biology) and the *statistical theory* from experimental psychology. The pathological theory defines impairments according to the presence or absence of observable biological symptoms. Biological processes that interfere with system preservation are bad, or pathological; those that enhance the life of the organism are good, or healthy. The pathological theory is bipolar: At one pole is normal, the absence of pathological symptoms and a healthy state; at the other pole is abnormal, the presence of pathological symptoms and an unhealthy state. Thus, the pathological theory is evaluative: To be abnormal is to be unhealthy; this is bad and should be prevented or alleviated.

The statistical theory is based on the construct of the normal curve—in essence, the notion that an individual's attributes can be described by his or her relative position in a frequency distribution of other persons measured on the same attributes. Whereas the pathological theory defines abnormality as the presence of observable pathological symptoms, the statistical theory defines it according to the extent to which an individual varies from the average of a population on a particular attribute. Unlike the bipolar pathological theory, which defines only one type of abnormality, the statistical theory, according to Mercer, defines two types: abnormally large and abnormally small amounts of the measured characteristic. As we know, the pathological theory is evaluative, it is always bad to have pathological signs. In contrast, the statistical theory of deviance is evaluatively neutral; whether it is good to be high or low depends on society's definition of the attribute being measured. As far as the attribute of intellectual capacity is concerned, in our society it is good to be abnormally high and bad to be abnormally low.

Mercer explained that both theories are used to define mental retardation—the pathological theory for assessing biological manifestations and the statistical theory for assessing behavioral manifestations, which are not comprehensible within the pathological theory. Although instances of moderate to profound mental retardation are associated with observable patterns of biological symptoms (syndromes), and are thus comprehensible under the pathological theory, the majority of individuals who are considered to be mentally retarded do not show any biological signs. In these instances, according to Mercer, the statistical theory is used and a low score on an intelligence (IQ) test is accepted as a symptom of pathology. Thus, the problem is that when the models are used in conjunction with one another, the tendency is to transpose them, turning behavioral patterns into pathological signs. Mercer (1973) explained the implicit logic that underlies this transformation:

Low IQ = "bad" in American society: a social evaluation. "Bad" = pathology in the pathological model. Therefore, low IQ = pathology. Thus, IQ, which is not a biological manifestation but is a behavioral score based on responses to a series of questions, becomes conceptually transposed into a pathological sign carrying all of the implications of the pathological model. (pp. 5–6)

Although Mercer identified a number of negative implications of the conceptual transposition, its primary implication is that mental retardation is regarded as an attribute of the individual, an objective pathology that individuals have. And, although Mercer's criticism emphasized mental retardation, the same type of criticism, in less sophisticated form, has been leveled against the field of special education relative to the diagnostic categories of learning disabilities (e.g., Rist & Harrell, 1982; Schrag & Divorky, 1975) and emotional disturbance (e.g., Algozzine, 1977, 1977; Apter, 1982; Hobbs, 1975; Rhodes, 1970; Ross, 1980; Swap, 1978), which, together with mild mental retardation, represent over two thirds of all students identified as handicaped under the EHA (USDE, 1988).

### The Wrong Theory Claim

The third type of theoretical criticism is that the field of special education is guided by the wrong theory, or that it relies too narrowly on one or more theories to the exclusion of others. Although this is a common theme in the alternative theoretical discourse within the field, historically it has been leveled most often by social scientists who argue that special education relies too heavily on theory derived from the disciplines of psychology and biology. The argument is that, by their very nature, these disciplines locate the root cause of all disability within the person (as we have seen above) and exclude from consideration causal factors that lie in the larger social and political processes external to the individual. In addition, social scientists see diagnosis, intervention, and technology based in the behavioral and biological sciences as superficial and one-sided because they ignore the social, political, and cultural contexts of disability (see Skrtic, 1986, 1988a).

Whereas the tendency in the behavioral and biological sciences is to study organisms and treat disability as an *objective* condition that people have, the social sciences study social, political, and cultural systems and processes and tend to consider deviance to be a *subjective* condition that is socially constructed and maintained (see, e.g., Gould,

1982; Szasz, 1961; Scott, 1969; Braginsky & Braginsky, 1971; Lemert, 1967; Goffman, 1961; Davis, 1963). And this is more than an academic argument. Many of the social scientists who raise the issue are ultimately concerned with the impact of social and political processes on people and society. From their perspective, in the extreme, special education in industrialized societies is an arm of education that creates and works against the social-political interests of powerless groups (Sarason & Doris, 1979; Barton & Tomlinson, 1984; Tomlinson, 1982; Farber, 1968).

**The Impact of Criticism of Special Education Knowledge**

Practical criticism was successful in bringing about changes in the way special education is practiced, as those changes have been embodied in the EHA and mainstreaming. But, as we know, even though it resulted in changes in the field's practices, the new practices simply reproduced and extended old problems. Nevertheless, although practical criticism resulted in little more than surface changes, theoretical criticism has had virtually no impact on the field of special education.

As we have seen, people from a number of disciplines and fields, including special education, have criticized the field's grounding assumptions, or have attempted to convince the professional community to expand its disciplinary base to include social and political theories of deviance. But there has been no general movement to alter special education policy, practice, or applied research on the basis of these insights. For example, discussing the impact of external theoretical criticism on special education applied research, Bogdan and Kugelmass (1984, p. 173) summarized the state of affairs succinctly by saying that, "in short, most research has been *for* special education (serving the field as it conceived of itself), not *of* special education, that is looking at the field from an alternative vantage-point." Special education applied research leaves unanswered and treats as unproblematic fundamental questions about its grounding assumptions.

Thus, on one hand, practical criticism has resulted in surface changes in the way special education is practiced but has had no effect on the field's taken-for-granted assumptions. On the other hand, theoretical criticism has had virtually no impact on theory, research, or practice in special education. The EHA and mainstreaming models altered special education practices but only within the frame of reference of the field's traditional assumptions about the nature of disability, diagnosis, special education, and progress. Real progress in special education, of course, will require a different frame of reference, a different set of assumptions, theories, and metatheories. At a minimum, it will require the special education community to take seriously the critics of its theoretical and applied knowledge. It will require a self-reflective examination of the limits and validity of special education knowledge and its grounding assumptions. But, as we know from the discussion in previous chapters, the problem is that the professional community will have difficulty accepting this type of criticism, precisely because it contradicts its taken-for-granted assumptions. Moreover, the problem is more than an inability to accept theoretical criticism. It is also an inability to access its language in a way that it is comprehensible.

Referring back to the discussion of professional induction, professionals in all fields are prepared for practice through a process that shapes their thought and behavior to conform to the profession's established knowledge tradition. The process requires total submission to the profession's authority, an acceptance of the profession's knowledge on faith. Professional induction is the efficient inculcation of the inductee with a commitment to a particular way of seeing the world and operating in it. Special education professionals ordinarily will find it difficult to accept and comprehend theoretical criticism because it is based on a view of the world and special education that falls outside of special education's established knowledge tradition. People inside the professional community and their theoretical critics on the outside are literally inhabitants of different conceptual worlds. They slice up the social world differently; they speak different languages and employ different concepts.

Moreover, professional autonomy means that there has been nothing to compel the special education professional community to listen to its critics. All judgments as to the adequacy of special education knowledge are left to the profession itself. And, of course, there is nothing particularly unusual about special education's inability to comprehend the language of its theoretical critics, to see itself as they do; this is an inherent characteristic of all professional communities. They all construct and maintain their own conventionally based reality. Each is an insulated subculture of conventional knowledge. Each is a way of seeing.

## The Alternative Theoretical Discourse in Special Education

The significant thing about the current situation in special education, of course, is the emergence of the alternative theoretical discourse within the field. As noted in chapter 3, the theoretical discourse is critical; it questions the assumptions and theories that ground special education models and practices. As such, it represents a valuable resource to the field—the start of, what I will call in the next chapter, a *critical emergence*. Nevertheless, the theoretical discourse has two problems. As I noted above and in chapter 3, the first problem is that it is, at this point at least, incomprehensible to the field; it is written and spoken in alternative theoretical languages. The second problem, also introduced in chapter 3, is that, although the theoretical discourse is critical, it is not pragmatic.

### The Problem of Incomprehensibility

At this point I can illustrate the incomprehensibility problem more fully by considering the response of the special education community to two examples drawn from the theoretical discourse: Lous Heshusius's (1982) *holistic* (i.e., combined interpretivist and radical humanist) critique of the philosophical, or what we would call *metatheoretical*, grounding of the field; and Christine Sleeter's (1986) radical structuralist critique of the learning disabilities concept. These are particularly helpful examples because Heshusius's critique represents a view of special education and disability from the *subjectivist* perspective, whereas Sleeter's represents a reading from the *macro/conflict* perspective—which, together, represent the two opposite extremes of special education's traditional micro/order-objectivist outlook.

The reaction from the applied science level of the special education community to Heshusius's (1982) argument for grounding special education practices in the holistic world view, rather than the mechanistic world view of the functionalist paradigm, was to dismiss it entirely as unscientific superstition (see Ulman & Rosenberg, 1986). The defenders of the prevailing functionalist paradigm evaluated and dismissed her proposal exclusively on the basis of functionalist assumptions about the nature of reality, knowledge, and inquiry, which, operating from the functionalist perspective, they implicitly assumed to be foundational and, thus, the only criteria that exist. True to the functionalist outlook, there was no recognition of the possibility of alternative frames of reference, to say nothing of the possibility of antifoundational knowledge.

The field reacted to Sleeter's radical structuralist critique of learning disabilities by characterizing it as "ideological rhetoric . . . a distorted account of history" (Kavale & Forness, 1987, p. 7). In this case, the defenders of the traditional outlook considered Sleeter's analysis to be dangerous, in that, it could be "taken seriously because of its. . . . ready appeal to egalitarian 'instincts' and [its] warping of reality" (p. 7). Recall that, for the functionalist, there is only one reality—the functionalist world view; any other version of reality must be a distortion. Heshusius is unscientific to Ulman and Rosenberg because she is arguing for a subjectivist understanding of science, special education, and disability and they are reading her from an objectivist point of view. Sleeter appears to be dangerous to Kavale and Forness because she is characterizing learning disabilities from the conflict perspective and they are operating on the assumption of an orderly world.

Given the discussion to this point in the book, reactions such as these, of course, are completely understandable.[1] My point in presenting them is to illustrate the incomprehensibility problem and to demonstrate how difficult it will be for the theoretical discourse, on its own, to have an impact on the field. Recall that in chapter 2 I noted that an immanent critique involves a double burden: the burden placed on the receivers to confront the contradictions between their ideals and practices, and the burden placed on the senders to present the ideals and practices in a way that the receivers can comprehend and thus acknowledge.

### The Problem of Foundationalism

Whereas the theoretical discourse is critical but incomprehensible to the field, the REI debate is comprehensible but acritical. As I noted in chapter 2, however, the significance of the fact that the REI debate and the theoretical discourse have emerged together is that, by combining them, the potential exists for an expanded discourse in special education that is both critical and comprehensible. By making available for theoretical and critical analysis the evidence produced by the field itself, according to its own assumptions and standards and in its traditional language, such a discourse would provide the field with a variety of possible knowledges, alternative interpretations, and optional descriptions of itself, its clients, and its implications for ethical practice and a just society. As we know, however, one problem with this vision of an expanded discourse is that, although the theoretical discourse is critical, it is not pragmatic—it does not provide a way to choose among the various theories it puts forth. To be critical *and* pragmatic, such a discourse not only must be able to look behind practices to expose the assumptions and theories in which they are grounded, but it also must be able to look behind the theories themselves; it must be able to question the metatheories in which the various theories are grounded. That is, to be critical and pragmatic at the metatheoretical level, such a discourse must be *antifoundational*. And that is the problem with the theoretical discourse in special education: It is *foundational*.

Figure 5.2 locates several of the theoretical perspectives contained within special education's alternative theoretical discourse on the conceptual framework developed in chapter 1. As in the social sciences generally, the movement in the special education theoretical discourse is away from the micro-objective perspective of functionalism and into the other three paradigms, which, of course, had been underdeveloped. The significance of this movement is that we now have theories grounded in all four modern paradigms (see Skrtic, 1990a). The advantage is that, because special education is the type of social phenomenon that Weber (1949, p. 81) argued can be understood only from *"particular points of view,"* the special education community now has the conceptual resources to understand itself from each of the four "points of view" of the modern era. Moreover, the problem of the foundational nature of the theories contained in special education's theoretical discourse, a problem that arises "in the belief that the 'true' content . . . of . . . reality is portrayed in such theoretical constructs" (Weber, 1949, p. 94),[2] can be addressed by treating each of the theories as an ideal type, an exaggerated utopia based on the one-sided accentuation of the presuppositions contained in a particular paradigmatic perspective. The value of these ideal types is their utility as expository devices, as conceptual tools for comparing ideals with actual conditions, and thus as means for doing immanent critiques.

Given the conceptual resources of the theoretical discourse, the analytic device of the ideal type, and the empirical evidence of the REI debate, what the special education community needs to carry out these immanent critiques is a method of discourse and the conditions to sustain it. The method of discourse that I am proposing, of course, is criti-

## Figure 5.2

The Theoretical Discourse in Special Education

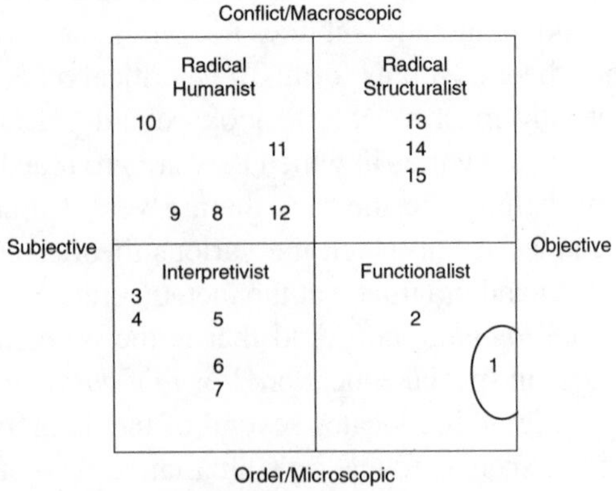

| | Conflict/Macroscopic | |
|---|---|---|
| | Radical Humanist | Radical Structuralist |
| | 10 | 13 |
| | 11 | 14 |
| | | 15 |
| | 9  8  12 | |

Subjective ——————————————————— Objective

| | Interpretivist | Functionalist |
|---|---|---|
| | 3 | |
| | 4  5 | 2 |
| | 6 | 1 |
| | 7 | |

Order/Microscopic

| | |
|---|---|
| 1 = special education knowledge tradition | 9 = Iano (1986) |
| 2 = Farber (1968) | 10 = Kiel (in press) |
| 3 = Heshusius (1982) | 11 = Tomlinson (in press) |
| 4 = Poplin (1984) | 12 = Sigmon (1987) |
| 5 = Ferguson (1987) | 13 = Carrier (1983) |
| 6 = Bogdan and Knoll (1988) | 14 = Tomlinson (1982) |
| 7 = Biklen (1985) | 15 = Sleeter (1986) |
| 8 = Janesick (1988) | |

cal pragmatism, which is the topic of the next chapter. The conditions for initiating and sustaining critical pragmatism as a mode of professional discourse are addressed in Part Three of the book.

## NOTES

1. For additional examples, see Simpson and Eaves' (1985) reaction to Stainback and Stainback's (1984a) call for broadening the research perspective in special education to include "qualitative methods," as well as the reactions of Forness and Kavale (1987), Carnine (1987), and Lloyd (1987) to Iano's (1986, 1987) theoretical treatment of the historical and philosophical grounding of special education.

2. I have had the good fortune to work with several of the participants in the theoretical discourse (see Skrtic, in press a), some of whom have shifted paradigms and none of whom are as foundational as I make them out to be. Nevertheless, their published works do represent particular theoretical points of view and, in this sense, represent valuable theoretical resources for the type of analysis I have in mind.

# 6

# Critical Pragmatism as a Mode of Professional Discourse

Ironically, over the last half of the modern era—a period in which the objectivist understanding of science was losing its relevance—the social disciplines fought to gain recognition as genuine sciences by modeling themselves after the very objectivist image that was falling out of favor. As we know, the subjectivist understanding of science as a paradigm-bound, communal activity that produces a series of possible knowledges is not a critique of science per se; it is a critique of objectivism (Barnes, 1985). Thus, although the subjectivist notion of possible knowledges leaves the physical sciences intact, it deconstructs the objectivist grounding of the social sciences, and therefore the social professions that draw their knowledge claims from them, because it undermines the very claim to legitimacy upon which the social disciplines are premised.

Until now the determination of a valid grounding for professional knowledge and practice has been left to the discretion of the professions themselves. It had been assumed, on the basis of the objectivist understanding of science and the positivist model of professional knowledge, that the validity of professional knowledge was unproblematic, and that, with the continuous, convergent, and cumulative growth of positive knowledge in the social sciences, periodic adjustments could be made to

**121**

refine and update what was at bottom a solid foundation of objective knowledge about social reality. But the philosophical and political implications of the paradigm shift to subjectivism and the meta-leap to antifoundationalism leave the social professions in the untenable position not only of having to choose a grounding for their practices and discourses without foundational criteria for making such a choice, but also of having to confront the fact that their past and future choices carry with them profound moral and political implications for their clients and for society. As we know, to be productive the social professions must have a paradigm; to be morally and politically viable in a democracy, they also must have a way to be critical about their paradigm and its implications for individuals and society.

Chapters 4 and 5 were devoted to the question of how special education professionals could have been so committed to ideas and practices that seem so wrong today. This chapter addresses the question of how such self-delusion can be avoided in the future. As I noted in chapter 2, I believe that critical pragmatism represents a way for the special education community to continually appraise and reorient its practices and discourses. In the chapters subsequent to that one, I have used critical pragmatism as a method of inquiry for looking behind these practices and discourses. My goal has been to bring a sense of crisis to the models, assumptions, theories, and metatheories in which they are grounded. Although the methods and procedures that I have used in Part Two, and that I will use again in Part Three, represent an example of critical pragmatism as a method of inquiry, in this chapter I address critical pragmatism as a mode of professional discourse, an approach to critical renewal in social professions such as special education.

Although such a renewal in special education is a necessary and worthwhile undertaking in its own right, ultimately it is a limited response without the same sort of critical renewal across the various subfields within public education. Thus, in this chapter I argue for and describe critical pragmatism as a mode of professional practice in the field of public education per se, recognizing, of course, that the process itself is applicable to any multiple paradigm profession.

## CRITICAL PRAGMATISM AND DIALOGICAL DISCOURSE

Because the social professions are multiparadigmatic endeavors, and because there are no foundational criteria to judge the adequacy of any given paradigm or knowledge claim, critical pragmatism requires dialogical discourse—that is, in the case of education, a dialogue among the multiple voices of the various theories, disciplines, and paradigms of the social sciences, as well as among social scientists, professional educators, students, and the public. I will return to the notion of a dialogical discourse among social scientists, educators, students, and the public. At this point, however, I want to concentrate on the idea of a dialogical discourse among the multiple voices of the various paradigms, theories, and disciplines of the social sciences.

Such a discourse appropriates C.S. Peirce's (1931–35) pragmatist notion of intersubjective communities of inquirers—the idea that scientific knowledge is a social product of normatively regulated intersubjective communication. Using the framework developed in Part One, we can understand scientific knowledge, according to this conceptualization, as a product of the paradigm-bound, communal activity and discourse associated with normal science. Thus, from the pragmatist perspective, the theories produced by members of the various disciplines are the social constructions of particular historically situated communities of inquirers—theories shaped by the particular set of implicit value assumptions these communities presuppose relative to the metatheoretical dimensions of the four paradigms of modern social scientific thought.

Using Weber's (1904/1949) insights and terminology, each theory can be understood as an ideal type, an exaggerated, one-sided profession of faith grounded in a particular paradigmatic value orientation. Although this is the subjectivist notion of science that Kuhn (1970) and other philosophers of science (e.g., Feyerabend, 1975) have used to reconceptualize the growth of scientific knowledge in the single-paradigm sciences, the idea of normatively regulated scientific communities takes on a different meaning relative to the multiple-paradigm sciences. Rather than attempting to understand the growth of knowledge as a revolutionary overthrow of one paradigm by another, as in the single-paradigm sciences, the emphasis in the case of multiple-paradigm sciences is on the growth in understanding that results from being open to multiple perspectives, from being open to the "moments of truth" in various ideal-typical interpretations of a single phenomenon (see Skinner, 1972; Geertz, 1983; Rorty, 1982, 1989).

As such, given adequate methods and conditions of discourse, the growth of knowledge in the multiple-paradigm sciences can be conceptualized as *hermeneutical understanding* (see Gadamer, 1975; Rorty,

1979), a form of knowledge that results when we are exposed to, and come to understand, to one degree or another, the knowledge traditions of other cultural groups. Hermeneutical understanding is a form of practical wisdom that develops under methods and conditions of dialogue, questioning, and conversation, and that leads to "a more sensitive and critical understanding of our own [knowledge tradition] and of those prejudices that may lie hidden from us" (Bernstein, 1983, p. 36).

Such a discourse, of course, does not expect to discover the ultimate true theory of social life. Indeed, it recognizes from the start that this is conceptually impossible, because, by their very nature, paradigms, theories, and disciplinary perspectives are merely ways of seeing that simultaneously reveal and conceal. The concern of such a discourse, instead, is to bring together, in a single dialogical analysis, a number of perspectives or optional descriptions to see what we can learn from them, individually and in combination, as well as from the hermeneutical growth in understanding that results from being exposed to them under open conditions of dialogical conversation and critical questioning. As an act of inquiry, dialogical discourse:

> . . . does not mean that there are not better or worse arguments in support of a hypothesis or theory . . . [only that] there is no need to presuppose that there is some ultimate foundation or ultimate standards that must be presupposed to make [the] activity intelligible. . . . This is how we can escape from the parochialism of assuming that what we now take to be paradigmatic forms of argumentation are the only legitimate forms. (Bernstein, 1983 pp. 72–73)

Such an approach to inquiry provides a means for continually evaluating and reappraising what the members of the social sciences and social professions think, do, say, write, and read, as well as a means of evaluating and reappraising the manner in which such appraisals are conducted. Again, the goal is not certainty; it is edification. Such a discourse is educative, self-formative; it is a pedagogical process of continually searching for optional descriptions—new and more interesting ways of describing and expressing ourselves, our practices, and our institutions, and thus a continual search for new and more interesting ways of coping with the world. It is a way to help us avoid the delusion that somehow our conventional outlook is the only true one (Rorty, 1979, 1989).

As a mode of professional practice and discourse, critical pragmatism is a way of incorporating the imaginative and creative aspects of

Kuhn's notion of revolutionary science and Rorty's notion of utopian politics into normal operating procedures. As such, by accepting the fact that the metatheoretical and theoretical presuppositions that ground our practices and discourses themselves require evaluation and reappraisal, it is a method for bringing a sense of crisis to our pragmatic choices, which is necessary to actualize Cherryholmes' (1988) notions of *critical practice*—the continual construction, deconstruction, and reconstruction of professional practices—and *critical discourse*—the continual construction, deconstruction, and reconstruction of a method for critically appraising practices. Critical pragmatism is a method for actualizing Rorty's (1989) notion of redescribing ourselves and our practices and discourses in the field of education. It is a method that says "'try thinking of it this way' . . . 'try to ignore the apparently futile traditional questions by substituting the following new and possibly interesting questions'" (p. 9).

At the broadest level, the futile questions that critical pragmatism ignores are the traditional foundational questions of whether an objectivist or subjectivist orientation, or a microscopic/order or macroscopic/conflict outlook, is the correct posture for the social sciences and the professions. Thus, ultimately, critical pragmatism ignores the traditional monological question of whether the functionalist, interpretivist, radical structuralist, or radical humanist paradigm is the correct frame of reference. Instead, it assumes the antifoundational posture that no single paradigm has cognitive authority over the others, and, on this basis, substitutes the dialogical question of what we can learn by viewing ourselves and the social world from multiple perspectives, as well as the pragmatic question of how we can use what we learn from this hermeneutical experience to reconcile our practices, discourses, and institutions with our ideals.

The claim that no paradigm can assume cognitive authority over the others—that there is no inherently correct conceptualization—does not mean that our choice of a frame of reference to guide our professional practices and discourses is arbitrary. The point is that until now the professional practices and discourses of the field of education have been grounded in its history, in the unquestioned assumptions and conventions of its knowledge tradition. Of course, to be productive in an ambiguous world, the professional culture of education must have a paradigm for unrandomizing complexity. Although we can never escape the need for a paradigm, we can be reflective about our frames of reference and their implications for ethical practice and a just society. The crisis in modern knowledge is providing new ways to understand the paradigms, theories, and disciplinary perspectives of the social disciplines. The important thing about recognizing the possibility of optional descriptions is that we now have the opportunity—and the moral obligation—to ground our professional practices and discourses in our *values* rather than our *history*. Critical pragmatism is a way to begin this process in the field of education.

## CRITICAL PRAGMATISM AND CRITICAL INQUIRY

My approach to describing the methods for actualizing critical pragmatism as a mode of professional discourse will be to compare them to the methods proposed by Sirotnik and Oakes (1986, in press) for actualizing *critical inquiry*—a mode of professional discourse aimed at professional renewal and school restructuring that is based on Habermas' notion of critical theory (1970a, 1968/1970b, 1970c, 1968/1971, 1976/1979). As we know from the discussion in chapters 1 and 2, critical theory, like American pragmatism, is a form of emancipatory social analysis. As such, both approaches are critical; both employ the technique of immanent critique with the hope of freeing us from the unquestioned assumptions embedded in our ideologies (critical theory), or conventions (American pragmatism).

Ultimately, both approaches are interested in promoting a more self-reflective and emancipated form of social life—one in which our social practices are consistent with our social values. A key difference between the two approaches, however, is that critical theory is grounded in the modern social knowledge of the radical humanist paradigm, whereas philosophical pragmatism is postmodern. Thus, the most fundamental difference between critical inquiry and critical pragmatism is that critical inquiry, like critical theory, is premised on a foundational, or at best, quasifoundational, epistemology (see Antonio, 1989; Rorty, 1989), whereas critical pragmatism, like philosophical pragmatism, assumes an antifoundational epistemological stance. This, of course, has a number of substantive, methodological, and political implications, some of which are taken up below.

Beyond providing a way to explain what I mean by critical pragmatism as a mode of professional discourse, a presentation format in which critical pragmatism is described by comparing it to critical inquiry has several additional advantages. First, it permits me to use critical pragmatism *as a method of inquiry* for describing critical pragmatism *as a mode of professional discourse*. The advantage of such a presentation format is that using critical pragmatism (as a method of inquiry) to critique Sirotnik and Oakes's notion of critical inquiry illustrates Cherryholmes' (1988) notion of a critical professional discourse—"continual movement between the constitution of a methodology designed to [carry out the construction and deconstruction of practices] and subsequent criticism of that approach" (p. 97). As such, my comments on critical inquiry as a mode of professional renewal and school restructuring in education can be read as a deconstruction of a methodology that has been proposed for carrying out the deconstruction of professional practice in the field of education.

Second, comparing critical pragmatism to critical inquiry permits me to highlight what I believe to be several methodological and political blind spots in critical theory, which has two advantages. By comparing critical inquiry and critical pragmatism as modes of emancipatory professional discourse, I am able to compare their epistemological groundings—critical theory and American pragmatism, respectively. The advantage here is that such a comparison permits me to reinforce and extend some of my earlier arguments about the necessity of an antifoundational grounding for the social sciences and social professions. Moreover, because critical theory is beginning to be recognized in the field of education as an important method of inquiry, largely as a result of the insightful work of educational theorists such as Apple (1982), Giroux (1983a, 1988), and Popkewitz (1980) and applied researchers such as Sirotnik and Oakes (1986, in press), a comparative presentation also allows me to comment on the adequacy of critical theory as a method of social analysis, and thus as a grounding for a critical renewal in education.

In the analysis to follow, I will again employ the ideal-typical technique. That is, I will exaggerate certain aspects of critical inquiry and critical pragmatism to accentuate their respective value orientations. On this basis, I will argue that both approaches profess the same ideals, but that the methods for actualizing critical inquiry contradict these ideals, whereas the methods of critical pragmatism are consistent with them. Ultimately, I will argue that the approach for actualizing this value orientation should be grounded in the postmodern or antifoundational philosophy of pragmatism rather than the modern or foundational sociology of critical theory.[1]

## CRITICAL INQUIRY

Sirotnik and Oakes's (1986, in press) proposed critical inquiry as a form of educational evaluation geared to professional renewal and school restructuring.[2] Ultimately, Sirotnik and Oakes are interested in promoting social justice and an emancipated form of social life through a cultural transformation in public education and society. Grounded in the normative epistemology of critical theory, critical inquiry is carried out by resident educators in local school settings, with the assistance of external collaborators drawn from the ranks of applied scientists in education, who serve an *educative* rather than an *evaluative* function. As such, critical inquiry, like critical theory, can be located in the radical humanist or macro-subjective paradigm of social scientific thought. Given its paradigmatic grounding, critical inquiry represents a radical departure from all previous forms of educational evaluation in several respects.

From a metatheoretical perspective, it represents a radical turn in educational evaluation because of its stance on the place of values in inquiry. That is, unlike any of the preceding generations of evaluation research, it assumes a *normative stance*. As Sirotnik and Oakes pointed out, all previous evaluation approaches, regardless of their philosophical assumptions and methodological procedures, "share one critical feature. They *advocate* no value position" (in press, p. 1).

Referring to the conceptual framework, we can understand the history of evaluation research as taking place exclusively in the two microscopic paradigms, beginning in the functionalist paradigm and gradually moving into the interpretivist paradigm (see Guba & Lincoln, 1987; Stake, 1967). Functionalist approaches to evaluation, which continue to dominate evaluation practices in education, eschew values because they fall outside the realm of objectivist science, according to the epistemological and methodological assumptions of the paradigm. And whereas interpretivist approaches (e.g., ethnography, naturalistic inquiry) (see Lincoln & Guba, 1985) recognize the role of values in inquiry, their metatheoretical assumptions about science and society call for a value-relative posture based on a negotiated consensus among research participants. Because they share the subjectivist view of science with the interpretivists, Sirotnik and Oakes recognize that inquiry is value-bound. But because they also subscribe to the macroscopic or conflict perspective of society, they insist that some values simply cannot be negotiated away. Given the radical humanist grounding of critical inquiry, for Sirotnik and Oakes social justice is one of these values (1986, in press).

The second way that critical inquiry departs radically from the historical development of evaluation research is in its *perspective on truth*. By recognizing both empirical and interpretive knowledge as necessary and useful, it deemphasizes the traditional epistemological debate over the question of whether truth is to be found through expert consensus (functionalist perspective) or through participant consensus (interpretivist perspective). This is a topic that, under the names of "the quantitative-qualitative debate" and "the compatibilist-incompatibilist debate" (see Firestone, 1989; Howe, 1988; Skrtic, in press b; Smith & Heshusius, 1986), occupied much space in the educational inquiry literature in the late 1980s. More important, however, the radical turn to the humanist perspective shifts the attention of the evaluation community for the first time to the order-conflict debate, which, of course, is a familiar and ongoing discourse in the social sciences. As we know, this debate pits conflict against order or consensus, and thus questions the value of consensus itself as an orientation to social analysis, while emphasizing conflict as a more appropriate basis for inquiry (see Mitroff & Pondy, 1974; chapter 1).

Finally, critical inquiry represents a radical break from previous evaluation approaches in its *conceptualization of knowledge*—a move away from monological knowledge and toward dialogical knowledge, which has both a methodological and a political implication. Methodologically, the dialogical stance of critical inquiry, in principle, opens it up to the voice of other paradigms, a matter to be taken up more fully below. The political implication is that, whereas interpretivists attempt to negotiate a consensus among the multiple voices of *participants* within a particular social context, and functionalists attempt to negotiate a consensus among the multiple voices of *experts* (researchers) within a particular data set, radical humanists, although open to interpretive and empirical knowledge, are not concerned primarily with negotiating a *consensus* among participants or experts. Their ultimate aim is immanent critique—an attempt to negotiate a *reconciliation* between normative ideals and actual social practices (see Kloppenberg, 1986; Skrtic, in press b; chapter 2).

Characteristic of the radical humanist perspective, critical inquiry ultimately seeks reconciliation between the normative standard of social justice and the social practice of public education. As noted, this normative posture is methodologically radical because it is unprecedented in evaluation research; it is politically radical because it serves an educative and emancipatory function aimed at cultural transformation through a critical emergence in inquiry participants, which is an approach to educational inquiry most often associated with the work of Freire (1970, 1973).

The most paradigmatically distinctive and politically important feature of critical inquiry is its normative stance. The most methodologically interesting and useful concept introduced by Sirotnik and Oakes is the notion of "dialogical validity," which they described as "the capability of information to nurture, stimulate, or otherwise provoke rigorous discourse" (Sirotnik & Oakes, in press, p. 14).

## BEHIND CRITICAL INQUIRY

Although the educative, emancipatory, and transformative ideals of critical inquiry represent a radical turn in evaluation research, its methods contradict such a value orientation. This is so because, although it calls for critical reflection through dialogical discourse, it excludes from the critical dialogue important *paradigmatic, substantive,* and *political* voices.

### Paradigmatic Voices

In terms of paradigmatic voices, although critical inquiry is multivocal, in the sense of including the functionalist, interpretivist, and radical humanist perspectives, it violates its own methodological standard of dialogical validity because it excludes the structuralist perspective. This exclusion is understandable, however, because critical theory, the epistemological and methodological grounding of critical inquiry, also tends to exclude the structuralist perspective (see Antonio, 1989; Giroux, 1983a).

The methodological implications of this omission are obvious: The modes of analysis characteristic of the structuralist paradigm are precluded from use in critical inquiry. More important, the targets of analysis (material structures such as law and bureaucracy) and the extant insights gained from applying structuralist inquiry to these targets are lost to the critical inquirer—a matter to be taken up at some length below. The political implications of excluding the structuralist perspective are even more troubling because Sirotnik and Oakes, like critical theorists generally, assume that change will occur through a cultural revolution—a revolution in consciousness premised on a critique of culture.

Although such an approach is intellectually and emotionally attractive and, I believe, politically and practically essential for professional renewal, school restructuring, and cultural transformation (see Skrtic, 1988b; Part Three), it runs the risk of ignoring, and thus leaving intact, the material structures of the profession and of school organization. In any event, if such a cultural revolution were successful in raising the level of critical consciousness in the profession of education, a major practical outcome undoubtedly would be recognition of the need for restructuring school organizations. But, as we will see in Part Three, restructuring will require knowledge of material structures such as law, bureaucracy, and professionalization itself, as well as their implications for ideational structures such as professional and political culture and ideology. All of this will require insights from the structuralist paradigm, which has no voice in critical inquiry. In a Foucauldian (1980b) sense, critical inquiry misses the oportunity to uncover certain forms of buried knowledge.

### Substantive Voices

As in the case of critical theory, critical inquiry advocates using theory to interpret and reinterpret empirical and interpretive data. Thus, Sirotnik and Oakes described critical inquiry as an "approach, driven by a critical theoretical stance, that makes use of appropriate information gathered from naturalistic [interpretivist] and empirical analytic [functionalist] inquiries" (Sirotnik & Oakes, in press, pp. 13–14). In addition, because it is a method for achieving critical understanding of the social, cultural, political, organizational, and economic circumstances of the development and institutionalization of current schooling practices, it also must employ a multidisciplinary orientation. And, of course, because each social discipline is a multiple paradigm science, critical inquiry, in addition to being theoretical and multidisciplinary, must also be multiparadigmatic. Thus, to raise the level of critical consciousness of participants, it must introduce into the critical discourse at each school site various theories drawn from the multiple paradigms of the multiple disciplines of the social sciences.

Although critical inquiry calls for a substantively dialogical orientation, it fails to establish one in three respects. First, although use of insights from critical theory will permit some disciplinary and theoretical perspectives to enter the discourse, critical theory alone does not address adequately the range of disciplinary and theoretical perspectives necessary. This is so because it tends to exclude theoretical insights from the structuralist perspective, as noted, and because, as Geuss (1981) argued, the range of disciplinary theories considered as "critical" theories tends to be limited to the sociological theory of the early (Hegelian) Marx and the psychoanalytic theory of Freud.

Second, although a multidisciplinary approach is required and implied, only a single disciplinary perspective—that of organization analysis—is explicitly indicated in the description of critical inquiry.[3] Finally, rather than a dialogical or multiparadigmatic approach for draw-ing theory from the discipline of organization analysis, critical inquiry actually reverts to a monological posture, in that, it only considers organization theory from one of the four paradigms. Because the methodological implications of limiting the number of *disciplines* included in the discourse are obvious for a methodology premised on a critical theoretical analysis of the historical, social, cultural, political, organizational, and economic circumstances of schooling, let us focus our attention on the implications of a substantively monological approach to selecting a disciplinary *paradigm* from which to draw organization theory.

Apparently influenced most heavily by Goodlad's (1975) and Sarason's (1971, 1982) thoughtful analyses of school organizations as cultures, Sirotnik and Oakes tend to overemphasize the cultural perspective at the cost of ignoring other paradigmatic conceptualizations of organization and change.[4] As we will see in chapters 8 and 9, culture is a powerful and, until recently, relatively underutilized, perspective for understanding organizations. But an exclusively cultural perspective has several disadvantages, which will become apparent in Part Three. At this point, it will be sufficient to note that the major problem created by exclusive use of the cultural perspective on school organization and change is that it minimizes the search for other barriers to change, such as structural, behavioral, and interpretive factors. Thus, in the case of Sirotnik and Oakes, the search for noncultural barriers to change is virtually precluded because culture is assumed to "determine . . . organizational structures, patterns of behavior, and ways of interrelating" (in press, p. 7).

As we will see in Part Three, although culture is a viable way to think about organization and change, depending on one's paradigmatic perspective, one could just as well argue, for example, that cognition shapes structure (Weick, 1985), that structure shapes culture (Mintzberg, 1979) or, in fact, that organizations are the continuous and reciprocal interaction of activity, cognition, structure, and culture (see Skrtic, 1988b; Part Three). The point is that a substantively monological view of school organization and adaptability limits understanding and thus limits unnecessarily the educative and emancipatory capabilities of critical inquiry and, ultimately, its transformative potential.

Turning to a more practical issue regarding theoretical and disciplinary perspectives, and assuming that a full range of such perspectives were identified and slated for entry into the critical discourse, it is not clear who in the process of critical inquiry would have the capacity to serve as the bearer and explicator of these disciplinary and theoretical perspectives. One might logically look to the outside collaborator to serve in this capacity, but Sirotnik and Oakes's implication that these collaborators be drawn from the ranks of "university-based educators" (in press, p. 25) doesn't seem tenable at present. This is particularly the case when we consider the fact that the field of educational evaluation is hardly producing evaluators with even an interpretivist perspective (Guba & Lincoln, 1987), much less a critical theoretical perspective.

Of course, there is some potential for drawing collaborators from foundations of education departments, or from the ranks of the relatively few education faculty members involved in critical studies, or perhaps from among those who are students of organization in departments of educational administration, most of whom, in any event, are likely to hold an exclusively micro-objective or functionalist view (see Clark, 1985; chapter 7). The problem with respect to drawing the collaborators from the ranks of university-based educators is that, generally speaking, neither the field of education, in general, nor the field of educational evaluation, in particular, can be considered theoretical or critical.

### Political Voices

Perhaps the most troubling absence of voices in critical inquiry is the omission of students and community members from the critical discourse. Clearly, the "participants" in critical inquiry are professional educators and educational evaluators. Although Freire's (1973) notion of emancipation through the development of critical consciousness is a pervasive theme in critical inquiry, the people in need of emancipation, according to the approach, do not include students and community members who, in addition to professional educators, are Freire's principal targets for emancipation. Following Freire (1973), Sirotnik and Oakes (1986) recognize that the process of critical emergence requires a self-effacing guide. But by converting his idea of the "teacher-student/student-teacher" relationship to a "collaborators-teachers/teachers-collaborators" (p. 47) relationship, they distort the integral relationship among the teacher, students, and community members—which has negative methodological and political implications.

Methodologically, the possibility of a critical emergence in educators depends heavily on the dialogical discourse between teachers and students. Responding to a question about the ways in which professional educators can become critical and reflective, Freire indicated the key role of his students in his own critical emergence by noting that, "from the beginning . . . [my emergence depended on my] dialogue with the students" (Shor & Freire, 1987, p. 28). With regard to the role of community members in his critical development, Freire added that "the more I discussed with them the problems of schools and kids, the more I became convinced that I should study their expectations" (Shor & Freire, 1987, p. 28). And, although one could argue that the voices of students and community members will be heard through the interpretivist research that will be analyzed as part of the critical inquiry, the only voices involved in the critical discourse—that is, the critical interpretation and reinterpretation of the empirical and interpretive knowledge that is produced through these methods—are those of professional educators and educational evaluators. This, of course, is not a dialogue among educators, students, and community members, and, thus, in a methodological sense, it minimizes the possibility of a critical emergence in educators and their collaborators.

In principle, of course, one can appreciate the logic of emancipating professional educators first and, presumably, students and community members later, once the educators have emerged as critical thinkers. Furthermore, there is little doubt that the questions Sirotnik and Oakes (1986, in press) pose as illustrative of the kinds of issues to be addressed within the critical inquiry are sensitive to the interests of students and community members in general, and to those of marginalized groups in particular. But politically, we must not lose sight of the fact that the ultimate end is a just system of public education and a just society. In this regard, if students and community members are neither present in the critical discourse nor, more important, the beneficiaries of critical emergence, there is the real danger that they may be liberated from certain forms of professional and social domination only to be placed under new forms of domination. As clients and constituents of public education, students and community members possess valuable forms of disqualified knowledge, which, in Foucault's (1980b) sense, provides profound insight into social institutions and disciplinary practices.

As Freire (1970, p. 74) noted, "in the [transformative] process, the leaders cannot utilize the [traditional methods of schooling] as an interim measure, justified on grounds of expediency, with the intention of later behaving in a genuinely [transformative] fashion. They must be [transformative]—that is to say, dialogical—from the outset." By limiting the dialogical discourse to resident educators and external collaborators, and excluding the voices of students and community members, critical inquiry fails to appreciate fully the political moment of the critical project.


## THE CASE FOR CRITICAL PRAGMATISM

As we have seen, critical inquiry represents a radical turn in evaluation research in both a political and a methodological sense. Politically it is radical because it seeks social transformation through a cultural revolution in public education, a revolution in consciousness that is grounded in and sustained by a dialogical discourse conducted within and focused upon the institutional practices of the profession of education. Thus, because it is a means to a negotiated reconciliation between the ethical ideal of social justice and the actual institutional practice of public education, critical inquiry is a substantively rational, normative political act. In all of these ways, the value orientation of critical inquiry and critical pragmatism is virtually identical.

Methodologically, critical inquiry is radical because it advocates a normative stance relative to the place of values in educational inquiry, and a dialogical conceptualization of truth, knowledge, and method. Given its ethical posture and dialogical epistemology, it is a method that, in principle, is premised on a democratized discourse among the multiple voices of paradigmatic perspectives, academic disciplines, substantiative theories, and political interests. As such, the politics and methodology of critical inquiry cannot be separated; it is a political methodology. In this sense, it is a form of radical democracy carried out in and through the institution of public education and the profession of education. Here again, the value orientation of critical inquiry and critical pragmatism are, in principle, virtually identical.

Although critical inquiry is a means to critical renewal and transformation through dialogical discourse, its actual methods, while multivocal, fail to meet its own standard of dialogical validity in terms of paradigmatic perspectives, substantive theories, and political interests. As a result, the practices of critical inquiry are inconsistent with its educative, emancipatory, and transformative value orientation. The source of the distortion is its grounding in critical theory. Referring to the conceptual framework in Part One, the problem with critical theory is that, even though it is normative, radical, and multivocal—and thus consistent with the aims of critical inquiry—it is also modern. The problem with being modern is that, ultimately, critical theory is foundational. The danger here, of course, is that, for the radical humanist, as for the functionalist, interpretivist, and radical structuralist, methodology can become ontology. And this is not merely an academic concern. Referring back to the discussion of the link between the missing paradigmatic and substantive voices, the problem of methodology becoming ontology is more than a tendency in critical inquiry.

Sirotnik and Oakes's assertion that "during the process of critical inquiry . . . participants come to view schools from the cultural perspective that . . . is essential for change" (in press, p. 16) is an indication that their allegiance to critical theory, and thus to the view that inquiry *is* a critique of culture, already has begun to shape their ontology. The point is that anything less than a fully developed dialogical perspective—methodologically, substantively, politically—can become ideology and thus distort inquiry and social action in unconscious ways.

Because it is grounded in the philosophy of pragmatism rather than the sociology of critical theory, critical pragmatism retains the normative value orientation of critical inquiry and, at the same time, provides the dialogical conceptualization of knowledge, truth, and method that it requires. By replacing the modern or monological perspective of critical theory with the postmodern or dialogical perspective of philosophical pragmatism, critical pragmatism as a mode of professional and educational renewal increases the possibility of an educative, emancipatory, and transformative discourse while it decreases the danger of methodology becoming ontology.

Another advantage of grounding critical professional discourse in philosophical pragmatism is related to the practical problem of providing collaborators who are capable of performing in an educative and emancipatory capacity. If my earlier comments about the readiness of education faculty members are accurate, a good deal of developmental work has to be done. The advantage of pragmatism in this regard is that, in addition to being a theory of knowledge, truth, and method, it is also a theory of education. As Dewey (1899/1976a) explained, the pragmatist theory of education calls for a pedagogy that engages humans' natural capacity to think by using concrete problem solving to develop critical reflective thought.

Applied to the problem of the acritical and atheoretical nature of the field of education, critical pragmatism, grounded in philosophical pragmatism, draws on the pragmatist theory of education as a means of achieving a critical emergence in inquiry participants and collaborators. That is, the minds of participants and would-be collaborators are put to work by using the method of critical pragmatism to conduct inquiries in schools and colleges of education—with education faculty members, graduate and undergraduate students, and community members as participants, and faculty members and students from the social disciplines as collaborators—coincidentally with inquiries in public school settings in which the participants are educators, students, and community members, and the collaborators are the faculty members, students (in education and the social sciences), and community members who are participating in the higher education inquiries.

In addition to addressing the practical problem of providing the requisite collaborators, as well as the political and methodological problems associated with the need to include the voices of students and community members at public school and higher education sites, this would prepare a corps of education students who are oriented to and capable of participating in and mounting critical inquiries at other public school and higher education sites in the future.

And in addition to including these voices, of course, it would be necessary for the expanded discourse to include the voices of the other social professions that participate directly or indirectly in public education. This would include the related professional fields that work in schools, as well as those that work in the community at large, such as social work, community psychology, health, and criminology, with whom educators often share a common set of clients. Finally, it goes without saying that such an expanded discourse would include students who have, or have been treated as though they have, disabilities, and their most immediate advocates, their parents and siblings. Given my arguments in Part Three, the insights of these students and constituents of public education represent ideal typical cases of disqualified knowledge—the most profound insights on professional and institutional injustice in education and thus the most useful knowledge for critical renewal.

A final advantage of critical pragmatism over critical inquiry is that, in addition to being a theory of knowledge, truth, method, and education, philosophical pragmatism is also a theory of ethics. From the vantage point of philosophical pragmatism, the basic problem with traditional utilitarian theories of ethics, as well as the formalistic (e.g., Rawls, 1971) and universalistic (e.g., critical theory) ones that criticize them, is that they all favor rules over intelligence for determining the right and the good. The pragmatist theory of ethics, of course, is based on the opposite preference. Faced with difficult choices, Dewey (1927/ 1988c; Dewey & Tufts, 1932/1989) advised, justice can best be discerned by applying the pragmatic method rather than searching for the applicable rule. For the pragmatists, the way to social justice, like the way to knowledge, truth, education, and democracy itself, is dialogical inquiry.

To this point in my ideal-typical characterization of critical pragmatism, I have addressed only the methods for conducting such a discourse. But as Dewey (1929–30/1988b) noted, an approach to emancipation based on the pragmatist notion of dialogical inquiry requires, in addition to methods of discourse, adequate conditions in which to initiate and sustain the discourse. Of course, like Sirotnik and Oakes, I am recommending that critical pragmatism be carried out in educational institutions, primarily in public schools, in collaboration with schools of education and universities. The problem, however, is that, while such a discourse requires dialogue, questioning, and conversation, these activities are characteristically lacking in traditional school organizations (see Sirotnik & Oakes, 1986; Sarason, 1982).[5] Thus, critical pragmatism as a method for deconstructing and reconstructing the practices and discourses of the professional culture of education must remain a utopia until the conditions for its realization have been addressed, which, in conjunction with looking behind special education as an institutional practice, is a matter taken up in Part Three.

## NOTES

1. Although Sirotnik and Oakes (1986) recognize critical theory's debt to philosophical pragmatism and the Deweyan intellectual tradition (also see Benhabib, 1986; Habermas, 1968/1970b; Rorty, 1989), ultimately they reject Dewey for his antifoundational and pragmatic stance because he "failed (or was unwilling) to explicitly acknowledge the profound *moral* universal in his philosophy" (1986, p. 30). The problem here is that Sirotnik and Oakes' understanding of emancipatory theorizing is premised on Habermas' (1968/1970b) "ethical universalism and evolutionary normative justification" (Antonio, 1989, p. 736), that is, the evolutionary form of emancipatory theorizing in which the normative standard of emancipation is a moral universal and thus nonfalsifiable. Dewey, of course, employed the historical form of emancipatory theorizing in which normative standards emerge out of historically situated critical discourses (see chapter 2). Thus, Dewey did not fail to acknowledge a moral universal in his philosophy; he explicitly avoided it because he believed that moral universalism distorts morality by substituting rules for intelligence in moral matters (see Dewey & Tufts, 1932/1989). For Dewey, moral universalism diminishes morality of its spontaneity and relevance for life, degrades practical activity, and, ultimately, is impractical because it establishes "ends without means for their realization" (Dewey & Tufts, 1932/1989, p. 344).

According to Dewey (1930/1988a, 1929/1988d), all normative content is culturally and historically specific, and thus universalistic claims are usually elitist and impervious to critical dialogue, which diminishes normative dialogue about social issues. Thus, critical theory, by insisting on a universalistic normative standard— "*unrestrained* human reason as the backbone of experiential knowledge and action" (Sirotnik & Oakes, 1986, p. 30)—paradoxically contradicts its own standard for unrestrained, dialogical, emancipatory discourse (see Antonio, 1989; Rorty, 1989). Ultimately, on the basis of its normative stance, critical theory must reject the other three paradigms, because they have no such standard, which makes it and Sirotnik and Oakes' notion of critical inquiry monological and foundational, which, in turn violates their own methodological standard of "dialogical validity" and introduces several serious negative implications, matters that are taken up in the text.

2. Sirotnik and Oakes (1986) provide a comprehensive discussion of methodological procedures and issues relative to critical inquiry. Along with Cherryholmes (1988), Freire (1970, 1973), Giroux (1988), and Greene (1978), I recommend their work highly to anyone interested in pursuing such a critical project in public education, with the caveats noted in this chapter, of course.

3. As we will see in Part Three, the field of organization analysis is a multidisciplinary endeavor, in that it attracts theorists from all of the social sciences. The problem here is that, although organization analysis as a disciplinary orientation is an extremely important perspective (or variety of perspectives), it does not on its own provide the the-

oretical insights to address the social, cultural, political, and economic circumstances of the development and institutionalization of current schooling practices, even though it does, of course, provide theoretical insights on their organizational circumstances.

4. Although Sirotnik and Oakes (1986) recognize other theories of organization (e.g., Meyer & Rowan, 1978), which (as we will see in Part Three) represent other paradigmatic perspectives to one degree or another, their reading of these theories ultimately is dominated by the cultural perspective. Thus, although referring to Sirotnik and Oakes as monological in this regard is an exaggeration in a technical sense, the fact that they implicitly select theory from paradigms other than the radical humanist paradigm, but read them as having only cultural implications, further illustrates my point about the monological and foundationalist tendency of critical theory.

5. Of course, Sirotnik and Oakes and I are not the first people to argue that schools should be sites of critical discourse. Indeed, in addition to the contemporary authors listed in note 2 above (among others), Dewey made the same argument earlier in this century, during what I will call the "social reconstructionists" phase of the progressive era (see chapter 7, note 2; chapter 10). Nevertheless, although the idea of social reconstruction and cultural transformation through education has had a great deal of emotional appeal for many people in this century, it has always suffered from the same problem—the inherent circularity in the argument that an institution that both reflects and, in part at least, transmits the cultural sensibility of society can be used to transform it (see chapter 10). We will see in the concluding chapter that, although Dewey and his contemporaries had adequate methods of discourse, what they lacked were the conditions within public education for such a discourse to emerge and flourish. What is different today, I believe, and thus why critical pragmatism is more than just another romantic notion of social progress, is that the emerging historical conditions of the 21st century both require and make possible the type of school organizations in which a reflective discourse can arise and sustain itself.

# PART THREE
# School Organization

# 7

# Two Discourses on Organization and Change

Young people today will have to learn organization the way their fore-fathers learned farming.

Peter Drucker[1]

Traditionally, organizations have been viewed merely as social tools, as mechanisms that societies use to achieve goals that are beyond the reach of individual citizens (Parsons, 1960). But Drucker's comment refers to the fact that organizations have become much more than tools; they have become the dominant characteristic of modern societies. For example, in addition to doing things *for* society, organizations do things *in* society. Like citizens, they can act, enter into contracts, use resources, own property, and transact with natural persons. As such, organizations have become social actors in their own right; they have become corporate persons, and thus have altered the very structural elements of which society is composed (Coleman, 1974).

In addition to doing things for society and in society, organizations do things *to* society. Historically, they have been criticized for dominating the political process, bureaucratizing human existence, causing alienation and overconformity, and distorting personality development (e.g., Argyris, 1957; Galbraith, 1967; Goodman, 1968). More recently, however, organizations have been recognized as having an even greater effect on society: The very goals society uses organizations to achieve are shaped by the nature of the organizations that are used to achieve them (Scott, 1981). Consider these examples:

> In his crucial decision on how to react to the installation of Russian missiles in Cuba, President Kennedy had to select from among a naval blockade, a "surgical" air strike, and a massive land invasion, not because these were the only conceivable responses, but because these were the principal organizational routines that had been worked out by the Pentagon. (Allison, 1971)

> Although we seek "health" when we visit the clinic or the hospital, what we get is "medical care." Clients are encouraged to view these outputs as synonymous although there may be no relation between them. In some cases, the relation can even be negative: more care can result in poorer health. (Illich, 1976)

> Products manufactured by organizations reflect the manufacturing process. They often reflect the need to subdivide work and to simplify tasks, and the manufacturing pressures toward standardization of parts and personnel. . . . Customization—in the genuine sense, not in the Detroit sense—becomes prohibitively expensive. Metal replaces wood and plastic replaces metal in many products to satisfy organizational, not consumer, needs. (Scott, 1981, p. 6)

Like defense, health, and consumer goods, education is a social goal shaped by the medium of an organization. Society wants education, but what it gets is a particular kind of schooling, one shaped by the particular kind of organization used as the mechanism to provide it. Although, as such, the organizational context of schooling should be an important topic of study for educators, historically they have neglected it. Part of the problem has been that, until relatively recently, school organization has been the exclusive domain of the field of educational administration, which, as we will see, not only has taken a narrow view of school organization but historically has avoided research topics related to school effects and student outcomes (Erickson, 1979; Bridges, 1982).

## ORGANIZATIONAL ANALYSIS AND EDUCATIONAL ADMINISTRATION

Understanding the history of the study of organizations is essential for understanding school organization and the field of educational administration. This is so because for most of this century, the practices and discourses in educational administration have been dominated by the broader discourse on organization, which is actually two discourses: the *prescriptive* and the *scholarly*. The prescriptive discourse emerged around the turn of the century and, since then, has been carried out by practitioners in business and industry who have been concerned primarily with controlling people who work in organizations (Edwards, 1979). The scholarly discourse emerged after World War II, at which point organizations became a legitimate area of academic study in the various social disciplines (Scott, 1981). As such, the scholarly discourse on organization is carried out by theorists in the multidisciplinary field of organization analysis. Although the field of organization analysis also is influenced by the needs of business and industry and thus by the prescriptive discourse, it is concerned primarily with understanding the nature and functioning of organizations and their effects on people and society (Pfeffer, 1982).

It is helpful to think of the study of organizations, including school organizations, as progressing over three interrelated and overlapping time periods and corresponding schools of thought: the *classical period*, the *human relations era*, and the *theory movement*.

### The Classical Period

During the first quarter of this century, the prescriptive discourse was dominated by two overriding organizational concerns: the division of labor and the coordination or control of work, which gave rise to two complementary schools of thought on organization and management (see Mintzberg, 1979). The first was Frederick Taylor's notion of scientific management (Taylor, 1911/1947), an elaborate and detailed set of prescriptions for standardizing work processes in industrial organizations. The second school of thought (Fayol, 1916/1949; Gulick & Urwick, 1937) was premised on administrative prescriptions for bringing work under the formal control of managers. The major accomplishment of the classical period was the synthesis of the notion of standardization of work processes with those of formal authority and direct supervision, which yielded the basic hierarchical organizational form that will be referred to in subsequent sections and chapters as the *machine bureaucracy*. This is the familiar pyramid-shaped, top-down structure of formal control relations that is depicted in most organizational charts (Mintzberg, 1979).

The machine metaphor dominated the prescriptive discourse during the classical period. It guided organizational design and shaped the approach to management, which was premised on the notion of man-as-machine (Worthy, 1950). Managers were concerned with the division of labor, the specification of work processes and roles, and the allocation of power. They were virtually oblivious to the social dynamics of people at work, as well as to the influence of the environment on organizations (Scott, 1981). The overarching goal was efficiency, and the guiding conceptualization of organizations was that they were rational—purposeful and goal-directed. Organizations were understood as physical entities, as machines whose structures and processes could be rationally fine-tuned to achieve virtually endless efficiency (see Haber, 1964).

Given that they emerged during the progressive era, interest in and enthusiasm over scientific management and the machine bureaucracy configuration did not stop on the shop floor. The progressive era had given rise to "an efficiency craze—a secular Great Awakening, an outpouring of ideas and emotions in which the gospel of efficiency was preached without embarrassment to businessmen, workers, doctors, housewives, and teachers" (Haber, 1964, p. ix). Although scientific management and the machine bureaucracy were intended as methods for organizing and managing the mass production process in business and industry, reformers during the "social efficiency" phase of the progressive movement waged and won a vigorous campaign for their use as means to maximize the efficiency of social organizations, including schools (Haber, 1964, p. 58; Callahan, 1962).[2] Educational administrators were particularly vulnerable to the push for scientific management and the machine bureaucracy structure because of the unfortunate timing of several events:

> First, by 1910 a decade of concern with reform . . . had produced a public suspicious and ready to be critical of the management of all public institutions. Second, just at this time Taylor's system was brought dramatically before the nation, not with a mundane label such as "shop management" but with the appealing title of "scientific management." By 1912 the full force of public criticism had hit the schools. Third, by 1912 Americans were urging that business methods be introduced into the operation of government and were electing businessmen to serve on their school boards. Fourth, and of basic importance, was the fact that the "profession" of school administration was in 1910 in its formative stage, just being developed. If America had had a tradition of graduate training in administration—genuinely educational, intellectual, and scholarly, if not scientific—such a tradition might have served as a brake or restraining force. As it was, all was in flux. (Callahan, 1962, p. 245)

As a result, the professional grounding for educational administration became the prescriptive discourse of scientific management and the machine bureaucracy rather than, say, history, philosophy, or curriculum. Instead of becoming social, moral, or instructional leaders, school administrators became "experts in how to administrate and control organizations" (Spring, 1980, p. 100). Moreover, rather than a restraining force or a corrective, inquiry in the field also emphasized efficiency, and toward that end, school organization and management were analyzed much like work in the factory (see Bobbit, 1913). In effect, the value orientation behind the machine model and the efficiency mentality reinforced and shaped the functionalist view of education—teaching and learning as routinized drill and practice (Getzels & Jackson, 1960) and schools as mass producers of socialized workers (Bakalis, 1983; Spring, 1980)—and, as we will see below and in subsequent chapters, its associated theories of human pathology and organizational rationality.

### The Human Relations Era

Ironically, the classical period's lack of attention to the social dynamics of the work place was what ushered in the human relations era. Beginning in the 1920s (Follett, 1924, 1940) and coming to fruition in the 1930s and 1940s as a result of the Hawthorne studies (Mayo, 1933; Roethlisberger & Dickson, 1939), the key insight of the human relations orientation was the idea that an informal (social, cultural, or nonrational) structure of unofficial worker relations existed within the formal (rational) structure of organizations. The message for managers was that worker behavior did not conform to the official specifications of the organization but, rather, was determined by the norms, values, and sentiments of the workers in the informal structure. Proponents of the human relations approach argued against the classical notion of man-as-machine, and instead recommended increased attention to the relations of work groups and worker satisfaction and motivation, to the virtual exclusion of formal (rational or structural) organizational considerations. But the human relations approach, in this pure form, was short-lived, giving way to the most significant outcome of this period: Chester Barnard's (1938) attempt to synthesize the classical notion of formal (rational) structure with the human relations notion of informal (nonrational) structure.

In this synthesis Barnard (see also Simon, 1947) argued that organizations are essentially cooperative (rational) systems that can become uncooperative (nonrational) in the absence of certain management practices intended to maintain them in a state of equilibrium. To maintain the cooperative state, he urged managers to alter or condition the behavior and attitudes of workers through training, indoctrination, and the manipulation of incentives. Ultimately, however, Barnard considered humans to be inherently cooperative and regarded those who were "unfitted for co-operation" (1938, p. 13) to be "pathological cases, insane and not of this world" (Burrell & Morgan, 1979, p. 149). Appearing roughly a decade before the English version of Max Weber's theory of bureaucracy (see below), Barnard's synthesis was the first attempt to explicate an academic theory of organization. As such, it became extremely influential in the history of organizational studies (Perrow, 1972), and subsequently in the development of the field of educational administration, as we will see.

The impact of the initial phase of the human relations movement in industry was not lost on the field of educational administration. In the 1940s and early 1950s it was translated by educational administrators into the notion of *democratic practices*, an approach to school management that emphasized democracy and participation in all aspects of school organization—democratic teaching, supervision, decision making, and administration. Although on the surface greater attention was paid to the interpersonal aspects of life in schools, democratic practices were more apparent than real. Most often they meant little more than a new set of prescriptions for school administrators to follow (Campbell, 1971). As in the case of business administration, the most significant outcome of the human relations era for educational administration was Barnard's synthesis of the classical and human relations perspectives, a matter taken up below.

### The Theory Movement in Organizational Analysis

Scott (1981) marked the emergence of the formal study of organizations in the social disciplines with the publication in English of Max Weber's analysis of bureaucratic organizational structure in the late 1940s (Weber, 1922/1946a, 1924/1947). Writing during the classical period, Weber chronicled the advance of organizational rationality in the industrialized world by tracing the emergence of the bureaucratic organizational form and documenting the way its rational-legal type of authority relation was replacing more traditional (nonrational) forms. It is true, of course, that today "the terms bureaucracy and bureaucrat are epithets—accusations connoting rule-encumbered inefficiency and mindless overconformity" (Scott, 1981, p. 23), but in the 1940s, when Weber's work was published in English, the bureaucratic form was held in high regard within the prescriptive discourse. The irony was that, although Weber intended to warn his readers of the negative effects of bureaucracy, his ideal-typical analysis was misinterpreted within the prescriptive discourse and the emerging scholarly discourse as an endorsement of the bureaucratic form as the "ideal" organizational configuration, one that was capable of attaining the highest level of efficiency (see Burrell & Morgan, 1979; Mommsen, 1974). We will return to Weber's warning about bureaucracy and its misinterpretation in the social sciences and educational administration below and again in chapter 10. At this point, let us return to the discussion of the theory movement in organization analysis and the more positive effects of Weber's work on the scholarly discourse.

Weber's theory of bureaucracy—in essence, a sociology of organization—was precisely what was needed to launch the theory movement in the academic disciplines. For the first time American social scientists had what they needed to study organizations *as* organizations. The availability of Weber's treatise spurred interest among social scientists in the work of other relevant intellectual forebearers, including the authors of the classical and human relations eras. This body of work became the initial intellectual foundation for the emerging field of organization analysis and the scholarly discourse on organization. Expansion of the scholarly discourse into other disciplines occurred rapidly, and its first journals and texts appeared between the mid-1950s and the early 1960s, which began to provide some integration of the ever increasing volume of theoretical and empirical work (Scott, 1981).

Forty years of development in the field of organization analysis has produced what appears to be a bewildering array of competing and contradictory theories of organization (Pfeffer, 1982). One source of variability stems from the fact that the history of organizational analysis has been inextricably bound up with the history of organizational management. Thus, approaches to organization analysis have varied depending on whether the analyst is grounded in the scholarly or the prescriptive discourse (Edwards, 1979; Braverman, 1974). Another source of variability is the field's multidisciplinary nature. As we might expect from the discussion of professional induction, the various disciplinary specializations involved in the study of organizations tend to emphasize different aspects of organization.

A further source of variability stems from the fact that, in addition to being a multidisciplinary field, organization analysis is a multiparadigmatic intellectual endeavor. It is multiparadigmatic because, as we know, the various social disciplines involved in organization analysis are multiple-paradigm sciences. And, though its multiparadigmatic status has added to the apparent confusion in the field, it also provides a powerful source of clarification.

Because the field of organization analysis is grounded in the disciplines of the social sciences, the theories it produces reflect the various modes of theorizing found in the social disciplines, which can be understood in terms of the four paradigms of modern social scientific thought presented in chapter 1. As we will see in chapter 8, the paradigm shift to subjectivism and the meta-leap to antifoundationalism have affected the field of organization analysis in parallel ways, methodologically and substantively. For now, however, it is sufficient to note that virtually all of the thinking about organization and management contained in the prescriptive discourse, both prior to and after the emergence of the scholarly discourse in the social sciences, is characteristic of the functionalist or micro-objective paradigm. Although the human relations movement contained the seeds for what were to become nonrational (and thus nonfunctionalist) theories of organization, these insights were lost in Barnard's synthesis, which is a purely functionalist formulation (Burrell & Morgan, 1979).

Moreover, because the functionalist paradigm has been, and continues to be, the dominant framework for the social sciences, most of the work in organization analysis over its entire history has been done from the functionalist perspective. This is particularly true for the initial work done in the late 1940s and early 1950s, including the misinterpretation of Weber's theory of bureaucracy. In fact, although Weber's work is so rich and insightful that in subsequent years it has been claimed by all four paradigms, its misinterpretation during this period, by participants in both the prescriptive and the scholarly discourses, is largely the result of reading it from the functionalist perspective (Burrell & Morgan, 1979; Mommsen, 1974).

### The Theory Movement in Educational Administration

During the early 1950s the leading professors of educational administration rejected the prescriptive discourse as a grounding for their field. In effect, they argued that the atheoretical nature of the prescriptive discourse had precluded the development of a research base in the field, which, in turn, was responsible for the intellectual provincialism of its professional education programs and, ultimately, for the inadequate state of practice (see Griffiths, 1983). They argued for a more scientific and theoretical grounding and, toward that end, adopted the emerging field of organization analysis as a parent discipline in the mid-1950s, with the hope of drawing from it the growing body of theoretical and empirical research on organizations (Griffiths, 1959, 1983; Hayes & Pharis, 1967).

In addition, they adopted logical positivism, the dominant mode of inquiry in the field of organization analysis at that time, as well as the prevailing conceptualization of organizations as rational, machine bureaucracies—all of which, of course, meant that they had adopted from the field of organization analysis the functionalist approach to a social science (Griffiths, 1983; Clark, 1985). Furthermore, because the field of educational administration had been a participant in the prescriptive discourse prior to the mid-1950s, and thus already had been operating from the functionalist perspective, adopting the field of organizational analysis as a grounding discipline at this point in its development did not mean a change in perspective on organization and management. It merely meant a shift from a *prescriptive* and *experiential* approach to functionalism to a more *scientific* and *positivistic* approach to functionalism.

Over the next 10 years the leading professors of educational administration published several textbooks that attempted to integrate the prevailing organizational and methodological insights of organization analysis into the field of educational administration (Coladarci & Getzels, 1955; Campbell & Gregg, 1956; Halpin, 1958; Griffiths, 1959, 1964). Although the authors clearly advocated for the prevailing positivist orientation of the social sciences and the notion of theory as a guide to practice, the emphasis in the textbooks was on administration, not organization. In fact, material on schools *as* organizations was noticeably absent, which is understandable because the first theoretical treatment of schools as organizations within the scholarly discourse (Bidwell, 1965) appeared after the first theory-oriented texts on educational administration had been published. At the time, however, this was not recognized as a problem. It was assumed that all organizations were rational, machine bureaucracies (Clark, 1985) and that, as such, insights on organizing and managing schools could be drawn directly from research on and scientific expositions of any type of organization, including the machine bureaucracies of business and industry (Erickson, 1979; Griffiths, 1983).

The theory movement in educational administration suffered from several additional problems. First, it was based exclusively on the functionalist perspective on organization, which, given contemporary thinking in organization analysis, is an extremely narrow view of organization. During the first 10 years of the theory movement in educational administration, when the major work was done to appropriate organizational insights from the scholarly discourse, the field of organization analysis itself had a narrow functionalist view of organization—a perspective that, although still dominant, has been radically enriched by theoretical insights from the other three paradigms over the last 30 years, as we will see in the next chapter. The problem in this regard is that, after their initial engagement with the scholarly discourse, participants in the theory movement in educational administration became disengaged from the field of organization analysis, and thus have not been a part of the revolutionary developments in the field. Although there are notable exceptions (e.g., Bates, 1980, 1987; Foster, 1986), virtually all of the work on school organization in the field of educational administration has been done from the functionalist perspective (see Griffiths, 1983, 1988; Clark, 1985).

Second, for a number of social, political, and organizational reasons within the field of educational administration, the theory movement in educational administration never really captured the imagination of the vast majority of the professorate, or that of practicing administrators. Virtually everyone in the field, except for the leading professors who had initiated the theory movement, remained tied to the prescriptive discourse (Cunningham, Hack, & Nystrand, 1977; Halpin, 1970; Halpin & Hayes, 1977).

Finally, given the inability of the theory movement to influence either the applied science or the practitioner level of the field, the ultimate goal of improved administrative practices was not met (Campbell & Newell, 1973; Immegart, 1977). Thus, although the field of organization analysis continued to mature in its perspectives on organization and management from the late 1940s until today, the field of educational administration remains today essentially as it was in the mid-1950s, particularly with respect to domination of the field by functionalist conceptualizations of inquiry, school organization, and the practice of school administration (see Clark, 1985; Griffiths, 1988).

The theory movement did have at least two effects, however. First, it introduced Weber's theory of bureaucracy into the field, which, given the functionalist misreading it received, further reinforced the functionalist notion of organizational rationality (see Clark, 1985). Second, it appropriated Barnard's theory of administration and introduced it into the educational administration knowledge tradition by way of the Getzels-Guba model of administration (Getzels & Guba, 1957), which Griffiths characterized as "the most successful theory in educational administration" (1979, p. 50), thus reinforcing the functionalist notion of organizational rationality in the field and, more important, linking it directly with the functionalist theory of human pathology.

## EDUCATIONAL ADMINISTRATION AND SPECIAL EDUCATION

In several important ways the genealogies of the fields of educational administration and special education parallel one another. First, both are products of the social efficiency phase of the progressive era. As we will see in the following two chapters, the same efficiency craze that forced scientific management and the machine bureaucracy on the developing field of educational administration created the need for a field such as special education. Second, both fields have been in a virtually constant state of self-criticism since the 1960s. As we saw in chapter 3, except for a lull just before and after enactment of the EHA, special education has operated under a cloud of uncertainty regarding its practices during this entire period. In educational administration the uncertainty over its practices that existed before the theory movement reemerged in the 1960s and 1970s when the leading professors realized that few of their colleagues were following them (see Cunningham et al., 1977; Halpin, 1970), and it piqued again in the 1980s in the wake of the excellence movement (see National Policy Board, 1989).

Finally, and most important for present purposes, both fields are grounded in functionalism and the mutually reinforcing theories of human pathology and organizational rationality. And, because these theories are two sides of the same coin, the fields of special education and educational administration are flip sides of the same conceptual confusion that has plagued the profession and institution of education throughout the 20th century.

## SCHOOL ORGANIZATION AND THE PROBLEM OF CHANGE

The most significant development in the field of education relative to school organization has been the emergence of a research tradition on educational change. Although one can find attempts to study school organizations and change throughout most of this century (see, e.g., Miles, 1964; Mort & Cornell, 1941), the most sustained and concentrated effort began in the 1950s, when the National Science Foundation began funding what was to become a series of curriculum development projects (see Elmore & McLaughlin, 1988). Organizationally, the research tradition is largely a loose confederation of applied researchers representing virtually every field in education (see Lehming & Kane, 1981), including educational administration and special education. Although most of the tradition's pioneers were from educational administration (see Miles, 1964), special educators became involved to a degree in the 1960s relative to efficacy studies on the special classroom, and more earnestly in the 1970s and 1980s relative to EHA implementation (see, e.g., Biklen, 1985; Skrtic, Guba, & Knowlton, 1985).

Emergence of the research tradition of educational change has had both political and methodological implications for organizational studies in education. Politically, it ended the exclusive grip of educational administration on the study of schools. As we know, educational administration had tended to avoid the topics of school effects and student outcomes (Bridges, 1982; Erickson, 1979). Moreover, concern was expressed about the political implications of a process in which the persons who are accountable for education were also evaluating it (see Becker, 1983; Erickson, 1977; Skrtic, 1985). There have been several methodological advantages, the first of which relates to the fact that, over the decades since the research tradition emerged, the central issue in the literature has been the apparent inability of planned change efforts to actually bring about change in school organizations. For example, Boyd and Crowson (1981) summarized the educational change research of the 1960s and 1970s by saying that:

> One of the great paradoxes of American public education is how little . . . our schools have changed over the past two decades of unprecedented ferment, turbulence, and systematic efforts at reform. In many of their most obvious features, schools have scarcely changed at all. Indeed, American public schools have become notorious for their ability to resist change and innovation. . . . In most schools, the methods and character of instruction, the organization of schooling and, in many respects, the curriculum itself are little different in appearance than they were many years ago (Cuban, 1979). And the public schools seem no more effective now than before the federal- and state-funded reform efforts of the 1960s and 1970s. Indeed, many infer from declining achievement test scores that the schools have become less effective. (p. 311)

And even though the same argument is being made today relative to the planned change efforts associated with the excellence movement (see Cuban, 1989; Wise, 1988), the significant thing about the first 20 years of failed attempts at change is that it forced school change researchers to change perspectives—from a narrow rational-technical concern for the innovation itself in the 1960s, to a broader concern for the innovation-in-context in the 1970s, and finally, by the end of the 1970s, to an even broader concern for understanding the culture of the implementation context itself (House, 1979). Thus, while the field of educational administration remained tied to the functionalist outlook, the research tradition of educational change made the shift from objectivism to subjectivism, paralleling the course of development in the social sciences.

Although the shift from the rational-technical to the cultural perspective provided a new way to understand the nature of change in school organizations, it did not improve efforts to change them (see Elmore & McLaughlin, 1988). For example, although the new cultural insights on educational change were available early in the excellence movement and the REI debate, they have had very little impact on change strategies in either reform movement. As I have noted, the REI continues to follow the rational-technical orientation (a major topic in chapter 9). Moreover, the same rational-technical approach has been the principal change strategy of the excellence movement, as Wise (1988) and Cuban (1989) have noted, and as we will see in chapter 10.

Although in itself the cultural perspective has not led to more successful change efforts, it has begun to focus attention on the heretofore neglected cultural dimensions of schools. The problem, as we saw in the last chapter, is that today culture is overemphasized at the expense of structure. Although the emphasis on culture has led to important new insights, such as those of Sarason (1982) and Sirotnik and Oakes (1986), it also has led to an increasing sense of despair among educational change researchers. For example, after recognizing the centrality of school culture in the problem of change and the apparent inability to influence it in any substantive way, some educational change researchers have begun to recommend abandoning the traditional system of public education (Sarason, 1983; Everhart, 1990).

In part, I believe that this sense of despair stems from approaching the study of change in organizations monologically—from a *particular* perspective, regardless of which perspective one chooses. Therefore, in the next chapter I attempt to look behind school organization from more than one perspective. Like any other social phenomenon, school organization is best understood dialogically—from a variety of points of view. And because the more points of view we can bring into the picture the more we will be able to see, I will build two ideal types—one structural and one cultural—from a number of theoretical and paradigmatic perspectives. Among other things, I will use the ideal types in chapter 9 to look behind special education as an institutional practice of public education from the perspective of school organization and change.

## NOTES

1. Cited in Scott (1981, p. 1).
2. I want to emphasize and differentiate two major forms and phases of progressivism during the progressive era that are relevant to public education and my analysis. The earlier *social efficiency* phase was grounded in the prescriptive discourse of scientific management and the machine bureaucracy configuration. Although a variety of "progressive" ideas emerged during this period that, to one degree or another, had an impact on social and educational practices (see Haber, 1964; Kliebard, 1988), there were two dominant segments within the social efficiency movement, each of which was concerned with the apparent decay of society but was premised on a different and largely contradictory motivation and thus use for the principles of scientific management and the standardization and formal authority of the machine bureaucracy. "To one segment, what seemed most important was the projection of the Christian moral code onto society as a whole, while to [the other] social efficiency was tied to social control, which was somewhat harder to reduce to moral terms" (Harber, 1964, p. 59). The social efficiency phase of the progressive era began in 1910 and disappeared with America's entry into the war. The moralistic segment was quickest to fade, but "efficiency as a technique of industrial management and as a form of social control found a small but steadfast following and had more lasting effects," particularly on the profession and institution of education (Harber, 1964, p. 74; Callahan, 1962; Cherryholmes, 1988; Oakes, 1985; Spring, 1980). Noting this is important at this point because, as we will see here and in chapter 9, the fields of educational administration and special education emerged from and were shaped by the social efficiency phase, with profound negative consequences. The later *social reconstruction* phase of the progressive era (1920s and early 1930s), which was grounded in the political discourse of progressive liberalism (and, thus, the antifoundational discourse of philosophical pragmatism), has had very little, if any, effect on the profession or institution of education (see Kliebard, 1988; Kloppenberg, 1986). It will be important in chapter 10, relative to my concluding arguments.

# 8

# Toward an Antifoundational Theory of School Organization and Adaptability

Because the field of organization analysis is grounded in the disciplines of the social sciences, the theories it produces reflect the various modes of theorizing found in the social disciplines, which can be understood in terms of the four paradigms of social scientific thought presented in Part One. As we know, the four paradigms are formed by the interaction of two dimensions of metatheoretical assumptions: an objective-subjective dimension, which reflects various metatheoretical assumptions about the nature of science; and a microscopic-macroscopic or order-conflict dimension (hereafter microscopic-macroscopic), which reflects various metatheoretical assumptions about the nature of society.

Applying this conceptual framework to theories of organization, the objective-subjective dimension corresponds to the question of the nature of action in organizations, ranging from the extremes of *rational action* (prospective and goal-directed) to *nonrational action* (quasi-random and emergent within evolving systems of meaning or cultures). The microscopic-macroscopic dimension corresponds to the question of the level at which organizational activity is most appropriately analyzed.

*Individualist* theories of organization emphasize the micro-level of individuals and small groups and are concerned with organizing processes; *structuralist* theories emphasize the macro-level of total organizations and are concerned with organization structure (Pfeffer, 1982; Scott, 1981). Thus, we can think of theories of organization as being grounded in one of the four paradigms of social scientific thought—functionalist (micro-objective), interpretivist (micro-subjective), structuralist (macro-objective), and humanist (macro-subjective)—which represent four fundamentally different ways to understand organization and change (Burrell & Morgan, 1979; Ritzer, 1980, 1983).

## ANTIFOUNDATIONAL ORGANIZATION ANALYSIS

Because the functionalist paradigm has been the dominant framework of the social sciences, most of the work in organization analysis has been done under the rational perspective on action at the individual level of analysis—that is, from the functionalist or micro-objective paradigm. But over the past 30 years there have been three shifts in emphasis that correspond to the shifts in the social sciences discussed in chapter 1. The shifts are: (a) one in the 1960s within the rational perspective on action from the micro-objective to the macro-objective paradigm, (b) one in the 1970s at the individualist level from the rational to the nonrational perspective on action, and (c) one in the 1980s at the structuralist level of analysis from the rational to the nonrational perspective (see Burrell & Morgan, 1979; Pfeffer, 1982; Scott, 1981).

As in the social sciences per se, one result of these shifts has been the development of a number of new theories of organization grounded in the other three paradigms, which had been underdeveloped. More significant, however, over the last half of this period, several theories have appeared that *bridge* paradigms by combining insights from more than one perspective (see Skrtic, 1987b, 1988b). Methodologically, the trend in organization analysis over this latter period, as in the social sciences generally, has been away from foundationalism and toward antifoundationalism. Thus, although discourse in the field of organization analysis had been dominated by the functionalist perspective and premised on the foundational view of knowledge, today it is characterized by theoretical and paradigmatic diversity, if not pluralism (Burrell & Morgan, 1979; Pfeffer, 1982; Scott, 1981), and, at the margins at least, by antifoundationalism (see Morgan, 1983). As a result of these substantive and methodological developments in the social disciplines and the field of organization analysis, multiple theories of organization and change can be considered in a single, antifoundational analysis (see Skrtic, 1987b, 1988b), a version of which is presented in this chapter as a basis for an organizational analysis of the institutional practice of special education in the next chapter.

Because organization analysis is a multiparadigmatic endeavor, and because there are no foundational criteria for adjudicating the question of the correct paradigm or knowledge claim, in the analysis to follow, I bring together a number of theoretical perspectives, drawn from each of the four paradigms, in an antifoundational dialogical analysis of school organization and adaptability. As we know from chapter 6, a dialogical analysis draws on the pragmatist notion of intersubjective communities of inquirers in which knowledge is a social product of normatively regulated intersubjective communication (Peirce, 1931–35). Thus, in this application of the concept, the various theories of organization from each of the four paradigms will be viewed as the social constructions of communities of organization theorists, each of which has been shaped by its value assumptions with respect to the metatheoretical dimensions of the conceptual framework developed in Part One.

In the analysis I treat each theory as an ideal type and attempt to create two larger heuristics on the basis of the insights gained from the various theories. I do not expect to discover or create the ultimate, true theory of school organization and adaptability, of course. Rather, I am interested in using what I can from each of the theories, as well as from the hermeneutical growth in understanding that results from being open to multiple perspectives in a single analysis, to create two new ideal types, which I will combine into a single heuristic in the next chapter, to analyze special education as an institutional practice.

In the analysis to follow, the theoretical territory is divided into two general frames of reference, the *structural* and the *cultural*, each of which includes two theoretical perspectives that bridge two or more of the four paradigms. As illustrated in Figure 8.1, the structural frame of reference includes *configuration theory* (Miller & Mintzberg, 1983; Mintzberg, 1979), which bridges the micro-objective and macro-objective paradigms, and what I will call *institutionalization theory* (Meyer & Rowan, 1977, 1978; Meyer & Scott, 1983), which bridges the macro-objective and macro-subjective paradigms.

**Figure 8.1**

The Structural Frame of Reference: Configuration and Institutionalization Perspectives

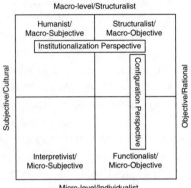

Configuration theory is important for organization analysis because it synthesizes the individualist's concern for *organizing processes* with the structuralist's concern for *organizational structure* under the rubric of organizational structur*ing*. It is important for an analysis of school organization because it provides several ideal typical organizational configurations, two of which, the *machine bureaucracy* and the *professional bureaucracy*, are particularly helpful for understanding the structure and functioning of school organizations, and a third configuration, the *adhocracy*, which is important for understanding special education and educational restructuring (see Skrtic, 1987b; 1988b).

Institutionalization theory is important for organization analysis because it combines the subjectivist's concern for *normative structures* (norms, beliefs, values, culture, ideology) and the objectivist's concern for *material structures* (actual organizational elements such as formalization and professionalization). The basic idea behind institutionalization theory is that, in addition to having a material structure that conforms to the technical demands of their work, school organizations maintain a normative structure that conforms to institutionalized beliefs and prescriptions. By combining the two theories, we can understand school organization as a *nonadaptable* two-structure arrangement.

The two theoretical perspectives within the cultural frame of reference are *paradigmatic theories* of organization (Brown, 1978; Golding, 1980; Jonsson & Lundin, 1977; Rounds, 1979, 1981), which bridge the macro-subjective and micro-subjective paradigms, and *cognitive theories* of organization (Weick, 1979, 1985), which bridge three paradigms—micro-subjective, macro-subjective, and macro-objective. Figure 8.2 illustrates the cultural frame of reference.

**Figure 8.2**

The Cultural Frame of Reference: Paradigmatic and Cognitive Perspectives

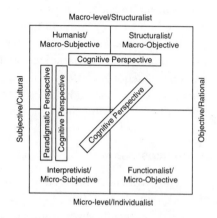

Paradigmatic theories of organization are important because they address the ways in which organizational cultures orient the thought and action of their members. They are important for understanding school organizations as cultures or systems of meaning, as well as the implications for changing such systems. From this perspective, organizational change is understood as a Kuhnian paradigm revolution.

Cognitive theories of organization emphasize the ways in which organizational members create and recreate organizational paradigms. They are important for organization analysis because they not only bridge the two subjective perspectives but also bridge the cultural and structural frames of reference. The cultural frame of reference is important for education because it provides a way to understand school organizations as *corrigible* systems of meaning.

## SCHOOL ORGANIZATION AND CHANGE: STRUCTURAL FRAME OF REFERENCE[1]

The central idea in configuration theory is that organizations structure themselves into somewhat naturally occurring configurations according to the type of work they do, the means they have available to coordinate their work, and a variety of situational factors such as age, size, and environment. Accordingly, school organizations structure themselves as professional bureaucracies, even though in this century they have been managed and governed as machine bureaucracies. By combining insights from configuration theory and institutionalization theory, we can think of school organizations as two organizations, one inside the other. On the outside, the formal structure of schools conforms to the machine bureaucracy configuration. This is the conceptual or normative structure of schools, the structure that people expect because it has been institutionalized in industrialized societies. On the inside, the informal structure of schools conforms to the professional bureaucracy configuration, which corresponds to the technical requirements of their work, means of coordination, and situational conditions.

### Differences Between the Machine and Professional Bureaucracies

The differences between the two organizations stem from the type of work they do and, thus, the means each has available to coordinate its work. Organizations configure themselves as machine bureaucracies when their work is *simple*, which (as we know from chapter 4) is work that can be rationalized into a series of precise, routine tasks that can be fully prespecified and done by separate workers. Simple work can be coordinated by standardizing the *work processes*, which is accomplished through *formalization*—detailed job specifications, precise instructions, and rules. Organizations configure themselves as professional bureaucracies when their work is *complex*—that is, when it is too ambiguous to be rationalized and prespecified and thus formalized. Complex work is coordinated by standardizing the *skills of the worker*, which (as we know from chapter 4) is accomplished through *professionalization* (i.e., education and socialization). Whereas the logic of formalization rests on *minimizing discretion* and *separating theory from practice*, professionalization, in principle, is premised on *increasing discretion* and *uniting theory and practice*, which is necessary because, as we know, complex work requires the adaptation of general theories or principles to variable cases or clients (Perrow, 1970; Schein, 1972; chapter 4).

The means of coordination in an organization influences the nature of the interdependency or *coupling* among its workers (March

& Olsen, 1976; Thompson, 1967; Weick, 1976, 1982). Because machine bureaucracies coordinate their work by rationalizing and formalizing it so that each worker does one part of the total job, their workers, like links in a chain, are *tightly coupled*. The workers in a professional bureaucracy, however, are *loosely coupled* because standardization of skills creates a form of interdependency in which professionals share common facilities and resources but do the entire job alone with an assigned client group. Coordination, which is loose at best, is accomplished by everyone knowing roughly what everyone else is doing by way of their common professionalization. Tightly coupled workers are highly dependent on one another because they each do one part of a larger work activity (e.g., building an automobile on an assembly line), whereas loosely coupled workers are not highly dependent on one another because each one of them does the entire work activity alone. Teachers working in a school are the ideal typical case of loosely coupled workers (see Mintzberg, 1979; Thompson, 1967).

## Managing Professional Bureaucracies Like Machines

Given the social norm of organizational rationality and the prescriptive discourse of educational administration, school organizations are conceptualized, managed, and governed as if they were machine bureaucracies, even though the technical demands of their work configure them as professional bureaucracies. As such, schools are forced by managers (Weick, 1982) and by their institutionalized environment (Meyer & Rowan, 1978; Mintzberg, 1979) to adopt all the trappings of the machine bureaucracy (rationalization of work, standardization of work processes, formalization of worker behavior), even though they are ill suited to the technical demands of doing complex work. In principle, the effect is that the professional bureaucracy configuration of schools is driven to be more like the machine bureaucracy. And, as Weick noted:

> When conventional management theory [i.e., management based on the machine bureaucracy structure] is applied to organizations that [are not machine bureaucracies], effectiveness declines, people become confused, and work doesn't get done. That seems to be one thing that is wrong with many schools. They are managed with the wrong model in mind. (Weick, 1982, p. 673)

Perhaps the most serious outcome of this drive toward the machine bureaucracy configuration is the violation of the discretionary logic of professionalization. Managing and governing schools as if they were machine bureaucracies misconceptualizes teaching as simple work that can be rationalized and formalized. This reduces professional discretion, which, in turn, lessens the degree to which teachers can personalize instruction to meet the particular needs of their students. Complex work cannot be formalized through rules:

> . . . except in misguided ways which program the wrong behaviors and measure the wrong outputs, forcing the professionals to play the machine bureaucratic game—satisfying the standards instead of serving the clients. . . . The individual needs of the students—slow learners and fast, rural and urban—as well as the individual styles of the teachers have to be subordinated to the neatness of the system. (Mintzberg, 1979, p. 377)

Fortunately, however, formalization doesn't work completely in school organizations because, from the institutionalization perspective, the machine bureaucracy structure, in which the formalization is inscribed, is *decoupled* from the professional bureaucracy structure, where the work is done. That is, the formal machine bureaucratic structure of school organizations functions as a myth that is created and maintained through symbols and ceremonies. This decoupled, two-structure arrangement permits schools to do their work according to the localized judgments of professionals—the essence of the professional bureaucracy configuration—while protecting the organization's legitimacy and resources by giving the public the appearance of the machine bureaucracy that it expects.

> Thus, decoupling enables organizations to maintain standardized, legitimating, formal structures while their activities vary in response to practical considerations. The organizations in an industry [broad sense] tend to be similar in formal structure—reflecting their common institutional origins—but may show much diversity in actual practice. (Meyer & Rowan, 1977, p. 357)

From the configuration perspective, however, decoupling doesn't work completely either. No matter how contradictory it may be, formalization requires at least overt conformity to its precepts and thus circumscribes professional thought and action (Mintzberg, 1979; cf. Dalton, 1959).

## Similarities Between the Machine and Professional Bureaucracies

Although the machine bureaucracy and the professional bureaucracy are different in these fundamental ways, because they use the principle of standardization to produce standard products or services, they are similar in two important respects: Both are *performance organizations*, and therefore both require a *stable environment*. Thus, in principle, both are inherently nonadaptable structures at both the micro level of workers and at the macro level of the organization.

Nonadaptability at the micro level of the worker results from the use of standardization as a coordination mechanism. Although in the machine bureaucracy the standardization of work processes is intended to eliminate as much worker discretion as possible, in the professional bureaucracy the standardization of skills, in principle, is intended to permit enough discretion to accommodate client variability. From the configuration perspective, however, professional practice is circumscribed because the standardization of skills produces professionals with a finite repertoire of standard programs that are applicable to a finite set of contingencies or perceived client needs. Although this pigeonholing process simplifies matters greatly for the professional, clients whose needs fall at the margins or outside the available standard programs tend to get forced artificially into the ones that are available, or forced out of the system altogether (see Perrow, 1970; Simon, 1977; Weick, 1976). A fully open-ended process—one that seeks a truly creative solution to each unique need—requires a *problem-solving organization*. But the professional bureaucracy, like the machine bureaucracy, is a performance organization; instead of accommodating heterogeneity, it screens it out by forcing its clients' needs into one of its standard programs, or by forcing them out of the system altogether (see Segal, 1974).

The professional and machine bureaucracies are nonadaptable at the macro level of the organization because both use the principle of standardization to produce standard products or services. When their environments become dynamic—requiring them to do something other than what they have been standardized to do—they are potentially devastated. Nevertheless, change in the machine bureaucracy can be approached in a more or less rational-technical manner because change in this type of organization is largely a technical matter of *re*standardizing the work processes—*re*rationalizing the work and *re*formalizing worker behavior. But, when its environment becomes dynamic, the professional bureaucracy cannot respond by making rational-technical adjustments because its coordination rests within each professional worker by way of professionalization.

At a minimum, change in a professional bureaucracy requires a change in what each professional does because each professional does the entire job individually and personally with his or her clients. But, because school organizations are managed and governed as if they were machine bureaucracies, attempts to change them typically follow the rational-technical approach (House, 1979), which assumes that additions to or changes in the existing formalization will result in changes in the way the work gets done. This fails to bring about the desired changes because the existing formalization is located in the mythical machine bureaucracy structure, which is decoupled from the work activity. Nevertheless, it does act to extend current formalization and, in so doing, drives school organizations further toward the machine bureaucracy structure.

Thus, managing and governing schools as if they were machine bureaucracies forces them to be more like machine bureaucracies, which reduces teacher discretion and leaves students with less personalized and thus less effective services. Rational-technical change efforts extend this push, driving schools to be even more like the machine bureaucracy, which reduces teacher discretion even further, leaving students with even less personalized and thus even less effective services. As in the case of management by rules, the inner professional bureaucracy structure of schools cannot be changed by adding more rules, except in misguided ways that force the professionals to play the machine bureaucracy game even more.

The institutionalization perspective on change assumes that professional bureaucracies are nonadaptable structures that use their outer machine bureaucracy structure to deflect change demands to ensure their survival in dynamic environments. Because schools are public organizations and therefore must be responsive to public demands for change, they relieve pressure for change by signaling the environment that a change has occurred. That is, they create the illusion that they have changed when, in fact, they remain largely the same (see M. W. Meyer, 1979; Meyer & Rowan, 1977, 1978; Meyer & Scott, 1983; Rowan, 1980; Zucker, 1981). In this way, schools maintain their legitimacy and support—their very survival—in the face of being unable to conform to environmental demands for change.

One way that school organizations signal change is by building symbols and ceremonies of change into their formal machine bureaucratic structure, which, of course, is decoupled from the informal professional bureaucratic structure where the actual work is done. Another important signal of change can be understood by extending the idea of decoupling to the internal structure of school organizations. Not only is the formal structure of the school decoupled from its informal structure, but its various units (classrooms and programs) are decoupled from one other as well (see Meyer & Rowan, 1977; Zucker, 1981). This is possible, of course, because coordination through standardization of skills creates precisely this sort of loosely coupled interdependency within the organization.

The advantage of a decoupled internal structure is that it permits schools to respond to change demands by adding on separate programs or specialists to deal with them. This makes any substantial reorganization of activity unnecessary, and thus buffers the existing organization of activity from dynamic environments. This is particularly efficient because, once they are created, these add-on units are simply allowed to float free, decoupled from the basic operation, which continues much as it had before the change demand emerged (Meyer & Rowan, 1978; Zucker, 1981).

## CULTURAL FRAME OF REFERENCE

Organization theorists working from the cultural frame of reference think of organizations as bodies of thought, as schemas, cultures, or paradigms. Their theories are premised on the idea that humans construct their social realities through intersubjective communication (see Berger & Luckmann, 1967). As such, the cognitive and paradigmatic perspectives on organization and change are concerned with the way people construct, deconstruct, and reconstruct meaning and how this relates to the way action and interaction unfold over time in organizations. Cognitive theories emphasize the way people create and recreate their organizational realities; paradigmatic theories emphasize the way organizational realities create and recreate people. Together, these theories reflect the interactive duality of the cultural frame of reference—people creating culture; culture creating people (Pettigrew, 1979).

## Organizations as Paradigms

The constructivist position at the macro-subjective level translates into the idea of organizations as paradigms, an approach to analysis concerned with understanding the way existing socially constructed systems of meaning affect and constrain thought and action in organizations. From Kuhn (1970) we know that a paradigm is a general guide to perception, a map, a way of viewing the world. Applied to organizations, a paradigm is a technology, a system of beliefs about cause-effect relations and standards of practice and behavior (Brown, 1978).

Regardless of whether these paradigms are true, by consolidating disorder into an image of orderliness, they provide a sense of collective identity and a justification for action (Brown, 1978; Clark, 1972). The process of organizational change from this perspective is similar to a Kuhnian paradigm revolution: long periods of stability maintained by the self-reinforcing nature of the organization's current paradigm—what Kuhn would call the long period of normal science—and occasional periods of change in which unreconcilable anomalies eventually destroy the prevailing paradigm—what Kuhn would call revolutionary science and the shift to a new paradigm (see Jonsson & Lundin, 1977; Golding, 1980).

From the paradigmatic perspective, an organizational change requires a paradigm shift, which is a slow and traumatic phenomenon because, once in place, the paradigm self-justifies itself, and thus the thought and action of organizational members, by distorting new information so that it is seen as consistent with the prevailing view (Golding, 1980). Nevertheless, when sufficient anomalies build up to call the prevailing paradigm into question, a new paradigm emerges, and action proceeds again under the guidance of the new organizing framework (Jonsson & Lundin, 1977).

Anomalies are introduced into organizational paradigms in different ways. One way is through the availability of technical information showing that the current paradigm is not working, which, according to the paradigmatic perspective on change, can bring about a paradigm shift in one of two ways. The first way is through a confrontation between an individual (or a small constituency group) who rejects the most fundamental assumptions of the current paradigm, on the basis of information that the system is not working, and the rest of the organization's members who are acting in defiance of the negative information to preserve the prevailing paradigm. The second way technical information can introduce an anomaly is the case when an initially conservative action is taken to correct a generally recognized flaw in what otherwise is assumed to be a viable system. Here, the corrective measure exposes other flaws that, when addressed, expose more flaws, and so on, until enough of the system is called into question to prepare the way for a radical reconceptualization of the entire organization. In this scenario, what were initially conservative attempts to protect the system act to undermine it and ultimately usher in a new paradigm (Rounds, 1981).

Another explanation for an organizational paradigm shift is the situation in which the anomaly is introduced because of shifting values and preferences in society, rather than because of availability of new technical knowledge (Rounds, 1979). In this case, the paradigm falls into a crisis because the social theory and values underlying it change. To the degree that the new social values are inconsistent with the members' prevailing organizational paradigm, however, resistance emerges in the form of political clashes and an increase in ritualized activity, which act to reaffirm the paradigm that has been called into question (see Rounds, 1979; Zucker, 1977).

## Organizations as Schemas

The essence of the cognitive perspective on organization is perhaps best expressed by Weick's (1979) assertion that "an organization is a body of thought thought by thinking thinkers" (p. 42), which bridges the micro- and macro-subjective perspective by emphasizing that, although an organizational paradigm orients the thought and action of its members, the thought and action of the members creates and recreates the organizational paradigm. Moreover, Weick bridged the cultural and structural frames of reference by arguing that the constructions of organizational members contain "grains of truth." That is, something is going on independent of the members even though they embellish and elaborate their organizational reality. A bewildering array of information and activity is present in the field of action, "but what happens is that the actor in the organization plays a major role in unrandomizing and giving order to the bewildering number of variables that constitute those grains" (Weick, 1979, p. 45).

Through activity, selective attention, consensual validation, and luck, people in organizations unrandomize streams of experience enough to form a sensemaking map or paradigm of the territory. Of course, the paradigm is not the territory; it is only a *re*presentation. But, for Weick (1979), "the map *is* the territory if people treat it as such" (p. 45). Organizational paradigms—correct or not—structure the territory sufficiently so that members can initiate activity in it, out of which may emerge a workable order.

Members' sampling of the environment and thus the paradigms they construct also are dominated by prior beliefs and values, which act as filters through which they examine their experience. Although this assertion is consistent with the paradigmatic perspective, Weick stressed *action* as the pretext and raw material for sensemaking, and therefore bridged the structural and cultural frames of reference. According to Weick (1979), actual structural elements—such as formalization, professionalization, and bureaucracy itself—are real to the extent that they shape the contingencies (contacts, communication, commands) that effect the grains of truth, maps, beliefs, and actions that constitute organizational paradigms.

Weick (1979), however, noted that the causal arrow goes the other way as well: "Maps, beliefs, and thoughts that summarize actions, themselves constrain contacts, communication, and commands. These constraints constitute and shape organizational processes that result in structures" (p. 48). Thus, from the cognitive perspective, structural contingencies shape the work activities of organizational members which, in turn, shape their value orientation and thus the organizational paradigms they create to understand the organization and interpret its structural contingencies. From this perspective, an organization is a human schema, "an abridged, generalized, corrigible organization of experience that serves as an initial frame of reference for action and perception. A schema is the belief in the phrase, I'll see it when I believe it" (1979, p. 50).

Although school organizations have been characterized as chaotic, unorganized systems (see Cohen, March, & Olsen, 1972), Weick (1985) argued that "underorganized systems" is a more appropriate metaphor because, although schools are ambiguous and disorderly, there is some order. More important, anything or anyone that can create more order in an underorganized system can bring about change. Thus, the very underorganized nature of schools that prevents change (from the structural perspective)—loose coupling, professionalization, decoupled structures and units—is the precise condition that can create the opportunity for change.

Weick (1985) used the ideas of superstitious learning and self-fulfilling prophecy (cf. Jones, 1977) to explain change in underorganized systems such as schools. Superstitious learning occurs when organizational members mistakenly see a change in the environment as caused by their own action. As a result, they build into their cause maps or paradigms the belief that they are able to change environments. Of course, this is an error in the sense that it is an incorrect interpretation of what actually happened. But Weick argued that when environments are sufficiently malleable, like they are in underorganized systems, acting on this mistaken belief can set in motion a sequence of activities that allows people to construct the reality that the belief is true. That is, in changeable environments, an apparent efficacy can transform a superstitious conclusion into a correct perception.

> An original prophecy is incorrect and may result from a mistaken perception that an environmental outcome was caused by an individual action. Later, when the person acts as if the prophecy were correct, the prophecy can become correct and the environment becomes responsive to the individual action rather than to some other exogenous factor. Thus, the incorrect theory of action becomes self-correcting. It sets into motion a set of events that validate what was originally an invalid belief. (Weick, 1985, p. 124)

According to Weick (1985), ambiguity in loosely coupled, underorganized systems is reduced when people can incorporate into their paradigms an inference—rightly or wrongly—about cause and effect. When they act on the stored inference as if it were true, a previously loose relationship between cause and effect becomes tightened and the uncertainty surrounding the effect is reduced. Confident action based on a presumption of efficacy can reinforce the inference about efficacy stored in the paradigm. In short, from the cognitive perspective, people in ambiguous, underorganized systems can make things happen.

When ambiguity is present, people who can resolve it gain power. And because ambiguity in organizations increases the extent to which action is guided by values and ideology (Weick, 1985), the values of these powerful people—the ones who can reduce ambiguity—affect what the organization is and what it can become. Weick explained that, when ambiguity increases, it sets the stage for ideology and values to be reshuffled—what we would call a paradigm shift. The people best able to resolve ambiguity gain power, as does their vision of the world and the organization. According to Weick, recognition of an important, enduring ambiguity—an unresolvable anomaly in the prevailing paradigm—is an occasion when an organization may redefine itself. Those who resolve the ambiguity for themselves and others can implant a new set of values in the organization, which creates a new set of relevancies and competencies and introduces a source of innovation.

Ambiguity sets the occasion for organizations to learn about themselves and their environments and allows them to emerge from their struggle with uncertainty in a different form than when they started the confrontation. But behind it all are people with ideas rooted in their values and vision of what can and should be. For Weick, the importance of presumptions, expectations, and commitments cannot be overestimated. Confident, forceful, persistent people can span the breaks in loosely coupled, underorganized systems with their presumptions, expectations, and commitments by encouraging interactions that tighten settings. *"The conditions of order and tightness in organizations exist as much in the mind as they do in the field of action"* (Weick, 1985, p. 128).

Now that we have two ideal-typical characterizations of school organization and adaptability—one structural and one cultural—I want to combine them in the next chapter to form a larger heuristic for looking behind special education as an institutional practice of public education. That is, I want to deconstruct the institutional practice of special education by using the heuristic to provide a critical reading of the EHA and REI reform proposals from an organizational perspective. Moreover, we will see that deconstructing the institutional practice of special education, in conjunction with a critical reading of the general education discourse on educational excellence, prepares the way for deconstructing the discourse on school failure, which, in turn, exposes the immanent contradiction between public education's bureaucratic practices and democratic ideals.

## NOTES

1. Except where noted otherwise, all of the material in this section on configuration theory (e.g., division of labor, coordination, internal coupling, management, and change) is drawn from Mintzberg (1979) and Miller and Mintzberg (1983); and all of the material on institutionalization theory (e.g., decoupled structures and units, and myth, symbol, and ceremony) is drawn from Meyer and Rowan (1977, 1978) and Meyer and Scott (1983).

# 9

# Special Education and Disability as Organizational Pathologies

The first right of any disabled person is not to be disabled, never to have been disabled.

Federico Mayor Zargoza[1]

Now that we have two ideal types for understanding school organization and change, I want to combine them in this chapter and use them as a heuristic to continue looking behind special education. In Part Two we looked behind special education as a professional practice from the perspective of professional culture. Here, I want to look behind it as an institutional practice of public education from the perspective of school organization.

Whereas in Part Two we were interested in that which conditioned, limited, and institutionalized the thought and action of special educators, one of our purposes here is to understand, from an organizational perspective, what has led educators to believe in the institutional practice of special education as a rational and just response to the problem of school failure. In this regard, we can think of student disability

**173**

as an ideal typical construct for understanding the problem of school failure—as the extreme case of school failure—and special education as the ideal typical institutional practice for containing the extreme case of school failure. As such, from a Foucauldian perspective, special education emerges as perhaps the most insightful vantage point for understanding the institution of public education and its professional and institutional practices and discourses.

A second purpose is to use the heuristic to analyze the EHA and the REI proposals and, by doing so, to shed whatever light we can on the problem of educational change. In this regard we can think of the EHA and the REI as ideal typical cases of school reform—measures that are intended to address, in an equitable way, the extreme case of school failure. Moreover, as we will see, by requiring school organizations to change their division of labor, means of coordination, and form of interdependency, the EHA and the REI require schools to change their fundamental organizational configuration. Given this, and the fact that the most insightful way to understand organizations is by observing their reaction to a change demand (Salancik, 1979; Van de Ven & Astley, 1981), the EHA and the REI proposals are extreme cases of educational reform and, as such, provide a particularly advantageous vantage point from which to analyze the institution of public education and its capacity for change.

Finally, although to this point in the book we have been concerned with special education and, relative to the presupposition of organizational rationality, with educational administration and educational change, we will reach a point in this chapter where we can expand the analysis to general education and public education itself. Given the claims I have been making throughout the book about the broader significance of the deconstruction of special education, the third purpose of the chapter is to deconstruct the 20th-century discourse on school failure and the contemporary discourse on educational excellence in general education. Moreover, by exposing the immanent contradictions between its democratic ideals and bureaucratic practices, the deconstruction of the discourses on school failure and educational excellence will allow me to accomplish my fourth purpose—deconstruction of the 20th-century institution of public education. This will prepare the ground for reconstructing public education for the emerging historical conditions of the 21st century in the closing chapter.

## THE NATURE OF DISABILITY AND DIAGNOSIS

From an organizational perspective, the professional bureaucracy is nonadaptable at the level of the professional because of the structural implications of professionalization as a coordinating mechanism and the conventional nature of professional cultures. As such, the set of instructional procedures and skills a teacher uses can be thought of as a repertoire of standard programs matched to predetermined contingencies, or a paradigm of conventional practices. This raises several questions relative to the notion of student disability, questions about the nature of these programs and practices and the manner in which they are applied in practice.

First there is the question of the source of these standard programs. As we saw in chapter 4, the positivist model of professional knowledge assumes that they are the end result of a rational system of knowledge production, a system in which the standard programs professionals use are engineered by applied scientists from objective knowledge about reality. Because the knowledge at each of the three levels of the hierarchy is subjective, however, the standard programs that professionals use in practice cannot be considered inherently correct in an objective sense; they are merely artifacts of a particular knowledge tradition grounded in the customs and conventions of a professional culture. Nevertheless, assuming for the sake of argument that these standard programs are the most effective ones available relative to the contingencies for which they have been engineered, let us consider the question of whether they are the standard programs that teachers actually use in practice.

Although in chapter 4 the argument concerning the nature of professional knowledge stopped at the level of a professional *culture* of conventions and customs, at this point we can extend it by considering the idea of two discontinuous *subcultures* within a given professional community: the subculture of applied scientists and the subculture of professional practitioners. Although the normative understanding of the professions assumes one continuous culture, the emerging conceptualization is that the applied science and practitioner subcultures within the professions, including the field of education, are largely discontinuous (Schön, 1983; Rudduck, 1977; Elliott, 1975). That is, although teachers leave their professional education programs with a repertoire of standard programs grounded in the conventions and customs of the applied science subculture, when they enter school organizations, they are inducted into the practitioner subculture, which has its own programs grounded in its conventions and customs. Thus, while the normative view of teacher education assumes that teachers learn their standard programs in professional schools and then apply and update them on the job, the emerging perspective is that, after initial professionalization, the two subcultures are decoupled—which is one way to explain why many professionals, including teachers, report that their professional education has little to do with their performance in professional work settings (Dornbusch & Scott, 1975; Schön, 1983).

We can find further evidence for the notion of decoupled subcultures in the educational change literature. Although we assume that the standard programs that teachers use are continually updated and modernized as new, knowledge-based procedures become available at the applied science level of the profession, this rarely occurs. This has been one of the painful lessons over the last 30 years of attempts to induce innovation into the public schools (see House, 1974, 1979; chapter 7). In most schools, the methods of instruction and the curriculum itself are much as they were earlier in the century (Cuban, 1979). Thus, even though the structural frame of reference assumes that the standard programs teachers use in schools derive from *professionalization*, we can think of the source of these standard programs as *acculturation*. That is, upon entry into school organizations, during the student teaching internship and later as employees, teachers are inculcated into an existing institutionalized subculture of practicing teachers, with its own set of norms, customs, and conventions.

Professional behavior in schools is governed more by institutionalized, cultural norms than it is by rational, knowledge-based actions designed to improve instructional effectiveness. Things are done in certain ways simply because they have always been done that way. To do anything else in these organizations would not make sense (Zucker, 1977, 1981). From this perspective, teaching is a ritualized activity that takes place in an institutionalized environment. Teachers learn to teach by modeling people they have seen teach—former teachers and cooperating teachers who got their programs from previous models (Lortie, 1975; Gehrke & Kay, 1984). The standard programs are passed on from one generation of teachers to another within an institutionalized context. There is nothing rational or inherently right or good (or, for that matter, wrong or bad) about these standard programs. They are simply artifacts of a professional subculture.

Another question we can ask about these standard programs concerns the manner in which they are applied. As we know, from the structural frame of reference, all professionals, including teachers, apply their standard programs by pigeonholing a predetermined contingency, or perceived client need, to an existing standard program. As Mintzberg (1979) noted, a common problem associated with pigeonholing is that "the professional confuses the needs of his clients with the skills he has to offer them" (p. 374). Pigeonholing is not a problem as long as the student's needs actually match what the professional has to offer. But, as we have seen, when the learning style and individual needs of a particular student do not match the professional's repertoire of standard programs, the student gets forced artificially into one program or another or forced out of the system altogether.

The professional bureaucracy is a performance organization, not a problem-solving organization configured to seek a creative solution to each unique need. The problem of innovation at the level of the professional, or what Mintzberg (1979, p. 373) called the "means-ends inversion," finds its roots "in convergent thinking, in the deductive reasoning of the professional who sees the specific situation in terms of the general concept. In the professional bureaucracy this means that new problems are forced into old pigeonholes" (p. 375). And it is important to recognize that this is not a dysfunction of the professional bureaucracy structure. It is configured precisely to screen out heterogeneity and uncertainty, to fit its clients' needs into one of its standard programs.

> The fact is that great art and innovative problem solving require inductive reasoning, that is, the induction of new general concepts or programs from particular experiences. That kind of thinking is divergent—it breaks away from old routines or standards rather than perfecting existing ones. And that flies in the face of everything the Professional Bureaucracy is designed to do. (Mintzberg, 1979, p. 375)

We can understand the means-ends inversion from the cultural frame of reference by thinking of a repertoire of standard programs as a paradigm, a technology of standard practices built on beliefs about cause-effect relations (Brown, 1978). From this perspective, a paradigm of standard programs comes to be embedded in the sagas and myths of the professional culture as the appropriate technology for doing the profession's work. Regardless of whether these stories are true, they persist because they provide a sense of certainty and a justification for action (Brown, 1978; Pfeffer, 1981; Clark, 1972). Once the paradigm of the professional culture is in place, it changes slowly because anomalies are distorted so as to make them consistent with the prevailing paradigm (Jonsson & Lundin, 1977). Although paradigm shifts can occur, resistance takes the form of political clashes between advocates of a new paradigm and defenders of the old one, conservative attempts to patch up the system incrementally, and an increase in ritualized activity (Rounds, 1979, 1981).

The arguments of the participants in the REI debate reject the assumptions that mild disabilities are pathological and that diagnosis is objective and useful. Instead, they recognize that many students are identified as handicapped simply because they have needs that cannot be accommodated in the regular classrooms of the general education system. This contradiction can be understood from an organizational perspective by redescribing student disability as an *organizational pathology* resulting from the inherent structural and cultural characteristics of traditional school organizations.

Structurally, schools are nonadaptable at the classroom level because professionalization ultimately results in convergent thinking. Given a finite repertoire of standard programs, students whose needs fall outside the standard programs must be forced into them, or out of the classroom—a situation compounded by the rational-technical approach to school management, which, by introducing unwarranted formalization, reduces professional thought and discretion and thus reduces the degree to which teachers can personalize their standard programs. The same phenomenon can be understood culturally by thinking of the standard programs as a paradigm of practice that persists because anomalies are distorted to preserve its validity. The principle distortion, of course, is the institutional practice of special education, which removes students from the general education system and thus prevents teachers from confronting uncertainty, thus eliminating it as a source of innovation. Moreover, formalization compounds and further mystifies the situation because it conflicts with the values that ground the paradigm and thus increases ritualized activity, which reduces thought and personalization (see below).

Thus, whether we think of schools from the structural or the cultural frame of reference, the implication is that student disability is neither a human pathology nor an objective distinction; it is an organizational pathology, a matter of not fitting the standard programs of the prevailing paradigm of a professional culture, the legitimacy of which is maintained and reinforced by the objectification of school failure as student disability through the institutional practice of special education.

## THE NATURE OF SPECIAL EDUCATION

The third grounding assumption is that special education is a rationally conceived and coordinated system of services that benefits identified students. One way to assess the rationality of special education is to ask what function it serves in public education. For example, consider the nonadaptability of school organizations in conjunction with their status as public organizations. As we know, schools are public organizations and therefore depend on the public for their support and legitimacy, their very survival. As such, schools must conform to the demands of their institutionalized environment. We have seen, for example, that schools must adopt the machine bureaucracy structure, not because it conforms to their technical needs or adds to their efficiency, but simply because it is what the institutionalized environment expects all legitimate organizations to look like (Meyer & Rowan, 1977, 1978). Thus, the institutionalized environment is a powerful source of fashion to which school organizations can hardly afford to be unresponsive (Mintzberg, 1979).

Although the institutionalized environment imposes a constant source of pressure on school organizations in this respect, on occasion it makes additional demands that require school organizations to change. As Rounds (1979) noted, changes are introduced into organizations when society's values and priorities shift. In some instances, school organizations are required to make incidental, add-on changes, which, as we have seen, they are able to do quite easily because of their loosely coupled internal structure. In other instances, however, the institutionalized environment requires schools to make fundamental changes, ones that require its teachers to do something different from what they were standardized (structural perspective) or acculturated (cultural perspective) to do. As we know, the standard programs or conventions teachers actually use can be thought of as a technology or paradigm of cause-effect relations and standards of practice and behavior (Brown, 1978). As such, the amount of resistance to a fundamental change requirement reflects the degree to which the values and beliefs embedded in the change demand run counter to those of the prevailing paradigm (Rounds, 1979).

From the institutionalization perspective we have seen how school organizations deal with demands from their institutionalized environments. We know, for example, that school organizations live with the contradiction of maintaining an inappropriate organizational structure by creating a mythical structure and decoupling it from their day-to-day activities. We know, too, that their decoupled internal structure allows them to respond to fundamental change demands by converting them to incidental changes, which can be dealt with by adding separate programs or specialists to the existing operation. Such a move permits the organization to respond without any substantial reorganization; it permits the organization to appear to be responsive to its institutionalized environment while buffering its fundamental operation from it.

The segregated special classroom—the exclusive model for special education from 1910 until the 1970s—is the ideal typical case of this process at work. During the social efficiency phase of the progressive era, when society required schools to both serve a broader range of students *and* to do so efficiently, the "ungraded" or special classroom emerged to deal with children that could not be squeezed into the available standard programs in the prevailing paradigm of the public education system (Sarason & Doris, 1979; Tweedie, 1983; Bogdan & Knoll, 1988). Thus, from an organizational perspective, the separate special classroom served as a legitimating device that allowed schools to signal the public that they had complied with the demand to integrate these new populations of students while at the same time allowing them to maintain their traditional paradigm of operation. Once special classes were created, they were decoupled from the internal workings of the school. Indeed, this lack of connection between the special class and the rest of the school enterprise was one of the major complaints in the 1960s and 1970s that led to passage of the EHA (see Dunn, 1968; Christophos & Renz, 1969; Deno, 1970; Johnson, 1962).

Another special education example is when schools were required to integrate children from minority groups in the 1950s. From an organizational perspective, the overrepresentation of these children in special classrooms in the 1960s (Chandler & Plakos, 1969; Dunn, 1968; MacMillan, 1971; Wright, 1967; Mercer, 1973; Janesick, 1988) can be understood as school organizations using an existing decoupling device—the segregated special classroom—to maintain legitimacy and public support in the face of failing to meet the needs of disproportionate numbers of these children in regular classrooms.

When one considers the function of special education within the larger organizational context of public education, one can hardly claim that it is a rationally conceived and coordinated system of services. Special education is not rationally conceived, because historically it has served as a myth and a legitimating device for school organizations to cope with the shifting value demands of their institutionalized environments. Special education services are not rationally coordinated because, by design, they are decoupled from the basic operation of the school, as well as from the other special needs programs, each of which has been added on incrementally as values have shifted in society.

Moreover, the rationality of public education itself is called into question when one understands that the inherent nonadaptability of the professional bureaucracy, which creates the need for myths and decoupling in the first place, produces as artifacts the "disabled students" that special education serves. Recall that Part Three began by noting that the unintended consequence of using organizations to provide services to society is that the services are shaped by the nature and needs of the organizations themselves. From an organizational perspective, student disability and special education are byproducts, unintended consequences of the particular kind of schooling that traditional school organizations provide.

The arguments of the participants in the REI debate reject the assumption that special education is a rational system. At best, it is characterized as a nonrational system for targeting otherwise unavailable educational services to designated students, even though the targeting process stigmatizes the students and the services do not necessarily benefit them. This contradiction can be understood from an organizational perspective by redescribing the institutional practice of special education as an organizational artifact that emerged to protect the legitimacy of a nonadaptable bureaucratic structure faced with the changing value demands of a dynamic democratic environment.

Even though the structural and cultural contingencies of the professional bureaucracy make schools nonadaptable, they maintain their legitimacy under dynamic social conditions by signaling the public that changes have occurred—including the addition of decoupled subunits. As such, the segregated special classroom emerged during the progressive era to preserve the legitimacy of the prevailing organizational paradigm by signaling compliance with the public demand to serve a broader range of students. Structurally, special education is a nonrational system, an organizational artifact that functions as a legitimizing device. Culturally, it distorts the anomaly of school failure and thus preserves the prevailing paradigm of school organization, which ultimately reinforces the presuppositions of organizational rationality and human pathology in the profession and institution of education and in society.

## THE NATURE OF PROGRESS

Participants on either side of the REI debate agree that most mild disabilities are not pathological, that diagnosis is neither objective nor useful, and that special education is not an instructionally rational system. But the two sides disagree fundamentally over an appropriate course of ameliorative action because of a conceptual confusion about the nature of progress, stemming from the assumption of organizational rationality. This confusion among REI opponents was evident in the way they reversed their position on the nature of progress in their criticism of the REI proposals. The same confusion can be illustrated for the REI proponents by considering the EHA and the REI proposals from an organizational perspective, which will require the introduction of a third organizational configuration—the adhocracy.

### Adhocracy

The professional bureaucracy is nonadaptable because it is premised on the principle of *standardization*, which configures it as a *performance* organization for *perfecting standard programs*. The adhocracy is premised on the principle of *innovation* rather than standardization; as such, it is a *problem-solving* organization configured to *invent new programs*. It is the organizational form that configures itself around work that is so ambiguous and uncertain that neither the programs *nor* the knowledge and skills for doing it are known (Mintzberg, 1979).

According to Mintzberg (1979), this type of organization was first recognized in the 1960s when analysts began to notice varying degrees of formalization across bureaucracies (Pugh et al., 1963). This eventually led to the recognition of what were referred to as "organic" organizations, which, because they operated in dynamic and thus uncertain environments where innovation and adaptation were necessary for survival, configured themselves as the *inverse of the bureaucratic form* (Burns & Stalker, 1966; Woodward, 1965). Mintzberg (1979) called the organic configuration adhocracy, following Toffler (1970), who had popularized the term in *Future Shock.*

Perhaps the best example of this configuration is the National Aeronautics and Space Administration (NASA) during its Apollo phase in the 1960s. Given its mission to land on the moon, it configured itself as an adhocracy because at that time manned space flight had no standard programs for achieving such a goal. At that point in its history, NASA had to rely on its workers to invent and reinvent these programs on an *ad hoc* basis, on the way to the moon, as it were. Moreover, although the Apollo project employed professional workers, NASA could not use *specialization* and *professionalization* to distribute and coordinate its work because there were no specialties that had perfected standard programs for doing the type of work that was assumed to be required, and thus no professional fields whose existing paradigms of standard programs could contain its uncertainty. Thus, its division of labor and coordination of work were premised on *collaboration* and *mutual adjustment*, respectively.

Under such an arrangement, division of labor is achieved by deploying professionals from various specializations on multidisciplinary project teams, a situation in which team members work collaboratively on the team's project and assume joint responsibility for its completion. Under mutual adjustment, coordination is achieved through informal communication among team members as they invent and reinvent novel problem solutions on an *ad hoc* basis, a process that requires them to adapt, adjust, and revise their conventional theories and practices relative to those of their colleagues and the teams' progress on the tasks at hand (Chandler & Sayles, 1971; Mintzberg, 1979). Together, the structural contingencies of collaboration and mutual adjustment give rise to a *discursive coupling* arrangement premised on reflective thought and thus on the unification of theory and practice in the team of workers (see Burns & Stalker, 1966).

By contrast, during its current Space Shuttle phase, NASA has reconfigured itself as a professional bureaucracy (see Romzek & Dubnick, 1987), as a performance organization that *perfects* a repertoire of standard launch and recovery programs, most of which were *invented* during its Apollo phase. This transformation from adhocracy to professional bureaucracy at NASA is a common organizational phenomenon in adhocracies. It begins when uncertainty is reduced, when the organization and its members begin to believe that they have solved all or most of their problems and thus that the programs they have invented can be standardized, perfected, and used as solutions in the future. The difference between the two configurations is that, faced with a problem, the adhocracy "engages in creative effort to find a novel solution; the professional bureaucracy pigeonholes it into a known contingency to which it can apply a standard program. One engages in divergent thinking aimed at innovation; the other in convergent thinking aimed at perfection" (Mintzberg, 1979, p. 436).

Finally, under the organizational contingencies of collaboration, mutual adjustment, and discursive coupling, accountability in the adhocracy is achieved through a presumed community of interests—a sense among the workers of a shared interest in a common goal, in the well being of the organization with respect to progress toward its mission—rather than through an ideological identification with a professional culture (professional bureaucracy) or a formalized relationship with an organization (machine bureaucracy) (see Burns & Stalker, 1966; Chandler & Sayles, 1971; Romzek & Dubnick, 1987). Thus, rather than the *professional-bureaucratic* mode of accountability that emerges in the professional bureaucracy configuration, the organizational contingencies of the adhocracy give rise to a *professional-political* mode of accountability, a situation in which work is controlled by experts who, although they act with discretion, are subject to sanctions that emerge within a political discourse among professionals and client constituencies (see Chander & Sayles, 1971; Burns & Stalker, 1966).

### The Education for All Handicapped Children Act[2]

From an organizational perspective, the basic problem with the EHA is that it attempts to force an adhocratic value orientation on a professional bureaucracy by treating it as if it were a machine bureaucracy.

The EHA is completely consistent with special education's third and fourth grounding assumptions; it is a rational-legal mechanism for change that assumes that schools are machine bureaucracies, that is, organizations in which worker behavior is controlled by procedural rules and thus subject to modification through revision and extension of formalization and supervision (see Elmore & McLaughlin, 1982). Moreover, as we saw in chapter 5, its requirements for nondiscriminatory assessments, parent participation, individualized education programs (IEPs), and placements in the least restrictive instructional setting are perceived to be new diagnostic and instructional technologies. Finally, its requirement for states to establish and implement a comprehensive system of personnel development—what Gilhool (1989) called "probably the most important provision of the act"—assumes that "there [are] known procedures for effectively educating disabled children," and that the problem is simply that "the knowledge of how to do so [is] not widely distributed" (p. 247). This, of course, assumes the possibility of rational-technical change through dissemination of practices and training.

Because its ends are adhocratic—a problem-solving organization in which interdisciplinary teams of professionals collaborate to invent personalized programs—they contradict the value orientation of the professional bureaucracy in every way, given that it is a performance organization in which individual professionals work alone to perfect standard programs. Culturally, this value conflict produces resistance in the form of political clashes, which undermine the ideal of collaboration, as well as an increase in ritualized activity which, by further mystifying the prevailing paradigm of practice, intensifies the problem of professionalization and thus deflects the ideals of problem solving and personalization (see Bogdan, 1983; Lortie, 1978; Martin, 1978; Moran, 1984; Patrick & Reschly, 1982; Singer & Butler, 1987; Skrtic et al., 1985; Weatherly, 1979).

Furthermore, because the EHA's means are completely consistent with the value orientation of the machine bureaucracy structure—rationalization and standardization of instructional programs (see below) and formalization of procedures—it extends and elaborates the existing formalization in school organizations. Structurally, this both deflects the adhocratic ends of the EHA from the actual work and further reduces professional thought and discretion, which intensifies professionalization and reduces personalization. This results in even more students who fall outside the standard programs, many of whom must be identified as handicapped (see chapter 3 and below). Also, because there is a legal limit on the number of students that can be identified as handicapped under the EHA, as well as a political limit on the amount of school failure society will tolerate, the EHA, in conjunction with other rational-technical reforms associated with the excellence movement in general education (see below), helped to create a new class of student casualties called "at-risk," which, at this point, is decoupled from both general education and special education.[3]

## Symbolic Compliance

Because the EHA requires at least overt conformity, a number of symbols of compliance have emerged. For example, the symbol of compliance for programs that serve students with severe and profound disabilities is the traditional decoupled subunit, the segregated special classroom. These programs are simply added to the existing school organization and, to one degree or another, decoupled from the basic operation. Because addressing the needs of students in these programs is beyond the repertoires or paradigms of practice of any single profession and thus requires an interdisciplinary approach, the efficacy of these programs depends on the availability of the requisite team of professionals. The degree of decoupling, as well as the availability of the requisite personnel, depends in large measure on the local history of special education services, which reflects values embedded in political cultures at the state, local, and school organization levels (see Biklen, 1985; McDonnell & McLaughlin,1982; Noel & Fuller, 1985; Skrtic et al., 1985).

Although there are exceptions to or variations on the traditional segregated classroom (see Biklen, 1985; Sailor et al., 1986; Thousand et al., 1986), the fact that the vast majority of students classified as having severe and profound disabilities and the professionals who serve them continue to be located in segregated settings is of great concern to special educators who work in this area of the field (e.g., Biklen, 1985; Gartner & Lipsky, 1987; Sailor, 1989; Stainback & Stainback, 1984b; Stainback et al., 1989; Thousand et al., 1986). Nevertheless, the complexity of the diagnostic and instructional problems that these professionals confront, in conjunction with their interdisciplinary orientation and decoupled status within school organizations, has important positive implications for the field of special education and for educational reform in general, a matter to be addressed in the concluding chapter.

The symbol of compliance for most students identified as mildly handicapped is the resource room, a new type of decoupled subunit. From an organizational perspective, the resource room is even more problematic than the traditional special classroom version because it violates the logic of the professional bureaucracy's means of coordination *and* its division of labor. Under the logic of mainstreaming, responsibility for the student's instructional program is divided among one or more regular classroom teachers and a special education resource teacher. This contradicts the division of labor because it requires that the student's instructional program be rationalized and assigned to more than one professional, which is justified implicitly on the assumption that the  professionals will work collaboratively to integrate the program.

But the collaboration required to integrate the student's instructional program contradicts the logic of professionalization and thus the form of interdependency among workers. In principle, teachers working collaboratively in the interest of a single student for whom they share responsibility violates the logic of loose coupling and the sensibility of the professional culture (Bidwell, 1965; Mintzberg, 1979; Weick, 1976), and thus should not be expected to occur as a generalized phenomenon in a professional bureaucracy. At a minimum, mainstreaming and the resource room model require reciprocal coupling (Thompson, 1967), which is not the type of interdependency that professionalization yields. Because professionalization locates virtually all of the necessary coordination within the teacher, there is no need for collaboration and thus it is rare, fleeting, and idiosyncratic (see Bishop, 1977; Lortie, 1975, 1978; Skrtic et al., 1985; Tye & Tye, 1984).

Moreover, although regular classroom placement, to the maximum extent possible, is required for these students under the EHA, they are identified as handicapped precisely because they cannot be accommodated within existing standard programs in particular regular classrooms (see Skrtic et al., 1985; Walker, 1987). As such, depending on the degree to which the particular school is adhocratically or bureaucratically oriented (see chapter 10), mainstreaming for these students more or less represents symbolic integration (Biklen, 1985; Skrtic et al., 1985; Wright et al., 1982).

Given the adhocratic ends of the EHA, it was intended to decrease the effects of student disability by increasing personalized instruction and regular classroom integration. But, given the bureaucratic value orientation of schools and of the means of the law itself, the result has been an increase in the number of students classified as disabled, disintegration of instruction, and a decrease in personalization in the regular classroom (Bryan et al., 1988; Carlberg & Kavale, 1980; Gartner & Lipsky, 1987; Gerber & Levine-Donnerstein, 1989; Keogh, 1988; Skrtic et al., 1985; USDE, 1988; Wang et al., 1986, 1987a; Walker, 1987).

### Policy Implications

Although the adhocratic ends of the EHA are distorted because of the bureaucratic nature of the law and its implementation context, schools appear to be complying with its procedural requirements because of the adoption of practices that, although they may be well intended and in some respects actually may result in positive outcomes, serve largely to symbolize (e.g., IEP's and resource rooms) and ceremonialize (e.g., IEP staffings and mainstreaming) compliance with the letter of the law rather than conformance with its spirit (see Carlberg & Kavale, 1980; Gerardi, Grohe, Benedict, & Coolidge, 1984; Schenck, 1980; Schenck & Levy, 1979). From a policy perspective, symbolic compliance with procedural requirements is problematic because it can lead monitors and implementation researchers to faulty conclusions. For example, Singer and Butler (1987) observed that "federal demands have equilibrated rapidly with local capacity to respond," and thus concluded that the EHA demonstrates that "a federal initiative *can* result in significant social reform at the local level" (p. 151). Although they are correct in asserting that such equilibration has resulted in "a basically workable system" (p. 151), they fail to recognize that equilibration is largely a process of institutionalizing the necessary symbols and ceremonies of compliance, which, given the limited capacity of bureaucratic school organizations to respond to the adhocratic requirements of the EHA, renders the system workable for school organizations, but not necessarily for the intended beneficiaries of the federal initiative.

And an even greater policy concern is that special education has itself conformed to the two-structure, machine-professional bureaucracy arrangement of general education to deal with the value contradictions between the EHA's adhocratic goal of personalized instruction and its bureaucratic means of uniform procedures (see Singer & Butler,

1987; Skrtic et al., 1985; Weatherly, 1979). As Singer and Butler noted, the EHA "has created a *dual* locus of organizational control," an arrangement in which information necessary for "legal or monitoring purposes, quick-turnaround defense of special education priorities . . . or public relations in the wider community" are managed centrally in the office of the special education director; whereas instructional decisions "have become or have remained more decentralized," in the hands of professionals (p. 139).

### The Regular Education Initiative[4]

The problem with the REI proposals is that each of them replicates the value contradictions of the EHA. Each proposal calls for an adhocratic value orientation while retaining the professional bureaucracy inner configuration of schools and extending their machine bureaucracy outer configuration. They retain the professional bureaucracy configuration because, by retaining the classroom teacher, each retains professionalization as the means of coordination. This, of necessity, yields loose coupling and thus deflects the ideal of collaboration. In principle, as long as the division of labor in schools is premised on specialization and coordinated through professionalization, teachers have no need to collaborate.

As we know, collaboration is a form of division of labor associated with the coordination mechanism of mutual adjustment, which is premised on a team approach to problem solving and yields a form of interdependency premised on reflective discourse. Although the REI proposals of Lilly and Pugach, Reynolds and Wang, and Stainback and Stainback call for collaborative problem solving between a classroom teacher and a support services staff, by retaining the notion of a classroom and placing the support services staff above it, they actually extend the formalization of the machine bureaucracy configuration and thereby undermine the ideals of problem solving and personalized instruction. Placing the support staff above the classroom teacher implies that the theory of teaching is at the support level, while the mere practice of teaching takes place in the classroom, which maintains the misplaced practice of separating theory and practice.

Moreover, this politicizes and thus undermines the ideal of collaboration, because placing support personnel above the practice context makes them technocrats rather than support staff. In an actual machine bureaucracy, technocrats are the people with the theory; they define and control the activities of the other workers (Mintzberg, 1979). This is not collaboration in an organizational sense; it is bureaucratic control and supervision. In professional bureaucracies, where the notion of a technocracy within the organization violates the logic of professional work, technocrats, particularly change agents and other school improvement personnel, are resisted (see Wolcott, 1977).

The same problems are inherent in the Gartner and Lipsky proposal, which retains the regular classroom and proposes to make it effective for all students by implementing the principles of effective schools research through school improvement projects. Here, the assumption is that the theory of effective teaching, which is known by the school improvement staff apart from and prior to the classroom context, is contained in the principles identified in the effective schools research, and that implementing these principles in the practice context is simply a matter of the teacher making a commitment to follow them (see Lezotte, 1989). In theory, imposing such standards from above, their apparent efficacy in some other context notwithstanding, can only lead to an extension of existing formalization, an increase in ritualized activity, and thus, ultimately, to an increase in professionalization and a corresponding decrease in personalization. In practice, this is precisely what has happened (see below and Clark & Astuto, 1988; Cuban, 1983, 1989; Slavin, 1989; Stedman, 1987; Timar & Kirp, 1988). As Cuban (1989) noted, under the effective schools formula many schools are returning to the 19th-century practices of standardized curriculum and instruction and thus ignoring individual differences.

Finally, the Stainback and Stainback proposal compounds both the problem of professionalization and formalization. Not only does it retain the notions of a classroom and the separation of theory and practice, thus politicizing and undermining the ideals of collaboration and problem solving, but, by creating a system of individual subject area courses, it disintegrates the student's instructional program by rationalizing it across even more teachers than under the mainstreaming approach.

Although the arguments put forth in the REI debate reject the presupposition of human pathology and thus represent progress relative to the mainstreaming debate, the outcome is the same. The adhocratic values of the REI proponents are distorted by the bureaucratic value orientation of public education and, because the REI proponents retain the presupposition of organizational rationality, by that of their own proposals. The ideal typical illustration of the distorting effect of the presupposition of organizational rationality on the REI proponents is the Stainback and Stainback proposal. Although it is by far the most adhocratically oriented REI proposal (total integration of students), it implies the most bureaucratically oriented system (near total disintegration of instruction).

In chapter 3 we saw that a critical reading of the REI debate rejected the presupposition of human pathology and thus left the legitimacy of special education as a professional practice hanging on the adequacy of the presupposition of organizational rationality. At this point, however, we have seen that a critical reading of the discourse on school organization and adaptability, in conjunction with an organizational analysis of the EHA and the REI proposals, rejects the presuppositions of human pathology *and* organizational rationality, which deconstructs special education, both as a professional practice and as an institutional practice of public education. In terms of the adequacy of its grounding assumptions, special education cannot be considered a rational and just response to the problem of school failure.

## PUBLIC EDUCATION AND THE DISCOURSE ON SCHOOL FAILURE

To this point in the book, we have been concerned with special education, first as a professional practice from the vantage point of professional culture, then as an institutional practice from the perspective of school organization. The focus of this section is on the implications of the deconstruction of special education for the discourse on school failure in the field of education and, ultimately, for the legitimacy of the institutional practice of public education itself. Considering these implications will require expanding the analysis to include the voice of the general education professional community and what it has to say (and not say) about school failure from the perspective of educational excellence. If we think of the mainstreaming and REI debates in special eduction as a *discourse on equity,* and of the "effective schools" and "school restructuring" debates in general education as a *discourse on excellence,* we can begin to see how the two discourses parallel, mirror, and, ultimately, converge upon one another.

By the effective schools debate I mean the early phase of the excellence movement, which was shaped by the thinking in *A Nation At Risk* (National Commission on Excellence in Education, 1983) and generally sought excellence through means that were quantitative and top-down. They were quantitative in that they simply called for more of existing school practices—more difficult courses, more homework, more time in school, and more rigorous standards. They were top-down in that they were bureaucratic and thus characterized by more "state control, with its emphasis on producing standardized results through regulated teaching" (Wise, 1988, p. 329), which ultimately distorted the goal of higher standards into more standardization (see, e.g., Bacharach, 1990; Cuban, 1983, 1989; Meier, 1984; Resnick & Resnick, 1985). Although well meaning, the advocates of the effective schools approach, like the proponents of mainstreaming, did not question the traditional bureaucratic structure of schools. As Cuban noted, "Their passion was (and is) for making those structures more efficient" (1989, p. 784).

By the school restructuring debate I mean the more recent phase of the excellence movement, which was shaped by the thinking in books such as *High School* (Boyer, 1983), *A Place Called School* (Goodlad, 1984), and *Horace's Compromise* (Sizer, 1984). The participants in this debate (see, e.g., Bacharach, 1990; Clark, Lotto & Astuto, 1984; Cuban, 1983, 1989; Elmore, 1987; Elmore & McLaughlin, 1988; Lieberman & Miller, 1984; McNeil, 1986; Oakes, 1985, Sergiovanni & Moore, 1989; Sirotnik & Oakes, 1986; Wise, 1988) generally seek excellence through means that are qualitative and bottom-up: qualitative in that they call for fundamental changes in the structure of school organizations; bottom-up in that they call for an increase in professional discretion, adult-adult collaboration, and personalized instruction.

The first parallel between the equity and excellence discourses is that the initial debate in each discourse is an extreme form of naive pragmatism that merely reproduces and extends the problems it sets out to solve. As in the case of mainstreaming and the EHA, the new practices that emerged out of the effective schools debate merely reproduced and extended the original problems (see Clark & Astuto, 1988; Cuban, 1983, 1989; Slavin, 1989; Stedman, 1987; Timar & Kirp, 1988; Wise, 1988). The second parallel is that the failure of the first debate gives rise to the second, which, although it is less naive, is also a form of naive pragmatism that promises to reproduce and extend current problems in the future. As we will see, although the restructuring debate is less naive than the effective schools debate, it does not explicitly recognize the connection between general education practices and the four assumptions. Like the REI debate in special education, it promises to reproduce and extend the general education problems of the 1980s in the 1990s and beyond (see below and Cuban, 1983, 1989; Wise, 1988).

Although the restructuring debate parallels the REI debate in this second respect, the effects of this pattern in the two debates are mirror images of one another. As we know, the REI debate implicates *school organization* in the problem of *student disability*. The mirror image of this in the restructuring debate is that, by pointing to the emergence and persistence of homogeneous grouping—curriculum tracking, in-class ability grouping, and compensatory pull-out programs—as an indication of deep structural flaws in traditional school organization (see Cuban, 1989; Oakes, 1985, 1986a, 1986b; Stedman, 1987; Wise, 1988), the participants in the restructuring debate have implicated *student disability* in the problem of *school organization*. The second way the REI and restructuring debates mirror each other is that, although both of them reject two of the four assumptions and question the other two, in the final analysis they retain the assumptions that they question. We saw this pattern for both the REI proponents and opponents relative to the question of the rationality and adaptability of school organizations. The mirror image of this contradiction in the restructuring debate is that, although it rejects the two assumptions about the rationality of school organization and change, it questions but retains the two about the nature of school failure and diagnosis. That is, although its participants criticize the institutional practices of tracking and compensatory pull-out programs, and even the overrepresentation of minority students in certain special education programs, they do not criticize special education as an institutional practice (see, e.g., Goodlad, 1984; Oakes, 1986a, 1986b; Sizer, 1984) and thus, in the end, retain the assumptions that school failure is pathological and that diagnosis is objective and useful.[5]

The restructuring debate does not recognize special education as a form of tracking because its criticism of homogeneous grouping stops at the point of presumed pathology, which is the third and, for present purposes, most important way that the two debates mirror one another.

Whereas the REI debate rejects the presupposition of human pathology but retains that of organizational rationality, the restructuring debate rejects organizational rationality but retains human pathology. The significance here, of course, is that the two debates—and thus the discourses on excellence and equity in public education—converge to reject both of the functionalist presuppositions that ground the 20th-century discourse on school failure and thus deconstruct it. The broader significance of the deconstruction of the discourse on school failure is that it provides the grounds for an immanent critique of the institution of public education. That is, given that education in a liberal democracy must be both excellent and equitable, public education must account for the fact that its practices are neither excellent nor equitable without recourse to the distorting and legitimizing effects of the functionalist discourse on school failure. Ultimately, to be able to continue making the claim that it embodies the ideal of democratic education, the institution of public education must reconstruct itself to be both excellent and equitable.

## EXCELLENCE, EQUITY, AND ADHOCRACY

We can turn from deconstruction to reconstruction by considering the moments of truth contained in the convergence of interests over excellence and equity in the REI and restructuring debates. As we know, the REI proponents call for (virtually) eliminating the regulatory requirements of the EHA. The corresponding argument among the proponents of restructuring is for eliminating scientific management as the approach to administration and change (see, e.g., Boyer, 1983; Cuban, 1983, 1989; Goodlad, 1984; Oakes, 1985, 1986a, 1986b; Sirotnik & Oakes, 1986; Sizer, 1984; Wise, 1988).

In organizational terms, the first convergence is that both sets of proponents are arguing for the elimination of rationalization, formalization, and tight coupling, the misplaced structural contingencies of the machine bureaucracy configuration. The second convergence is between the REI proponents' arguments for merging general and special education and those of the restructuring proponents for eliminating the various general education tracks. Here, in principle, both sets of proposals are calling for the elimination of specialization, professionalization, and loose coupling, the structural contingencies of the professional bureaucracy configuration. In practical terms, both sets of proponents seek an adaptable or innovative system in which increased teacher discretion leads to more personalized instruction through collaborative problem solving among professionals and client constituencies (see chapter 3 and Boyer, 1983; Cuban, 1983, 1989; Goodlad, 1984; McNeil, 1986; Oakes, 1985; Sizer, 1984).

Of course, because the restructuring proponents retain the assumption of pathology, there are differences between the two sets of proposals. But these are differences in degree, not in kind. In organizational terms, both debates argue for the introduction of collaboration, mutual adjustment, and discursive coupling, the structural contingencies of the adhocratic form. In principle, actualizing both sets of reform proposals will require an adhocratic school organization and professional culture.

As we know, the REI opponents' position on equity is that, given the nonadaptability of regular classrooms and school organizations, the targeting function of the EHA and the pull-out logic of mainstreaming must be maintained for political purposes, diagnostic and instructional inadequacies notwithstanding (Kauffman, 1988; Kauffman et al., 1988). The moment of truth in this position is the argument that, as long as resources are constant and students differ, no teacher, whether in a general or special education classroom, can escape the necessary choice between excellence (i.e., higher class means) and equity (i.e., narrower class variances), unless more powerful instructional technologies are available. In organizational terms, this is true because the structural contingencies of rationalization and formalization circumscribe a finite set of resources relative to a prespecified set of activities and outcomes, whereas those of specialization and professionalization circumscribe a finite repertoire of standard programs relative to a finite set of presumed client needs. Thus, students whose needs fall on the margins or outside of these standard programs must be either squeezed into them or squeezed out of the classroom.

Given the inevitability of human diversity, a professional bureaucracy can do nothing but create students who do not fit the system. In a professional bureaucracy, all forms of tracking—curriculum tracking and in-class ability grouping in general education, as well as self-contained and resource classrooms in special, compensatory, remedial, and gifted education—are symptoms of the organizational pathologies created by specialization and professionalization and compounded by rationalization and formalization. Students are subjected to—and subjugated by—these practices because, given their structural and cultural contingencies, traditional school organizations cannot accommodate diversity and so must screen it out.

The problem with the REI opponents' argument, however, is that it assumes that this sort of nonadaptability is inherent to *schooling*, rather than to its traditional bureaucratic *organization*. Student diversity is not an inherent problem for school organizations; it is a problem only when they are premised on standardization and thus configure themselves as performance organizations that perfect standard programs for known contingencies. As we have seen, the adhocratic form is premised on innovation. It configures itself as a problem-solving organization for inventing new programs for unfamiliar contingencies. Regardless of its *causes* and its *extent*, student diversity is not a liability in a problem-solving organization; it is an asset, an enduring uncertainty, and thus the driving force behind innovation, growth of knowledge, and progress.

The problem with the REI and restructuring proposals in this regard is that, although their ends require the adhocratic configuration, their means reproduce the professional bureaucracy configuration. This is so because, by retaining the notion of a classroom, they retain a specialized division of labor and a professionalized means of coordination, and thus retain a loosely coupled form of interdependency. Ultimately, both reform approaches eliminate rationalization and formalization and thus the misplaced machine bureaucracy outer structure of schools, while retaining specialization and professionalization and thus the professional bureaucracy inner structure.

From an organizational perspective, the argument for eliminating rationalization and formalization is an argument for uniting theory and practice in the professional, which, as we know from chapters 4 and 8, is the essence of professionalism and the logic behind specialization and professionalization. Beyond the fact that specialization, professionalization, and loose coupling contradict the goal of collaboration, by retaining the professional bureaucracy configuration, the REI and restructuring proposals unite theory and practice in the *individual* professional rather than in a *team* of professionals. As we know from the Apollo example, and as we will see again in the next chapter, this is a problem from a structural perspective because the type of innovation necessary to personalize instruction requires the formulation of new *multi*disciplinary knowledge and skills from the disciplinary knowledge and skills of existing professional specializations. This requires a collaborative division of labor, coordination premised on mutual adjustment, and a discursive form of interdependency. That is, it requires an adhocratic arrangement in which multidisciplinary teams formed around specific projects of innovation transcend the boundaries of conventional specializations. From a cultural perspective, we know that repertoires or paradigms of practice are *social* constructions; innovation occurs when new paradigms emerge through confrontations over uncertainty within social groups, a process that involves the deconstruction and reconstruction of existing paradigms (Brown, 1978; Rounds, 1981; Weick, 1979). From an organizational perspective, innovation or professional problem solving is not a solo performance; when it does occur, it is a social phenomenon that emerges out of a reflective discourse.[6]

Beyond the problem of innovation, eliminating rationalization and formalization while retaining specialization and professionalization creates a serious problem relative to accountability, one that is receiving increased attention in the school restructuring literature (see Conley, 1990; Murphy, 1989; Timar & Kirp, 1988, 1989). Although the advocates of school restructuring clearly reject the "hyperrationalist" position of the effective schools approach, concerns have been raised about the opposite extreme implicit in the school restructuring debate, the so-called "romantic decentralist" position (Timar & Kirp, 1988, p. 130).

The hyperrationalist approach, of course, is the *bureaucratic* mode of accountability associated with rationalization and formalization, the misplaced contingencies of the machine bureaucracy outer structure of school organizations. As we know, such an approach has serious negative consequences for educational excellence and equity because it decreases discretion and further separates theory from practice, thus decreasing the degree to which teachers can personalize instruction.

The decentralist approach is a *professional* mode of accountability associated with specialization and professionalization, the structural contingencies of the internal professional bureaucracy configuration of schools. In the extreme, it places virtually all decisions about the adequacy of practice in the hands of individual professionals. The advantage of this approach is that, by increasing discretion and uniting theory and practice in the professional, it *potentially* enhances the teacher's ability to personalize instruction. One problem with extreme forms of decentralization in any type of professional bureaucracy, of course, is that it places clients at risk of the most callous sorts of professional misconduct, such as racism, sexism, and handicapism, various forms of class, ethnic, linguistic, and cultural discrimination, and outright physical, emotional, and sexual abuse.

Notwithstanding the repugnance and seriousness of these abuses when they occur, a far more pervasive problem with decentralization in public education is its negative implication for instructional accountability relative to the structural and cultural characteristics of school organizations and the conventional nature of professional culture. From an organizational perspective, we know that decentralization is a problem in a structural sense because the convergent thinking and deductive reasoning of professionals and professions means that they tend to see clients' needs in terms of the skills they have to offer clients (Mintzberg, 1979; Segal, 1974; Perrow, 1970). In a cultural sense, professionals and professions tend to distort negative information about the adequacy of their practices to make it consistent with their prevailing paradigms of practice (Brown, 1978; Rounds, 1979, 1981; Weick, 1985).

The point is that, because modes of accountability are shaped by the logic of an organization's division of labor, means of coordination, and forms of interdependency (see Burns & Stalker, 1966; Kiel & Skrtic, 1988; Romzek & Dubnick, 1987), there is no way out of the professional -bureaucratic accountability dilemma as long as schools are configured as professional bureaucracies and managed as if they were machine bureaucracies. The advantage of the professional-political mode of accountability that emerges in the adhocratic configuration is that it avoids both extremes by assigning responsibility to *groups* of professionals. By democratizing and politicizing discretion within a community of interests—within a reflective discourse among professionals and client constituencies—it, at once, sharply reduces the potential for professional inadequacy and misconduct and greatly increases the possibility for divergent thinking and inductive reasoning among professionals.

From an organizational perspective, the REI and restructuring proponents are right about eliminating scientific management and the EHA. At a minimum, achieving their adhocratic ends will require merging theory and practice. If merging theory and practice is to have the adhocratic effect they desire, however, they will have to do more than eliminate general education tracks and merge the general and special education systems in the ways that they have proposed. Achieving the adhocratic ends of the REI and restructuring reform proposals will require merging theory and practice *in conjunction with* eliminating specialization and professionalization. Ultimately, this will require *eliminating the classroom*, which is an organizational artifact produced by the structural contingencies of specialization and professionalization and reinforced by that of loose coupling. From a structural perspective, the only way to introduce collaboration, mutual adjustment, and discursive coupling, the structural contingencies of the adhocratic form, is to eliminate rationalization, formalization, and tight coupling, the misplaced structural contingencies of the industrial machine bureaucracy, *and* specialization, professionalization, and loose coupling, the structural contingencies of the professional bureaucracy configuration.

Furthermore, from a cultural perspective, achieving these adhocratic ends will require that an adhocratically oriented professional culture emerge *and* be sustained within the field and institution of education. To emerge, such a culture will require the structural contingencies of the adhocratic form. Moreover, to be sustained, it will require an enduring source of uncertainty because, as we know, when uncertainties are reduced, adhocracies begin the transformation to bureaucracies, structurally and culturally.

In political terms, the institution of public education cannot be democratic unless its practices are excellent *and* equitable. In organizational terms, its practices cannot be excellent and equitable unless school organizations are adhocratic. In structural and cultural terms, school organizations cannot be adhocratic—and thus cannot be excellent, equitable, *or* democratic—without the uncertainty of student diversity. As such, educational equity is the precondition for educational excellence, school restructuring, professional renewal, and, as we will see in the final chapter, for the cultural transformation needed to restore the public for democracy in the 21st century.

## NOTES

1. Federico Mayor Zargoza is the current Director-General of UNESCO. The quote was taken from an exhibit at the United Nations complex in New York on March 3, 1990.

2. The citations appearing in this section are references to empirical and interpretive research evidence supporting my theoretical claims.

3. See Cuban (1989, p. 784) on the relationship among school reform, the at-risk category, and the graded school, "the core processes" of which are "labeling, segregating, and eliminating those who do not fit." The graded school, of course, is the actual case of the idealized professional bureaucracy configuration presented here.

4. The citations appearing in this section are references to empirical and interpretive research evidence supporting my theoretical claims.

5. Although the various special needs pull-out programs and all forms of tracking and ability grouping in general education are criticized in the restructuring debate, students with disabilities and special education as an institutional practice receive virtually no attention in it or in the effective schools debate (see Pugach & Sapon-Shevin, 1987; Shepard, 1987; Lilly, 1987). Furthermore, although Oakes's (1986b) criticism of "the all-too-frequent placement of black students with severe learning problems in programs for the 'educationally retarded' (sic), while whites with similar difficulties are placed in classes for the 'learning disabled'" (p. 150), indicates recognition of the problem of overrepresentation of minority students in *certain* special education programs, it does not criticize the historical problem of overrepresentation of minority students in special education per se (see text and chapter 3). More important (for present purposes), although Oakes is questioning the *accuracy* and *political neutrality* of special education diagnostic and placement practices, she is not criticizing special education as an institutional practice or rejecting the assumptions that school failure is pathological and that diagnosis is objective and useful.

6. The best articulation of the argument for uniting theory and practice in the professional is Schön's (1983, 1987, 1988, 1989) argument for developing reflective professional practitioners by eliminating (in what I have called the professional bureaucracy configuration) the "normal bureaucratic emphasis on technical rationality" (Schön, 1983, p. 338). As such, like the participants in the restructuring debate, he is calling for the elimination of the structural contingencies of rationalization and formalization. Given the importance of the idea of uniting theory and practice in the professional and the recognized significance of Schön's work on the topic, I devote a section in chapter 10 to a deconstruction of his idea of the reflective practitioner, drawing on the genealogical analysis of the special education knowledge tradition (chapter 5), as well as on a similar analysis of the field's value orientation in chapter 10, to support my theoretical and metatheoretical claims.

# 10

# The Special
# Education Paradox

The final result of political action often, no, even regularly, stands
in completely inadequate and often even paradoxical relation to its
original meaning.

Max Weber[1]

The unintended consequence of using organizations to provide services to society is that the services are shaped by the nature and needs
of the organizations that provide them. Although a democratic society
such as ours ideally wants and needs an adhocratic form of education,
we have had to settle for the bureaucratic type of schooling that traditional school organizations provide. Moreover, as we have seen, even
well-meaning attempts to change these organizations only make them
more bureaucratic and thus even less effective and less equitable. This
is not merely an educational problem, however. The contradiction
between democratic ends and bureaucratic means is the central fact of
the modern state.

According to Weber (1922/1978), democracy and bureaucracy
grow coincidentally because the actualization of democratic government requires development of the bureaucratic administrative form. As
such, the problem arises in the contradiction between the substantive
rationality of democracy and the formal rationality of bureaucracy
because, although democracy is intended to be dynamic, the bureau-

cratic form on which it depends resists change. Moreover, Weber believed that the contradiction between democracy and bureaucracy, although unintended, is inevitable and irresolvable.

## PUBLIC EDUCATION AND THE
## CONTRADICTION OF THE MODERN STATE

The adhocratic form of school organization is an unintended consequence of the contradiction between democracy and bureaucracy played out in public education. That is, under the democratic requirement of universal compulsory education, the nonadaptable bureaucratic school organization creates a separate organization within itself to contain the uncertainty of students whom it is compelled to serve, but who are resistant to its standard programs.

Paradoxically, out of this act of political and functional expediency, the nonadaptable bureaucratic form creates its inverse—an organization that, because it is faced with uncertain work and dynamic conditions, configures itself as an adaptable, problem-solving organization—the adhocratic form. As such, the problem-solving work activity of the adhocratic form creates the structural conditions necessary for the emergence of a professional culture of *special* education, which is grounded in the spirit of adhocracy and thus the inverse of the bureaucratically grounded professional culture of general education. Although the nature of its work activity permits special education to develop an adhocratic value orientation, the decoupled nature of its work environment precludes the conditions necessary for a reflective discourse and thus for the emergence of an adhocratic mode of professional practice. Therefore, its practices develop bureaucratically, which reproduces the contradiction between bureaucracy and democracy in the professional culture of special education.

The negative implication of this contradiction is that practices of the field remain more bureaucratic than adhocratic; the positive implication is that the contradiction between the field's adhocratic ideals and its bureaucratic practices creates a constant source of anomalies and uncertainty—and thus the grounds for an ongoing immanent critique that acts as a mechanism for change within the field and, ultimately, within public education itself. With time, professionalization and formalization, as well as situational factors such as age and size, drive the culture toward the bureaucratic form and value orientation, which has the dual effect of introducing more anomalies and crushing the adhocratic spirit.

In this concluding chapter I will argue that this spirit of adhocracy, so clearly evident in the value orientation of the EHA and the REI, is the value orientation necessary to deconstruct the schools of the 20th century and to reconstruct those of the 21st century, according to the ideals of education in a liberal democracy. In preparation for this argument, let us consider the American ideal of public education in greater depth.

## THE IDEAL OF PUBLIC EDUCATION IN AMERICA

The question of the value orientation, or cultural significance, of public education in America, of course, is one of those questions that Weber believed can be answered only from particular points of view. Thus, let us consider it in an ideal typical sense from the normative perspective. As we might expect, the normative view is democratic, progressive, and egalitarian through and through.

Public education is the democratic birthright of every American, as well as the prime vehicle for insuring good democratic government (Cubberley, 1919). As the institution through which America "sought to hold itself together and prepare its citizens for the greatest of all experiments in democracy" (Greer, 1972, p. 17), public education had to satisfy four inherently contradictory requirements. First, it had to be both *excellent and equitable*. If America was to remain democratic and avoid tyranny, Jefferson argued, public education must produce intelligent citizens and thoughtful leaders (Ford, 1904). Moreover, he insisted that, if it was to remain a free society—one in which positions of power were open to all on the basis of merit—public education had to ensure that "men of talent might rise whatever their social and economic origins" (Greer, 1972, p. 16).

Second, public education had to *promote stability and change*. Under conditions of a rapidly expanding political economy, and thus an increasingly diverse population, public education had to represent a stabilizing force, a mechanism for standardizing the thought and behavior of its citizens. At the same time, educational pioneers from Horace Mann to William Torrey Harris argued that public education in a rapidly expanding democracy had to be dynamic enough to change with the spiritual mood of the public and the material needs of society (see Cremin, 1961, 1965).

Third, public education had to *promote the development of reflective thought*. If students were to be prepared for full economic, political, and cultural participation in such a dynamic and changing democracy, they and thus their teachers must be reflective thinkers. For example, in his prototypical model for secondary schools, Benjamin Franklin argued for a curriculum of practical learning (concrete problem solving), because frontier life required that every student be "prepared to cope with the unexpected" (Greer, 1972, p. 15), and be capable of learning any business, calling, or profession. Jefferson charged the schools with the responsibility of educating the intelligent citizen in the interest of good democratic government; and Americans since the Jacksonian era have insisted upon an enlightened public capable of divergent thinking in the interest of social and cultural progress (Welter, 1962).

Finally, these same pioneers, as well as early 20th-century progressive reformers such as Dewey, argued that public education had to *promote cultural transformation* in the interest of social responsiveness to changing historical conditions associated with phenomena such as industrialization, urbanization, and immigration (see below and Cremin, 1961; Dworkin, 1959; Kloppenberg, 1986). Thus, not only did public education have to promote excellence and equity and stability and change; it also had to transform the cultural sensibility of the public when it was necessary for it to see itself and America in new ways.

Given the inherent contradictions in the democratic ideal of public education, it is not surprising that it has been called into question so often by critics representing the entire spectrum, from the conservative and neoconservative Right to the social democratic and critical Left (e.g., Bell, 1976; Bellah et al., 1986; Bloom, 1987; Bowles & Gintis, 1976; Giroux, 1981). In the following sections I compare the democratic ideals of American public education to its actual practices by considering the evidence on its capacity to be excellent, equitable, adaptable, and reflective, transformative in terms of the analysis of professional culture presented in Part Two and the analysis of school organization presented in chapters 8 and 9.

Ultimately, I will argue that, given its current professional culture and organizational structure, the institution of public education does not and cannot live up to the ideals of democratic education, but that it can live up to them with critical pragmatism as a mode of professional discourse and the adhocratic school organization as the conditions for critical practice and discourse. Moreover, I will argue that, given these methods and conditions, the profession and institution of education can resume the unfinished critical project contained in American pragmatism and work toward the type of professional renewal, school restructuring, and cultural transformation that will be necessary to resume the unfinished project of democracy.

## CAN SCHOOL ORGANIZATIONS BE EXCELLENT AND EQUITABLE?

Although the empirical evidence on the efficacy (e.g., Goodlad, 1984; Sizer, 1984) and equity (e.g., Edgar, 1987; Lipsky & Gartner, 1989; McNeil, 1986; Oakes, 1985; Skrtic, 1988b) of traditional school organizations is overwhelmingly negative, there are schools that are relatively effective and equitable (see Berman & McLaughlin, 1974–1978; Brophy, 1983; Clark, Lotto, & Astuto, 1984; Edmonds, 1979; Goodlad, 1975; Lieberman & Miller, 1984; McNeil, 1986), including some that have met or surpassed the intent of the EHA and the spirit of mainstreaming and the REI (see Biklen, 1985; Skrtic et al., 1985; Thousand, Fox, Reid, Godek, & Williams, 1986; Wright et al., 1982). We can confront this apparent contradiction from the perspective of professional culture and school organization by thinking of schools as underorganized systems—that is, as structural configurations that are ambiguous because of the nature of their work, division of labor, mode of coordination, and form of interdependency. Order in such a system is achieved by everyone knowing roughly what everyone else is doing, by way of socialization into a common professional knowledge tradition. Moreover, this tradition is grounded in a multiple-paradigm science and, furthermore, because it is actually two traditions that are, at best, only loosely coupled, the situation is made all the more ambiguous.

Because thought and activity in such a context require a paradigm for unrandomizing complexity, school organizations and the thought and action of their administrators and teachers are guided by ideology and values. Given the functionalist grounding of the professional culture of education and the bureaucratic work conditions and activities of school organizations, most often the value orientation of the organization and its members is bureaucratic. On occasion, however, someone, some group, or some event introduces or uncovers anomalies in the bureaucratic paradigm of practice that, because they violate the paradigm-induced expectations of the organization's members, increase the inherent ambiguity enough to cast doubt on the prevailing paradigm.

Under this condition of heightened uncertainty, in which the prevailing paradigm loses some of its ability to maintain its allegiances, someone or some group, acting on a different set of values, manages to convince itself and others to see things in a different way. This decreases the ambiguity by redefining the paradigm of practice in such a way that the original anomalies disappear—a subtle process of paradigm deconstruction and reconstruction in which the organization's members redefine the way they interpret its structural contingencies, and thus the constraints that shape their thought and action.

Although this is an idealized characterization, when one considers the empirical evidence, it is just this sort of organizational phenomenon that is found in successful schools. Their success turns on human agency, on the values, commitments, expectations, and actions of the people who work in them (see, e.g., Biklen, 1985; Brophy, 1983; Clark et al., 1984; Edmonds, 1979; Lieberman & Miller, 1984; McNeil, 1986; Singer & Butler, 1987; Skrtic et al., 1985; Thousand, Fox, Reid, Godek, & Williams, 1986). For example, in their reanalysis of much of the effective schools literature, Clark et al. argued that these factors are precisely what one finds working in a mutually reinforcing way in successful schools. Teachers affect student learning by their expectations for and commitment to their students' performance and their own teaching (see also Brophy, 1983; Edmonds, 1979). Students affect one another by their commitment to achievement and expectations for and valuing of learning.

Given these values, commitments, and expectations, teachers and students in these school organizations act toward one another in ways that reinforce and mutually shape their expectations for themselves and their values for and commitments to learning and one another. Administrators make a difference when they exhibit the same sort of values, commitments, and expectations for themselves, teachers, students, and the school organization itself. Clark et al. (1984) characterize this mutually reinforcing circle of thought and action as a "'syndrome' or 'culture'" (p. 58)—what we would call a paradigm of practice. According to their reanalysis of the empirical evidence, Clark et al. (1984) argued that the key for effective schools "lies in the people who populate particular schools at particular times and their interaction with these organizations. The search for excellence in schools is the search for excellence in people" (p. 50). And the same holds true for educational equity. As with educational excellence, equitable schools are best understood as a culture or a paradigm of mutually reinforcing values, commitments, expectations, and activities. People matter most in equitable schools (see Biklen, 1985; Biklen & Zollers, 1986; Edmonds, 1979; Skrtic et al., 1985).

As we know from previous chapters, the structural and cultural implications of the professional bureaucracy, particularly when it is managed and governed as if it were a machine bureaucracy, mean that, in principle, it is impossible for traditional school organizations to be excellent or equitable. Even though some schools seem to contradict the theory, the point is that these organizations are more effective and more equitable than one would expect because they operate more like adhocracies than professional bureaucracies. They operate more like adhocracies because the people who inhabit them think like problem solvers; they think like problem solvers because they act like problem solvers. And these people think and act like problem solvers because someone or some group tightened up an ambiguous setting with adhocratic values. As Weick (1985) noted, the cultural and structural conditions that provide the sense of order in underorganized systems, whether that order is more bureaucratic or adhocratic, exist as much in the mind as they do in the field of action.

## CAN SCHOOL ORGANIZATIONS CHANGE?

As in the case of educational excellence and equity, the empirical evidence on the capacity of school organizations to change is overwhelmingly negative (e.g., Cuban, 1979; Elmore & McLaughlin, 1988; Lehming & Kane, 1981). But here, too, there are schools that are relatively adaptable (see Berman & McLaughlin, 1974–1978; Clark et al., 1984; Goodlad, 1975; Lieberman & Miller, 1984; McNeil, 1986), including some, of course, that have implemented the adhocratic changes associated with the spirit of the EHA, mainstreaming, and the REI proposals (e.g., Biklen, 1985; Skrtic et al., 1985; Thousand et al., 1986; Wright et al., 1982), even though, in principle, the structural and cultural features of school organizations preclude these types of changes. Again, we can confront this contradiction by thinking of school organizations as underorganized systems of mutually shaping structures, conventions, ideas, and activities. Change in these organizations turns on the recognition of anomalies that violate conventionally based expectations and thus force educators to question their paradigm of practice.

Because the paradigm is the glue that holds everything together, most anomalies are distorted to be consistent with the network of theories, assumptions, and models contained within the prevailing paradigm. But when persistent anomalies sustain nagging uncertainties, or when the number of anomalies reaches some point of no return, the pieces come unstuck and the paradigm deconstructs. This forces those who had been committed to it to seek a new orienting framework. The new paradigm is a reconstruction; it puts the pieces back together in a different way, according to the value orientation that is presupposed in it, and activity resumes under the new guiding framework of structures, conventions, ideas, and activities. As such, the stage is set for new anomalies to emerge and thus for the process to repeat itself. Thus, the two essential elements in school organization change are *anomalies* that cause the paradigm to deconstruct, and *values* according to which the pieces are reconstructed.

When we consider the empirical evidence on educational change in terms of this idealized image, we find that change in school organizations follows the same organizational phenomenon that one finds working in effective and equitable schools. That is, the success of change efforts in schools also turns on human agency, on the values, commitments, expectations, and actions of the people who work in them (see Biklen, 1985; Brophy, 1983; Clark et al. 1984; Skrtic et al., 1985; Thousand et al., 1986). Referring again to the Clark et al., (1984) study, which also reanalyzed much of the educational change literature, we find that, "as with the effective school, effective school improvement programs are probably best represented as a 'syndrome' or 'culture' of mutually reinforcing expectations and activities. . . . People matter most in school improvement programs" (pp. 58–59).

And, again, the same holds true for change related to equity, such as that associated with the EHA, mainstreaming, and the REI. As with other successful school improvement programs, people matter most (see Biklen, 1985; Skrtic et al., 1985). Effective implementation of these programs is best represented as a culture or a paradigm of mutually reinforcing values, commitments, expectations, and activities. Thus, as in the case of effective and equitable schools, the bureaucratic form is what is nonadaptable, not school organizations per se. School organizations can be effective, equitable, and adaptable, but when they are, they are operating more like adhocracies than bureaucracies because their members are thinking and acting more like problem solvers than performers. They are thinking and acting this way because someone or some group reconstructed an ambiguous setting adhocratically.

This explanation of the relationship between structure and culture and, more important, of the power of human agency to resist the structural and cultural features of organization, does not provide sufficient insight to address in a more fundamental way the larger issues of professional renewal, school restructuring, or cultural transformation. An important limitation in this regard is the meaning or cultural significance of excellence, equity, and adaptability that is inherent in the explanation. The methodological problems inherent in operationalizing these concepts in educational research and evaluation notwithstanding, the degree to which these successful schools can be considered excellent, equitable, or adaptable, of course, can be understood only within the horizon of possibility established by current interpretations of excellence, equity, and adaptability embedded in the professional culture of education and the organization of schools. That is, even the successful school can be understood to be so only in terms of prevailing 20th-century definitions of success.

Moreover, the successful school, even if we could agree that it is truly successful, is successful only within the horizon of possibility established by the degree to which human agency can overcome the limiting conventions of professional culture and school organization. In the final analysis, today's successful school is an adhocractically oriented enterprise operating within the constraints of a bureaucratically oriented configuration. We do not know what is possible—in terms of excellence, equity, and adaptability—in an adhocractically oriented enterprise operating within the constraints of an adhocratically oriented configuration.

I will return to these issues in the three concluding sections. In preparation for those discussions, as well as to provide a longitudinal illustration of the relationship between structure and culture in schools, let us consider a genealogy of the special education professional value orientation, keeping in mind the genealogy of special education professional knowledge presented in chapter 5.

## GENEALOGY OF SPECIAL EDUCATION VALUES

From both the structural and the cultural perspectives, we know that, in principle, traditional school organizations are nonadaptable at the micro level of the classroom, and that, as a result, students who cannot be squeezed into the standard programs of the prevailing paradigm of practice must be squeezed out of the system. Because schools are nonadaptable at the organizational level, change demands must be transformed into symbols of change, such as decoupled subunits, which signal the public that a change has occurred, and at the same time buffer the organization from the need to change. We also know that, from the cultural perspective, change demands can arise externally, when values change in society, or internally, through an accumulation of anomalies, either by way of a confrontation among organizational members over the adequacy of the current paradigm or through a series of conservative reforms that expose even more anomalies and eventually undermine the entire paradigm of practice. The genealogy of the special education value orientation has been shaped by all of these scenarios of organizational change.

### Emergence of the Adhocratic Spirit

When society required schools to serve a broader range of students at the turn of this century, the special classroom emerged as a vehicle that, at once, contained the uncertainty of student diversity by decoupling it from the core of the system, and preserved the legitimacy of the prevailing paradigm by signaling the public that schools had complied with the democratic ideal of universal compulsory education. For all its moral, political, and pedagogical faults, however, the segregated special classroom created a set of contingencies that contained some, but not all, of the structural conditions necessary for the adhocratic form. By definition, students in these classrooms could not be squeezed into the standard programs of the prevailing general education paradigm and, because the teachers in these classrooms had been recruited from the ranks of the general education system and thus had only the traditional standard programs available to them, the first special classroom teachers had to invent new programs under conditions of uncertainty.

Further, because the special classroom was decoupled from the larger system, the teachers who worked in them were relatively protected from the structural contingencies of rationalization and formalization. And, because there were no special education professional education programs at the time, they were protected as well from those of specialization and professionalization. Although they were relatively free from the machine bureaucracy and professional bureaucracy configurations, however, the conditions for the adhocratic form were lacking because the decoupled subunit status of the special classroom meant that its teachers were, for all practical purposes, decoupled (rather than merely loosely coupled) from general education teachers as well as other special classroom teachers.

Thus, because these early special education teachers faced uncertainty and were relatively free from traditional bureaucratic contingencies, their work activity required reflection and innovation rather than convention and perfection. As such, their value orientation shifted from bureaucratic (perfecting standard programs for known contingencies) to adhocratic (inventing novel programs for contingencies never before encountered). But, because they worked alone, and thus did not have the advantage of a discursive community of inquiry, their practices, although they may have been innovative at the start, became routinized and bureaucratized over time.

With more time and increased size, as well as the standardization and formalization associated with professionalization and regulation of the field between 1910 and 1960, the special classroom model and its bureaucratic diagnostic and instructional practices became institutionalized as the field's paradigm of practice. As such, what began as an adhocratically oriented enterprise, was driven toward a bureaucratic process of delivering standard programs geared to presumed student needs—a situation that, in combination with other factors such as school desegregation, began to produce the anomalies that served as a basis for criticism of the diagnostic and instructional practices associated with the special classroom model in the 1960s.

## Emergence of the EHA Paradigm

Although they introduced empirical information that the prevailing special classroom paradigm was not working, those who criticized special education practices in the 1960s did not question the adequacy of the prevailing general education paradigm. They simply provided the negative technical information that eventually deconstructed the prevailing special education paradigm. Of course, the new paradigm that emerged was the EHA, which, on the basis of the value orientation of the field, seeks an adhocratic solution, but, on the basis of its functionalist knowledge tradition and bureaucratic practices, uses bureaucratic means. This, as we have seen, has had the effect of driving the field further toward the bureaucratic form and value orientation, which over the 1980s has produced enough anomalies to call the prevailing EHA paradigm into question.

As we have seen, at this point the REI proponents and opponents are arguing that the real flaw is in the general education system. In this instance, we can understand the EHA as an initially conservative effort to remedy a flaw in an otherwise viable system of general education—a measure taken to correct the flaw with the least possible increment of change. This, of course, led to the unanticipated consequence of raising new ambiguities about the diagnostic and instructional practices associated with the EHA and mainstreaming models, and, more important, with the overall system of public education. The important thing about the REI is not the actual reform measures that are being proposed. It is the fact that it is calling into question the prevailing general education paradigm. The EHA did more than provide students identified as handicapped with access to the general education system; it created opportunities for special educators to become more familiar with general education, which exposed more of its basic contradictions to people with an adhocratic value orientation.

The unfortunate, but genealogically interesting, thing about the situation today is that special education is losing its adhocratic spirit. This is particularly true for special educators in the mild disability areas because the EHA and mainstreaming have forced them to act and think bureaucratically. This waning of the adhocratic spirit is particularly evident among the REI opponents who, as we have seen, are defending the prevailing paradigm in the face of technical evidence that it is not working.

Moreover, as we have seen, even the REI proponents who represent the mild disability areas in the field of special education (Reynolds, Wang, Lilly, Pugach) are relatively conservative in their outlook compared to the REI proponents who represent the severe and profound disability area (Gartner, Lipsky, Stainback, Stainback). From an organizational perspective, this is so because professionals in the severe and profound disability area continue to work in separate settings, within but apart from the general education system. They have taken over the special classrooms, the decoupled subunits that historically have existed as adhocratic spaces outside the bureaucratic structure and culture of general education and, more recently, outside that of special education.

As noted in chapter 9, the needs of the students that the professionals in this area serve are so variable that the notion of a standard program is virtually precluded. Moreover, the complexity of the diagnostic and instructional problems is so great that interdisciplinary collaboration is required. Given their decoupled status and the extreme ambiguity and complexity of their work, in conjunction with the availability of an interdisciplinary team of professionals and what is ordinarily a close working relationship with students' parents, these programs conform to the adhocratic configuration in every respect (see Sailor & Guess, 1983). As such, they represent the actual case of the ideal typical adhocratic configuration in public education. These programs and the professionals that work in them are prototypical of the school organization and professional culture that are needed for education in the 21st century.

## Reappraisal and Reorientation of Professional Practices

The genealogy of the value orientation of the professional culture of special education is important in several respects. First, it supports Weick's (1985) notion that the value orientation of a professional culture is shaped by the nature of its work activity. This is important substantively because it addresses the problem of the culture of the school that Sarason (1971, 1982) highlighted. Given Weick's theory and the historical evidence provided by the genealogy, we can see that, although Sarason was correct in arguing that meaningful change in public education had to be based on changing the culture of the school, his subsequent despair over what he perceived to be the virtual impossibility of doing so (1983) is warranted only with respect to the bureaucratic structural contingencies of traditional school organizations. That is, his argument that meaningful change in schools (1971, 1982) and, ultimately, meaningful learning in classrooms (1983) are unlikely outcomes in public education is true only if the conventional notion of a classroom and the practice of separating theory from practice, are continued. But, if the classroom is eliminated (by eliminating specialization, professionalization, and loose coupling and replacing them with collaboration, mutual adjustment, and discursive coupling), the culture of the school, in principle, will reemerge in a form that is more adhocratic and less bureaucratic.

In theory, then, we can change the culture of the school by changing the structure of the school, a possibility that is supported empirically by the genealogy of special education values, in that (a) after an adhocratically oriented structural change, a previously bureaucratically oriented segment of the general education teacher population developed an adhocratic value orientation (as reflected in the spirit of the EHA and REI); (b) subsequent bureaucratically oriented structural changes (the professionalization of the field and, more recently, the bureaucratic procedural requirements of the EHA) have driven a portion of the historically adhocratically oriented special education professional community back toward the bureaucratic orientation (as reflected in the value orientation of the REI opponents); and (c) special education professionals that continue to work in adhocratic settings (severe and profound disability areas) have remained more adhocratically oriented than those who, since the EHA, work more within the bureaucratic structure of general education (the mild disability areas) (as indicated in the split within the REI proponent camp over which students should be integrated).

The second sense in which the genealogy of special education values is important is that it illustrates the inadequacy of conceptualizing educational excellence, equity, and change within the current cultural and structural horizon of public education. In the case of special education, we have seen that, even though the EHA, mainstreaming, and the REI are premised on the adhocratic spirit, their conceptualization and actualization are shaped almost entirely by a bureaucratic horizon of possibility, which has reproduced and extended the original problems and, ultimately, acted to crush the adhocratic spirit.

Finally, the genealogy of special education's adhocratic value orientation is significant because it illustrates that structural changes that merely free teachers from bureaucratic contingencies, although they may allow a spirit of adhocracy to emerge in a professional culture, do not assure that the new practices developed within this adhocratically oriented culture will be either more effective or more ethical than the practices they replace. As the case of special education demonstrates, even well meaning attempts to reform practices adhocratically can result in new bureaucratic practices that simply reproduce old problems in a new form. The point is that, although anomalies can cause a professional culture to recognize problems with its practices, merely recognizing and acting on these deficiencies pragmatically is insufficient. A professional culture must be pragmatic, but it also must be critical. That is, to be able to reappraise and reorient its professional practices, without simply reproducing them and their attendant problems, it must be able to engage in a critical reflective discourse that calls into question the implicit presuppositions embedded in the models, assumptions, theories, and metatheories that stand behind these practices, as well as behind the critical discourse itself.

And, of course, to carry out this type of continual deconstruction and reconstruction of professional practices and discourses, a profession must have methods and conditions for actualizing and sustaining a reflective discourse.  In the remaining sections I return to the discussion of the requirements for democratic education, drawing on the genealogy of special education values where I can as empirical support for my theoretical arguments. In these sections I will be particularly concerned with the issue of methods and conditions for reflective discourse, relative to teachers and students in schools in the next section, and then more broadly in subsequent sections relative to the implications of reflective discourse in public education for the emerging political and economic conditions of the 21st century.

## CAN SCHOOL ORGANIZATIONS PROMOTE REFLECTIVE THINKING?

As we know, the idea that schools should promote reflective thinking in students is fundamental to the American ideal of democratic education. And, though the idea that teachers should also be reflective is implicit in the notion of thinking students, it was made explicit in this century by subjectivists such as Dewey (1910/1989), Piaget (1948/1974), Wertheimer (1945/1959), and their followers (see Kloppenberg, 1986; Kohlberg & Mayer, 1972), who argued that education should be premised on reflective teachers engaged in the cultivation of reflective thinking in students. Of course, given the domination of objectivism, the ideas of reflective students and reflective teachers were buried under the educational prescriptions of objectivists such as Skinner (1953), Tyler (1949), Schwab (1983), and Bloom (Bloom, Engelhart, Furst, Hill, & Krathwohl, 1956).

Nevertheless, the general trend away from objectivism and toward subjectivism during the 1960s and 1970s led to reemergence of both of these ideas within the field of education during the 1980s. The reemergence of interest in the notion of the thinking student began as a reaction against the objectivist arguments of "Hirsch, Cheney, Ravitch, Finn, and Bennett . . . that disciplinary knowledge and cultural literacy are the primary ingredients for achieving an educated citizenry" (Costa, 1989, p. vi) and has been advanced by the subjectivist implications of cognitive psychology (Resnick & Klopfer, 1989). As a result, "thoughtful educators everywhere are calling attention to the importance of developing students' thinking skills through their experiences in school" (Resnick & Klopfer, 1989, p. 1).

The revival of interest in the progressive idea of the thinking teacher has been stimulated by Schön's (1983) critique of the objectivist understanding of professionalization and his proposal for a mode of professional practice premised on the apparently subjectivist notion of reflection-in-action. Although in his original work Schön only tangentially addressed teaching, he addressed the idea of reflective teaching directly in his subsequent writing (1987, 1988, 1989), in which he argued for reflection-in-action as a means for teachers to enhance their understanding of instructional practices and to see themselves as "builders of repertoire rather than accumulators of procedures and methods" (1988, p. 26).

I want to consider the recovery of both of these ideas—reflective students and reflective teachers—by comparing them, in an ideal-typical analysis, to their corresponding conceptualizations contained in Dewey's pragmatist notion of progressive education. I have several purposes in mind. First, I want to use the comparison to argue that neither Schön's notion of the reflective teacher nor the new cognitive science understanding of the reflective student goes far enough toward the type of reflective teachers and students that are needed today. Second, by addressing this shortfall, I want to extend my previous arguments about the advantages of antifoundationalism over subjectivism as a philosophical framework into the realm of curriculum and instruction. Third, I want to consider both the subjectivist and antifoundationalist conceptualizations of reflective teachers and reflective students in terms of their implications for the adhocratic school organization.

Finally, the discussion of Dewey's conceptualization of progressive education, in addition to providing a vehicle for comparison, will in itself prepare the way for my concluding comments about the implications of progressive education, critical pragmatism, and the adhocratic school organization for the ideas of professional renewal, school restructuring, and cultural transformation.

## Student Reflection: The Subjectivist Perspective

In its most articulated form in the field of education, the emerging conceptualization of student reflection is contained in Resnick and Klopfer's (1989) notion of "the thinking curriculum," which is premised on the belief that "the entire educational program must be reconceived and revitalized so that thinking pervades students' lives from kindergarten onward, in mathematics and history class, in reading and science, in composition and art, in vocational and special education" (p. 2). Such a reconceptualization is possible, they argued, because recent developments in cognitive psychology have resolved the fundamental conflict between the subjectivist and objectivist conceptualizations of curriculum and instruction.

Historically, the conflict emerged when objectivists rejected the subjectivist outlook because its "theories of thinking seemed to deny the importance of specific knowledge and to set cultivation of thinking skills apart from learning subject matter" (Resnick & Klopfer, 1989, p. 3). In its contemporary form, the conflict is at the center of the confrontation between objectivists and subjectivists over the question of whether greater emphasis should be placed on knowledge or on thinking—that is, a confrontation between objectivists "who assert that the new standards for literacy will best be met by increasing the emphasis on knowledge"—and subjectivists, who argue that "such knowledge in and of itself may be of little use. . . .[and thus] what is needed is to emphasize the teaching of thinking processes and skills" (Costa, 1989, p. vi).

As Resnick and Klopfer noted, however, "modern cognitive theory resolves this conflict. . .[because] it offers a perspective on learning that is thinking- and meaning-centered, yet insists on a central place for knowledge and instruction" (1989, p. 3). That is, cognitive science resolves the conflict between objectivists and subjectivists because "it combines . . . knowledge and thinking. Rather than polarize these two educational necessities, it integrates them" (Costa, 1989, p. vii). Thus, the *new* subjectivist position within the contemporary debate is that "the tools of inquiry by which one discovers and validates knowledge are . . . transferable . . . and, consequently, emphasis should be given to developing these skills using disciplinary and cultural knowledge as a means, not an end, for educating a literate citizenry" (Costa, 1989, p. vii).

### The Contradiction Between Subjectivist Values and an Objectivist Pedagogy

Given the new subjectivist position on the relationship between knowledge and thinking, the thinking curriculum is a combination of an instructional model "based on constructivist, self-regulated assumptions about the nature of learning" (Resnick & Klopfer, 1989, p. 4), drawn from recent developments in cognitive psychology, and a curriculum that uses knowledge of the physical, social, and cultural disciplines as a means to education rather than its end (Costa, 1989). The link between instruction and curriculum, according to Resnick and Klopfer (1989), is what educators have learned from cognitive psychology:

> Recent cognitive research teaches us to respect knowledge and expertise. Study after study shows that experts on a topic reason more powerfully about that topic and learn new things related to it more easily than they do on other topics. This is true for science, mathematics, political science, technical skills—for all fields of expertise. We learn most easily when we already know enough to have organizing schemas that we can use to interpret and elaborate upon new information. (pp. 4–5)

Thus, "a fundamental principle of cognition . . . is that learning requires knowledge" (Resnick & Klopfer, 1989, p. 5). But, because "cognitive research also shows that knowledge cannot be given directly to students," the thinking curriculum must provide students with a base of *generative* knowledge—that is, "knowledge that can be used to interpret new situations, to solve problems, to think and reason, and to learn" (Resnick & Klopfer, 1989, p. 5). According to Costa (1989), this base of generative knowledge is determined by "theorists, practitioners, and scholars" in particular fields of expertise, who are asked to "define the key concepts of their disciplines and link them to the modes of thinking, dispositions, and tools of inquiry that are basic to those disciplines" (p. vii).

Finally, the teacher's role in the thinking curriculum is to "help students get started in developing their base of generative knowledge so they can learn easily and independently later on"—which is based on the assumption that "key concepts and organizing knowledge structures . . . become generative [by being] called upon over and over again as ways to link, interpret, and explain new information" (Resnick & Klopfer, 1989, p. 5).

To the degree that it draws on Piaget's "picture of the 'natural' child as a scientist trying to make sense of the world, and of true learning as constructing ideas, not memorizing information in the forms given by teachers or texts" (Resnick & Klopfer, 1989, p. 3), the value orientation of the thinking curriculum is subjectivist; that is, it is grounded in the constructivist view of learning and development, which asserts that "people are not recorders of knowledge but builders of knowledge structures" (Resnick & Klopfer, 1989, p. 4).

Referring back to the discussions of Kuhn and of professionalization presented in previous chapters, however, we can see that the actual curricular and instructional practices of the thinking curriculum are grounded in the traditional objectivist conceptualizations of science and of professional induction.[2] Thus, rather than teaching the "facts" of a particular discipline, the cognitive science approach teaches its key concepts, modes of theorizing, method of inquiry, and paradigmatic dispositions, which, as we know, are presupposed in the discipline's models, assumptions, theories, and metatheories. Moreover, when Resnick and Klopfer say that these "key concepts and organizing knowledge structures . . . become generative [by being] called upon over and over again as ways to link, interpret, and explain new information" (p. 5), they are implicitly referring to the dogmatic and authoritarian approach to professional induction that is associated with the positivist model of professional knowledge.

The thinking curriculum is constructivist enough to recognize that the reconstruction of knowledge is central to the development of reflective thought. But its objectivist orientation distorts the subjectivist value orientation contained in the idea of "reconstruction," turning it into an objectivist mode of practice in which the goal of instruction is "restructuring" students' initial constructions into the constructions of particular disciplinary cultures.[3] This, of course, is completely consistent with the role that such restructuring plays in the induction of scientists and other professionals into scientific and professional cultures; "only after a number of such transformations of vision does the student become an inhabitant of the scientist's world, seeing what the scientist sees and responding as the scientist does" (Kuhn, 1970, p. 111). Although this is an effective approach for inducting students into a particular paradigm or way of seeing, it is not intended to promote reflective thought. Rather than promote thinking that is divergent and inductive, which is characteristic of the blurring of rules that takes place during episodes of revolutionary science, it promotes thinking that is convergent and deductive, which is characteristic of the (implicitly or explicitly) rule-governed activity of normal science (see Barnes, 1982; Kuhn, 1977).

Ironically, by missing Kuhn's distinction between normal and revolutionary science, advocates of the thinking curriculum also miss the central insight of Piaget, upon whom Kuhn leaned heavily for his notions of paradigms and paradigm shifts (see Kuhn, 1970). That is, they miss the insight that cognitive growth in humans, like the growth of knowledge in the sciences, is a *series* of deconstructions and reconstructions driven by the attempt to resolve anomalies. It is not simply a single "transformation of vision" from an intuitive construction grounded in personal experience to a received construction grounded in the historically situated and temporarily relevant knowledge tradition of a discipline and delivered in a dogmatic spirit. As such, the subjectivist value orientation and objectivist practices of the thinking curriculum are inconsistent and contradictory. Rather than resolving the conflict between the objectivists and the subjectivists, the thinking curriculum reproduces the conflict within its model of curriculum and instruction, and thus deconstructs itself.[4]

### Teacher Reflection: The Subjectivist Perspective

Whereas the objectivist practices of the new cognitive instructional researchers in education contradict the subjectivist value orientation, Schön's (1988) notion of teachers as creators of repertoires rather than performers of established procedures is consistent with it. By linking thought and action in the notion of reflection-in-action, however, Schön (1983) implicitly is expressing the antifoundational value orientation that lies at the very heart of philosophical pragmatism, which, as we will see below, is the notion of the interdependence between thought and action. Thus, my argument is that, although Schön's subjectivist conceptualization of reflective professional practice is completely consistent with his *explicitly* subjectivist value orientation, his *implicitly* antifoundational value orientation contradicts his subjectivist conceptualization of reflective professional practice. To achieve what he calls reflection-in-action would require an antifoundational rather than a subjectivist mode of professional practice. Given that he recommends a subjectivist mode of practice rather than the requisite antifoundational one, his value orientation and his practices are inconsistent, which deconstructs his proposal for reflection-in-action.

I want to carry out my treatment of Schön on three levels: *metatheoretically*, by comparing his subjectivist conceptualization of reflection with the antifoundational conceptualization of reflection contained in philosophical pragmatism; *theoretically*, by considering his proposal from the perspective of school organization and adaptability; and *empirically,* by using the genealogy of the special education value orientation as supporting evidence for my metatheoretical and theoretical analyses. In addition to allowing me to deconstruct Schön's notion of the reflective practitioner, this approach will permit me to reinforce some of my points about the nature of the adhocratic school organization and to conclude my arguments relative to the genealogy of the special education value orientation—all of which will set the stage for my concluding arguments.

### The Contradiction Between Antifoundational Values and Subjectivist Practices

As we will see, the conceptualization of reflection contained in Dewey's (1910/1977) notion of progressive education is premised on the antifoundational theory of knowledge (see also Freire, 1970; Rorty, 1979). As such, reflection is understood to be an intellectual process that begins with a perceived problem, which presupposes a set of shifting and historically situated interests, value orientations, or points of view, and obtains in social discourse. There is no difference between Schön's conceptualization of reflection and that of the pragmatists on the matter of a problem. For Schön, reflective thinking is a process set in motion "when people are presented with a surprise" (1989, p. 204), "a problematic situation that cannot be readily converted to a manageable problem" (1989, p. 201).

The difference between Schön's conceptualization and that of the pragmatists turns on the question of whether reflection is an *individual act* premised on volition, or a *social act* grounded in a dialogical discourse. Although Schön's (1983, 1989) principal examples of reflection-in-action are social—a jazz band improvising and a group of teachers reframing a problem—he consistently characterizes reflection as a solitary act, one in which the only discourse that takes place is between a practitioner and a problematic situation, a conversation in which "the situation talks back, the practitioner listens, and as he appreciates what he hears, he reframes the situation once again" (Schön, 1983, pp. 131–132). Keeping in mind this distinction between Schön and the pragmatists, let us consider his conceptualization of reflective teaching from the perspective of school organization.

Given my characterizations of traditional school organization, the idea of the reflective teacher immediately raises the question of the degree to which reflective teaching is a real possibility in schools as they are currently organized. Historically, of course, the argument that traditional school organization works against the possibility of teacher reflection is most often associated with Dewey (1910/1977, 1910/1989, 1928/1965), and more recently with Freire (1978). Schön (1983, 1988), too, has been clear about the organizational context required for reflective teaching.

> To the extent that an institution seeks to accommodate to the reflection-in-action of its professional members, it must meet several extraordinary conditions. In contrast to the normal bureaucratic emphasis on uniform procedures, objective measures of performance, and center/periphery systems of control, a reflective institution must place a high priority on flexible procedures, differentiated responses, qualitative appreciation of complex processes, and decentralized responsibility for judgement and action. In contrast to the normal bureaucratic emphasis on technical rationality, a reflective institution must make a place for attention to conflicting values and purposes (1983, p. 338).

According to Schön, then, reflective teaching requires a reflective school organization. In fact, although he says little more about the type of organization that will be required for reflection-in-action, his characterization of a reflective organization is completely consistent with what I have called the adhocratic form of school organization. Nevertheless, given his conceptualization of the reflective practitioner as an individual engaged in a discourse with a problem situation rather with other practitioners, Schön's notion of a reflective organization retains the structural feature of specialization, which is characteristic of the professional bureaucracy and thus, from an organizational perspective, contradicts his adhocratic value orientation of innovation through reflective problem solving. Innovation, or the creation of repertoires, is premised on:

> . . . the building of new knowledge and skills [which] requires the combination of different bodies of existing ones. So rather than allowing the specialization of the expert . . . to dominate its behavior, the adhocracy must instead break through the boundaries of conventional specialization . . . . Thus, whereas each professional of the professional bureaucracy can operate on his own, in the adhocracy the professionals must amalgamate their efforts. . . . Different specialists must join forces in multidisciplinary teams, each formed around a specific project of innovation. (Mintzberg, 1979, pp. 434–435)

Thus, from an organizational perspective, reflective teaching is a possibility in the adhocratic school organization. But, contrary to Schön's conceptualization of reflective practice as a solitary act, when it does occur, it is a social phenomenon. As such, reflective teaching, in the sense of inventing and reinventing (or constructing, deconstructing, and reconstructing) educational practices to solve unexpected problems, requires a reflective discourse within a community of interests, which, as we will see in the discussion of progressive education, is completely consistent with the pragmatist conceptualization of reflection.

My final argument against Schön's conceptualization of reflective teaching is that, as I noted in chapter 9 relative to the reform proposals of the REI and restructuring debates, freeing teachers from the centralized authority of rationalization and formalization while retaining the structural contingencies of specialization and professionalization may permit them to build repertoires, but it will not assure that the repertoires they build will be any more effective, or ethical, or even much different than their current ones. My evidence for this assertion, of course, is the genealogy of the special education value orientation. As we know, although freeing a small segment of the bureaucratically oriented general education teaching staff did result in the emergence of a new adhocratically oriented professional culture of special education, it did not result in the emergence of a better repertoire of practices. Referring to the organizational analysis above and the discussion of progressive education to follow, this is so because, although the special classroom required innovation and, therefore, reflection, it did not provide the reflective discourse within a community of interests that the pragmatists argued was necessary to develop reflective and ethical students, teachers, citizens, and, ultimately, democratic government and just social practices.

### Reflective Teachers and Students: The Antifoundational Perspective

Understanding Dewey's conceptualization of progressive education from the perspective of the field of education is difficult because, as Kloppenberg (1986) noted, it "has been so distorted by generations of well-meaning but ill equipped educational administrators that its original significance has been almost entirely lost" (p. 374). Of course, educational administrators were ill equipped for understanding Dewey's philosophy of education because, as in the case of Weber's theory of bureaucracy, they were inclined by their paradigmatic orientation to give it a functionalist reading. Thus, for a fair reading—one that is informed by the metatheoretical assumptions upon which it is premised—let us consider progressive education in its ideal typical sense. Let us consider it from Dewey's perspective, from the perspective of antifoundationalism and the pragmatist conceptualization of knowledge, truth, ethics, and inquiry.

In *The School and Society* Dewey (1899/1976a) argued that, prior to industrialization, children's daily experiences at home provided them with a multitude of problems and questions about self, nature, and community—questions they could answer through their own investigations and experiences with other children, or through encounters with adults who, at that point in our history, were themselves involved daily in concrete problem-solving activities. But when industrialization removed work from the home, and when its fruits reduced the need to solve problems, children lost the rich problem-solving context that had provided their parents and grandparents with ample opportunity to develop imagination and intelligence. Thus, he argued that industrialization, the very historical condition that created the need for public schools, also required that a particular type of education be provided in them. Dewey was an optimist, but he was not a romantic; he did not argue for a return to the days before industrialization. In fact, as we will see, he believed that industrialization was a positive force for an expanded notion of democracy. Rather than returning to the problem-rich context of the past, Dewey argued that the goal of public education should be to return problems to the lives of children by recreating a problem-rich context in which reflective teachers could put their students' minds to work instead of filling their heads with "facts."

Because Dewey wrote his philosophy of education during the period of the rationalization of school organizations according to the industrial model of the machine bureaucracy, he recognized that the sort of education he had in mind would require nothing less than complete reconstruction of the curriculum and the method of instruction. The approach he recommended, of course, was *progressive education*, which proposed that, instead of presenting abstract information to passive students, teachers should engage their students' native capacities and enthusiasm by linking learning to life through concrete problem solving, or what he called the "concrete logic of action" (1899/1976a, p. 69).

Dewey's conceptualization of progressive education was grounded in the pragmatist theory of knowledge, which conceives of thinking as arising "from the need of meeting some difficulty, in reflecting upon the best way of overcoming it, and thus leads to planning, to projecting mentally the result to be reached, and deciding upon the steps necessary and their serial order" (1899/1976a, p. 69). As such, he viewed education as a reflective process premised on a "reconstruction or reorganization of experience that adds to the meaning of experience, and . . . increases the ability to direct the course of subsequent experience" (1916/1980, p. 82). He favored problem solving as a pedagogical approach because he believed it provided the best means for developing the capacity to think reflectively. Kloppenberg (1986) summarized the implications of Dewey's philosophy of education in terms of its implications for teachers:

> The teacher's goal . . . is not to train students to perform familiar tasks in time-honored ways, but to help them learn to solve unanticipated problems with imagination, not to impart bodies of knowledge but to develop the capacity to think . . . [that is] the ability to reason independently, without

the assistance of inherited methods or the reassurance of knowing that a correct answer always exists. (p. 375)

## Dialogical Discourse Within a Community of Interests

Philosophically, the most distinctive feature of progressive education is its fusion of reflection and activity, which as Kloppenberg (1986) noted, is the cornerstone of philosophical pragmatism, the *via media* that cut through the objectivism-subjectivism dichotomy. Although the idea that thought and action are separate had dominated Western philosophy since the Greeks distinguished *theoria* from *praxis*, the pragmatists':

> . . . emphasis on the interdependence of contemplation and action, on the completion of *theoria* in *praxis*, signaled a dramatic departure from the image of the mind as mirror prevalent in Western thought since Descartes. . . . When the subject and object are perceived as related immediately rather than as two distinct substances, the gap separating external reality from the thinking process disappears. It is then only a short step to the conclusion that man must act upon his environment, not simply think about it. (Kloppenberg, 1986, p. 86)

But there is more to progressive education than reflection. In addition to the antifoundational theory of knowledge, progressive education rests on its corollary, the pragmatist theory of truth, which emphasizes the social construction and validation of knowledge through dialogical discourse within a community of interests. Politically, then, the most distinctive feature of progressive education is its fusion of the individual and the social, a *via media* that relates the microscopic/order and macroscopic/conflict extremes that have shaped modern knowledge.

Progressive education, like pragmatism itself, cuts a road between individual and collective interests. In *The Public and Its Problems* (1927/1988c) and *Individualism, Old and New* (1929–30/1988b), Dewey argued that the technological advances associated with industrialization had changed the historical conditions of the early 20th century. In turn, these changes had created a growing contradiction between the *possessive* form of individualism characteristic of the 18th and 19th centuries and the new *social* form of individualism that he believed was required for democratic life within the expanding network of regional, national, and international interdependencies that had emerged. He believed that the mounting social and political costs of this contradiction could no longer be ignored, and that the new conditions of interdependence made possible and begged for a way of developing in the public a new sense of itself as a community of interests, a new cultural sensibility premised on social individualism.

I will return to this topic below, but for now it is sufficient to say that Dewey saw public education, in general, and progressive education, in particular, as the vehicle to bring about the necessary change in cultural sensibility. As such, progressive education, grounded in the pragmatist conceptualizations of knowledge and truth, and thus a fusion among subject and object and individual and social, was designed to nurture the intellectual capacity of students to recognize and appreciate the uncertainty of knowledge and the interdependency of social life and so to prepare them for carrying out the necessary cultural transformation of society.

Finally, such a project of mediation and reconciliation cannot proceed without a theory of ethics, which, as we know, is also contained within philosophical pragmatism. Dewey's moral philosophy is completely consistent with his notion of progressive education and pragmatism; like all activity, he conceived of ethical activity in terms of problem solving—a process that begins with a "felt difficulty" and progresses toward resolution in praxis through inquiry within a community of interests (Dewey & Tufts, 1932/1989). Thus, "the central Deweyan outlook on ethics [is] that it is the concrete task of bringing the broadest lessons of experience and the resources of inventiveness to the solution of particular problems, not the application of a fixed and pre-set code of moral universals" (Edel & Flower, 1989, p. xxvii).

As Edel and Flower (1989) noted, for Dewey ethics was a way of "dealing with reconstruction and resolution of conflicts and problems in particular situations . . . not the application of rules that simply sum up past experience, nor the resistance to temptation to transgress established rules" (p. xxv). As such, Dewey considered the traditional conflict in the field of ethics between freedom and responsibility—that is, between individual interests and the common good, or between excellence and equity—to be a pseudo-problem created by the artificial split between the individual and the social in modern knowledge (Dewey, 1920/1982; Kloppenberg, 1986). Thus, the pragmatist theory of ethics, actualized through progressive education, contains the key to Dewey's analysis of freedom and responsibility:

Freedom is essentially the capacity to learn and to make creative and innovative use of learning in guiding conduct. The pragmatic emphasis is on
responsibility as prospective rather than retrospective . . . on sensitivity,
learning and self-development. (Edel & Flower, 1989, p. xxv)

## CAN PUBLIC EDUCATION TRANSFORM SOCIETY?

The first real test of the grounding idea that public education should
transform society occurred during the progressive era, a period in
which the notion of an orderly, democratic society was shaken by the
problems associated with industrialization. As we know from chapter
7, America's initial response to the problem of industrialization was
shaped by the idea of social efficiency, which was promoted by progressive reformers who, although they had different and conflicting
motivations, were grounded in the functionalist discourse of scientific
management and the machine bureaucracy configuration. Although the
social efficiency movement was short-lived, its intensity and timing
were sufficient to instill the idea in government, business, and education that the problem with democracy was that it was inefficient and,
more important, that things could be set right by adopting industry's
bureaucratic form and its science of emerging efficiency (see Callahan,
1962; Haber, 1964).

Nevertheless, the idea of social transformation through education
took on a new significance in the social disarray following World War
I, and particularly after the stock market crash of 1929. During this
period, a generation of progressive reformers who were grounded in
philosophical pragmatism contended that the problem with democracy
*was* bureaucracy. Drawing on Weber's sociology of bureaucracy and
Dewey's philosophy of education, they argued that nothing short of
social reconstruction was necessary to save democracy from the distorting effects of bureaucracy (see Kliebard, 1988; Kloppenberg,
1986). Of course, Weber believed that the inherent contradiction
between democracy and bureaucracy was the central and irresolvable
fact of the modern state. But the progressives tempered Weber's
(1922/1978) pessimism with Dewey's (1927/1988c) optimistic argument that, although industrialization had intensified the very real problem of bureaucracy, it also provided an opportunity for America to
recover democracy through a cultural transformation leading to a
social reconstruction of the modern state itself.

According to Dewey (1899/1976a, 1927/1988c), the problem of bureaucracy is intensified by industrialization because it places more of life—particularly work and education—under the bureaucratic form, which, by design, reduces the need to solve problems and to engage in discourse. Ultimately, this stunts the growth of reflective thought and thus undercuts the ability of the public to govern itself. As we know, Dewey (1929–30/1988b) believed that the opportunity posed by industrialization was that it created an expanding network of social interdependencies that made possible and required a new cultural sensibility, a shift from the possessive form of individualism that had served America well in the 18th and 19th centuries, to a social form of individualism that was more suited to the new historical conditions of the 20th century.

For Dewey, the concern over the decline of democracy was a twofold problem. Speaking of the new interdependence that had emerged with industrialization, he said:

> In spite of attained integration, or rather perhaps because of its nature, the Public seems to be lost; it is certainly bewildered. . . . The social situation has been so changed by the factors of an industrial age that traditional general principles have little practical meaning. They exist as emotional cries rather than as reasoned ideas. (1927/1988c, pp. 308–318)

Thus, the first problem for Dewey was a bewildered public which, because of changed social conditions, could no longer express its interests and thus was unfit for participation in democracy. The second problem was "the essential need . . . [for] improvement of the methods and conditions of debate, discussion and persuasion" (1927/1988c, p. 365), which were needed if the public was ever to develop a sense of itself as a community of interests and thus be able to reconstruct society.

For Dewey and the other reconstructionists (see Kloppenberg, 1986), the only meaningful response to the problem and opportunity of the industrial era was to restore the public for democracy through a cultural transformation, which was to be actualized by instituting progressive education in the public schools. Drawing once again on Dewey and his philosophy of education, which, of course, was grounded in the social epistemology of American pragmatism, they repudiated the prevailing idea that public education should serve as a vehicle for convincing individuals to restrain themselves and to follow the rules. Instead, they proposed the progressive theory that people should be freed from external restraints and expected to freely choose to be responsible. Education in a democracy, then, according to the progressive outlook, should cultivate a sense of *social responsibility* by developing an awareness of *interdependence*, and engender a critical attitude toward received knowledge by promoting an appreciation of *uncertainty* (see Bourgeois, 1896; Croly, 1909/1965, 1914; Dewey, 1897, 1899/1976a, 1916/1980, 1928/1965).

And it was here, of course, that the reconstructionists were confronted with the problem that ultimately blocked their reform efforts: the contradiction between the adhocratic value orientation of progressive education and the bureaucratic value orientation of the profession and institution of public education. Thus, the circularity in their argument for transforming society through education was, and continues to be, that:

> Education inevitably involves institutions as well as the ideas to be communicated, and unshackling students from a false individualism and a false subservience to [received knowledge] must therefore await the unshackling of their teachers. . . . If the problems facing society can be traced to its individualism, as these thinkers believed, and reform must proceed by means of education, how can reformers get around the awkward fact that the educational system is imbued with precisely the values that they have isolated as the source of the problem? (Kloppenberg, 1986, p. 377)

No one grasped the circularity problem better than Weber (1922/1978). Whereas the problem of an unreflective public could be traced to the contradiction between democracy and bureaucracy in the modern state, he argued that the circularity of trying to solve the problem through education turns on a more fundamental contradiction in the logic of modernity itself: the contradiction among *democracy, bureaucracy, education*, and *professionalization*.

Weber explained that the ever increasing push to further bureaucratize the economy and government creates the need for more and more experts and thus continually increases the importance of specialized knowledge. But the logic of expertise contradicts democracy because it creates "the struggle of the 'specialist' type of man against the older type of 'cultivated' man" (1922/1978, p. 1090). And because the progressive project is premised on restoring democracy by educating the cultivated citizen, it is stymied because public education itself becomes increasingly bureaucratized in the interest of training specialized experts for an increasingly bureaucratized economy. Thus, democracy continues to decline, not only because the bureaucratic form resists change but also because the cultivated citizen continues to disappear.

As more of life comes under the control of the specialization and professionalization of the professional bureaucracy, the need to solve problems and to engage in discourse diminishes even further. This stunts the growth of reflective thought in society *and* in the professions, which not only undercuts the ability of the public to govern itself democratically but further diminishes the capacity of the professions to see themselves and their practices and discourses critically.

More than any other American institution, public education, with its democratic ideals and bureaucratic professional cultures and school organizations, stands precisely in the center of this social phenomenon. And, of course, behind public education stands special education, with functionalism, objectivism, and, ultimately, modern knowledge and foundationalism standing behind it all.

## PROSPECTS FOR THE FUTURE

We can begin to assess the significance of the reconstructionist debate for contemporary society by comparing the emerging historical conditions of the 21st century to those of the early 20th century, the historical conditions in which the debate took shape.

> By 1932 . . . industrialism has moved into overdrive and an urban society is clearly in the making. . . . A new physics has replaced the Newtonian outlook and a new logic is shaking philosophy . . . . The social sciences have been staking claims for the study of human life and thrusting different perspectives of method and research into the arena. Ethics is in a particularly precarious position: formerly it had coasted on the comfortable assumption that people agreed about morality but only argued about how it was to be justified. Now it is startled into the perception that there are fundamental conflicts on moral questions. (Edel & Flower, 1989, pp. viii–ix)

In the late 20th century we have a better understanding of the implications of the "new physics," particularly for the social disciplines, which, on the basis of these implications, are beginning to question some of their earlier objectivist claims about epistemology, methodology, and social life. Moreover, we have had more than a century to think about antifoundationalism, the new logic of philosophical pragmatism that began shaking philosophy in the 1870s and has continued to shake it and social and political theory until today. And, as we know, this has produced new and reappropriated old methodologies for addressing fundamental conflicts on moral questions, particularly questions about the relations of power and knowledge in the emerging postmodern world. Finally, and most important in terms of determinate possibilities for the future, industrialism has stalled out in the late 20th century and is being overtaken by postindustrialism.

The significance of the emergence of postindustrialism is that it is premised on an even greater and more pervasive form of interdependence and social responsibility than industrialism. Whereas the network of social interdependencies of industrialization stopped at the boundaries of industrial organizations themselves, postindustrialization extends the network into the very core of the postindustrial organizational form (see Dertouzos, Lester, & Solow, 1989; Drucker, 1990; Kearns & Doyle, 1988; Naisbitt & Aburdene, 1985; Reich, 1983, 1990). The key difference is that industrial organization depended on the machine bureaucracy configuration and thus on the separation of theory and practice and an unreflective, mechanical form of interdependency among workers. Postindustrial organization, however, depends on the adhocratic form, on collaboration, mutual adjustment, discursive coupling, and a political form of accountability premised on a community of interests among workers and managers, and, ultimately, among the organization's members, consumers, and host community (Dertouzos et al., 1989; Drucker, 1990; Kearns & Doyle, 1988; Mintzberg, 1979; Reich, 1983).

Reich (1990) characterized the adhocracies of the postindustrial economy as "environments in which people can identify and solve problems for themselves" (p. 201), as contexts in which:

> . . . individual skills are integrated into a group. . . . Over time, as group members work through various problems . . . they learn about each others' abilities. They learn how they can help one another perform better, what each can contribute to a particular project, and how they can best take advantage of one another's experience. (p. 201)

The system of education that is needed for the postindustrial economy is one that prepares young people "to take responsibility for their continuing education, and to collaborate with one another so that their combined skills and insights add up to something more than the sum of their individual contributions" (Reich, 1990, p. 202). As such, educational excellence in the postindustrial era is more than basic numeracy and literacy; it is a capacity for working collaboratively with others and taking responsibility for learning (Dertouzos et al., 1989; Drucker, 1990; Kearns & Doyle, 1988; Naisbitt & Aburdene, 1985; Reich, 1983, 1990). Moreover, educational equity is the precondition for excellence, growth of knowledge, and progress in the postindustrial era, for collaboration means learning collaboratively with and from persons with varying interests, abilities, skills, and cultural perspectives, and taking responsibility for learning means taking responsibility for one's own learning *and* that of others (Dertouzos et al., 1989; Drucker, 1990; Kearns & Doyle, 1988). Ability grouping and tracking have no place in such a system because they "reduce young people's capacities to learn from and collaborate with one another" (Reich, 1990, p. 208). Moreover, such practices work against promoting social responsibility in students and developing their capacity for negotiation within a community of interests—outcomes that are unlikely unless "class unity and cooperation are the norm" (Reich, 1990, p. 208; Dertouzos et al., 1989).

Given the relevancies of the postindustrial era, the successful school in the 21st century will be one that produces liberally educated young people who can work responsibly and interdependently under conditions of uncertainty. It will do this by promoting in its students a sense of social responsibility, an awareness of interdependency, and an appreciation of uncertainty. It will achieve these things by developing students' capacity for experiential learning through collaborative problem solving and reflective discourse within a community of interests. The successful school in the postindustrial era will be one that achieves excellence and equity simultaneously—indeed, one that recognizes equity as the way to excellence. The successful school in the postindustrial era will be one that produces cultivated citizens by providing all of its students with a progressive education in an adhocratic setting.

Where do we stand today in relation to the problems that Dewey identified at the start of the century? It is certain that the problem of an unreflective public is still with us. One need do little more than consider the state of political and cultural life today to see that the public continues to be bewildered. Nevertheless, the prospects for reflective discourse have improved considerably. As we have seen, developments at the margins of the social disciplines are providing new intellectual and methodological resources, as well as recovering and recycling others. Not only are some of these developments finding their way into educational inquiry, but the methods themselves are premised on and aimed at education, edification, and self-formation. Moreover, beyond providing much useful information about school organization and adaptability, three decades of unsuccessful planned change, including the EHA and the first phase of the excellence movement, have resulted in enough uncertainty about public education to create a convergence of interests over school failure. And, of course, the most significant development is the emergence of postindustrialism, which, in principle, holds out the possibility of a convergence of interests over public education itself.

In the final analysis, however, cultural transformation and social reconstruction will depend on adequate methods and conditions for reflective discourse. Given the emerging historical conditions of the 21st century, and the fact that democracy *is* collaborative problem solving through reflective discourse within a community of interests, critical pragmatism and the adhocratic school organization provide us with the methods and conditions to resume the critical project of American pragmatism and thus with what is certainly our best—but perhaps our last—chance to save our democracy and ourselves from bureaucracy.

## NOTES

1. Weber (1919/1946b, p. 117).

2. For example, when Resnick and Klopfer (1989) say that "we learn most easily when we already know enough to have organizing schemas that we can use to interpret and elaborate upon new information" (p. 5), they are implicitly referring to the organizing scheme of a paradigm of normal science (see Kuhn, 1970; chapter 1).

3. For example, in one of the expositions of the cognitive science approach that Resnick and Klopfer (1989) refer to as an example of the type of restructuring that is necessary for developing generative knowledge, Minstrell (1989) noted that, given "the findings of cognitive research, restructuring students' existing knowledge has become the principal goal of instruction. . . . [because] students come to the classroom with strong initial conceptions. . . . [which] are often very different from what we want them to learn" (p. 142).

4. Although I will not address the topic in the depth it deserves, the idea of curriculum and instruction that is implied in the discussions of critical pragmatism in Part One, chapter 6, and in the remaining sections of this chapter (relative to Dewey's notion of progressive education) is different from that of the "thinking curriculum" in every respect. For example, instruction under the thinking curriculum approach is monological, a form of drill and practice that is carried out in a spirit of authoritarianism and aimed at restructuring the experiential knowledge of individual students into the conventional knowledge constructions of particular disciplinary cultures. Given an

approach to instruction that merely restructures and thus reproduces modern knowledge, the curriculum of the thinking curriculum approach begins and ends with modern knowledge. Conversely, instruction from the perspective of critical pragmatism is dialogical, a form of discourse that is carried out in a spirit of inquiry and aimed at developing the experiential knowledge of students through deconstruction and reconstruction of particular modern knowledge traditions. Thus, although it also begins with modern knowledge, in the end the curriculum of the critical pragmatism approach produces postmodern knowledge. More important than the type of knowledge produced or reproduced, of course, is the type of student that is produced under each approach. The goal of curriculum and instruction under the thinking curriculum approach is to produce experts, that is, deductive and convergent thinkers who are oriented to performance and perfection. This is achieved by extending professional and scientific education down into elementary and secondary education. As we will see in subsequent sections, however, the goal of curriculum and instruction under the critical pragmatism approach is to produce cultivated citizens, inductive and divergent thinkers who are oriented to socially responsible problem solving and innovation. This will require developing the spirit of critical pragmatism in elementary and secondary education and extending up into professional and scientific education and out into society. Whereas the thinking curriculum teaches students and teachers to "respect [modern] knowledge and expertise" (Resnick & Klopfer, 1989, p. 4), critical pragmatism teaches them to subject modern knowledge and expertise to "interrogation and critique" (Greene, 1978, p. 58).

# References

Abeson, A., & Zettel, J. (1977). The end of the quiet revolution: The Education for All Handicapped Children Act of 1975. *Exceptional Children, 44(2)*, 115–128.

Algozzine, B. (1977). The emotionally disturbed child: Disturbed or disturbing? *Journal of Abnormal Child Psychology, 5(2)*, 205–211.

Algozzine, B., & Korinek, L. (1985). Where is special education for students with high prevalence handicaps going? *Exceptional Children, 51(5)*, 388–394.

Allington, R. L., & McGill-Franzen, A. (1989). Different programs: Indifferent instruction. In D. K. Lipsky & A. Gartner (Eds.), *Beyond separate education: Quality education for all* (pp. 75–97). Baltimore: Paul H. Brookes.

Allison, G. T. (1971). *Essence of decision: Explaining the Cuban missile crisis.* Boston: Little, Brown.

Althusser, L. (1969). *For Marx.* Hamondsworth, England: Penguin.

Antonio, R. J. (1981). Immanent critique as the core of critical theory: Its origins and developments in Hegel, Marx, and contemporary thought. *British Journal of Sociology, 32(3)*, 330–345.

Antonio, R. J. (1989). The normative foundations of emancipatory theory: Evolutionary versus pragmatic perspectives. *American Journal of Sociology, 94(4)*, 721–748.

Apple, M. (1982). *Education and power.* London: Routledge & Kegan Paul.

Apter, S. J. (1982). *Troubled children, troubled systems.* New York: Pergamon Press.

Argyris, C. (1957). *Personality and organization.* New York: Harper.

Astuto, T. A., & Clark, D. L. (1988). State responses to the new federalism in education. *Educational Policy, 2*, 361–375.

Bacharach, S. B. (1990). *Education reform: Making sense of it all.* Boston: Allyn & Bacon.

Bakalis, M. J. (1983). Power and purpose in American education. *Phi Delta Kappan, 63(1)*, 7–13.

Ballard-Campbell, M., & Semmel, M. (1981, August). Policy research and special education: Research issues affecting policy formation and implementation. *Exceptional Education Quarterly, 2(2)*, 59–68.

Barnard, C. I. (1938). *Functions of the executive.* Cambridge, MA: Harvard University Press.

Barnes, B. (1982). *T. S. Kuhn and social science.* New York: Columbia University Press.

Barnes, B. (1985). Thomas Kuhn. In Q. Skinner (Ed.), *The return of grand theory in the human sciences* (pp. 83–100). Cambridge, England: Cambridge University Press.

Barton, L., & Tomlinson, S. (Eds.). (1984). *Special education and social interests.* London: Croom-Helm.

Bates, R. J. (1980). Educational administration, the sociology of science, and the management of knowledge. *Educational Administration Quarterly, 16*(2), 1–20.

Bates, R. J. (1987). Corporate culture, schooling, and educational administration. *Educational Administration Quarterly, 23*(4), 79–115.

Becker, H. S. (1983). Studying urban schools. *Anthropology and Education Quarterly, 31*(2), 99–108.

Bell, D. (1976). The cultural contradictions of capitalism. New York: Basic Books.

Bellah, R. N., Madsen, R., & Sullivan, W. M., et al. (1986). *Habits of the heart.* New York: Harper & Row.

Benhabib, S. (1986). *Critique, norm, and utopia: A study of the foundations of critical theory.* New York: Columbia University Press.

Berger, P. L., & Luckmann, T. (1967). *The social construction of reality.* New York: Doubleday.

Berman, P., & McLaughlin, M. W. (1974–1978). *Federal programs supporting educational change* (Vols. 1–8). Santa Monica, CA: Rand Corp.

Bernstein, R. J. (1976). *The restructuring of social and political theory.* Philadelphia: University of Pennsylvania Press.

Bernstein, R. J. (1983). *Beyond objectivism and relativism: Science, hermeneutics, and praxis.* Philadelphia: University of Pennsylvania Press.

Bidwell, C. E. (1965). The school as formal organization. In J. G. March (Ed.), *Handbook of organizations* (pp. 972–1022). Chicago: Rand McNally.

Biklen, D. (1985). *Achieving the complete school: Strategies for effective mainstreaming.* New York: Columbia University Press.

Biklen, D., & Zollers, N. (1986). The focus of advocacy in the LD field. *Journal of Learning Disabilities, 19*(10), 579–586.

Bishop, J. M. (1977). Organizational influences on the work orientations of elementary teachers. *Sociology of Work & Occupation, 4*, 171–208.

Blatt, B., & Kaplan, F. (1966). *Christmas in purgatory.* Boston: Allyn & Bacon.

Bledstein, B. J. (1976). *The culture of professionalism: The middle class and the development of higher education in America.* New York: W. W. Norton.

Bloom, A. (1987). *The closing of the American mind.* New York: Simon & Schuster.

Bloom, B. S., et. al. (1956). *Taxonomy of educational objectives: Cognitive domain.* New York: David McKay.

Bloor, D. C. (1976). *Knowledge and social imagery.* London: Routledge & Kegan Paul.

Bobbitt, F. (1913). Some general principles of management applied to the problems of city school systems. In *The supervision of city schools* (12th yearbook of the

National Society for the Study of Education) (Part 1, pp. 137–196). Chicago: University of Chicago Press.

Bogdan, R. (1983). Does mainstreaming work? is a silly question. *Phi Delta Kappan*, *64*, 425–434.

Bogdan, R., & Knoll, J. (1988). The sociology of disability. In E. L. Meyen & T. M. Skrtic (Eds.), *Exceptional children and youth: An introduction* (pp. 449–477). Denver: Love Publishing.

Bogdan, R., & Kugelmass, J. (1984). Case studies of mainstreaming: A symbolic interactionist approach to special schooling. In L. Barton & S. Tomlinson (Eds.), *Special education and social interests* (pp.173–191). New York: Nichols Publishing.

Bourgeois, L. (1912). *Solidarité* (7th ed.). Paris: Colin. (Original work published 1896)

Bowles, S., & Gintis, H. (1976). *Schooling in capitalist America*. New York: Basic Books.

Bowles, S., & Gintis, H. (1986). *Democracy and capitalism*. New York: Basic Books.

Boyd, W. L., & Crowson, R. L. (1981). The changing conception and practice of public school administration. In D. C. Berliner (Ed.), *Review of research in education* (pp. 311–373). Itasca, IL: F. E. Peacock.

Boyer, E. L. (1983). *High school*. New York: Harper & Row.

Boyer, E. L. (1987). *College: The undergraduate experience in America*. New York: Harper & Row.

Braaten, S. R., Kauffman, J. M., Braaten, B., Polsgrove, L., & Nelson, C. M. (1988). The regular education initiative: Patent medicine for behavioral disorders. *Exceptional Children, 55*, 21–27.

Braginsky, D., & Braginsky, B. (1971). *Hansels and Gretels*. New York: Holt, Rinehart & Winston.

Braverman, H. (1974). *Labor and monopoly capital: The degradation of work in the twentieth century*. New York: Monthly Review.

Bridges, E. M. (1982). Research on the school administrator: The state of the art, 1967–1980. *Educational Administration Quarterly, 18*(3), 12–33.

Brophy, J. E. (1983). Research in the self-fulfilling prophecy and teacher expectations. *Journal of Educational Psychology, 75*(5), 631–661.

*Brown v. Board of Education*. (1954). 347 U.S. 483, 74 S. Ct. 686, 98 L. Ed. 873.

Brown, R. H. (1978). Bureaucracy as praxis: Toward a political phenomenology of formal organizations. *Administrative Science Quarterly, 23*, 365–382.

Bryan, T., Bay, M., & Donahue, M. (1988). Implications of the learning disabilities definition for the regular education initiative. *Journal of Learning Disabilities, 21*, 23–28.

Burns, T., & Stalker, G. M. (1966). *The management of innovation* (2d ed.). London: Tavistock Publications.

Burrell, G., & Morgan, G. (1979). *Sociological paradigms and organizational analysis*. London: Heinemann.

Callahan, R. (1962). *Education and the cult of efficiency*. Chicago: University of Chicago Press.

Campbell, R. (1971, August). NCPEA—*Then and now*. Paper presented at NCPEA meeting, University of Utah, Salt Lake City.

Campbell, R. F., Fleming, T., Newell, L. J., & Bennion, J. W. (1987). *A history of thought and practice in educational administration*. New York: Teachers College Press.

Campbell, R. F., & Gregg, R. T. (Eds.). (1956). *Administrative behavior in education*. New York: Harper & Brothers.

Campbell, R. F., & Newell, L. J. (1973). *A study of professors in educational administration: Problems and prospects of an applied academic field*. Columbus, OH: University Council for Educational Administration.

Carlberg, C., & Kavale, K. (1980). The efficacy of special versus regular class placement for exceptional children: A meta-analysis. *Journal of Special Education, 14*, 295–309.

Carnine, D. (1987). A response to "False Standards, a Distorting and Disintegrating Effect on Education, Turning Away from Useful Purposes, Being Inevitably Unfulfilled, and Remaining Unrealistic." *Remedial & Special Education, 8*(1), 42–43.

Carrier, J. G. (1983). Masking the social in educational knowledge: The case of learning disability theory. *American Journal of Sociology, 88*(5), 948–974.

Champion, R. H. (1984). Faculty reported use of research in teacher preparation courses: Six instructional senarios. *Journal of Teacher Education, 35*(5), 9–12.

Chandler, J. T., & Plakos, J. (1969). *Spanish-speaking pupils classified as educable mentally retarded*. Sacramento: California State University, Department of Education.

Chandler, M. D., & Sayles, L. R. (1971). *Managing large systems*. New York: Harper & Row.

Cherryholmes, C. H. (1988). *Power and criticism: Poststructuralist investigations in education*. New York: Teachers College Press.

Chomsky, N. (1959). Review of Skinner's "Verbal Behavior." *Language, 35*, 26–58.

Christophos, F., & Renz, P. (1969). A critical examination of special education programs. *Journal of Special Education, 3*(4), 371–380.

Churchman, C. W. (1971). *The design of inquiry systems*. New York: Basic Books.

Clark, B. R. (1972). The organizational saga in higher education. *Administrative Science Quarterly, 17*, 178–184.

Clark, D. L. (1985). Emerging paradigms in organizational theory and research. In Y. S. Lincoln (Ed.), *Organizational theory and inquiry: The paradigm revolution* (pp. 43–78). Beverly Hills, CA: Sage Publications.

Clark, D. L., & Astuto, T. A. (1988). *Education policy after Reagan—What next?* (Occasional paper No. 6). Charlottesville: University of Virginia, Policies Studies Center, University Council for Educational Administration.

Clark, D. L., Lotto, L. S., & Astuto, T. A. (1984). Effective schools and school improvement: A comparative analysis of two lines of inquiry. *Educational Administration Quarterly, 20*(3), 41–68.

Cohen, M. D., March, J. G., & Olsen, J. P. (1972). A garbage can model of organizational choice. *Administrative Science Quarterly, 17*, 1–25.

Coladarci, A. P., & Getzels, J. W. (1955) *The use of theory in educational administration*. Stanford, CA: Stanford University.

Coleman, J. S. (1974). *Power and the structure of society*. New York: W. W. Norton.

Collins, R. (1979). *The credential society*. New York: Academic Press.

Costa, A. L. (1989). Foreword. In L. B. Resnick & L. E. Klopfer (Eds.), *Toward the thinking curriculum: Current cognition research*. Alexandria, VA: Association for Supervision and Curriculum Development.

Council for Children with Behavioral Disorders (CCBD). (1989). Position statement on the regular education initiative. *Behavioral Disorders, 14*, 201–208.

Cremin, L. A. (1961). *The transformation of the school*. New York: Knopf.

Cremin, L. A. (1965). *The genius of American education*. New York: Vintage.

Croly, H. (1914). *Progressive democracy*. New York: Macmillan.

Croly, H. (1965). The promise of American life. In J. W. Ward (Ed.), *The American heritage series*. Indianapolis: Bobbs-Merrill. (Original work published 1909)

Cuban, L. (1979). Determinants of curriculum change and stability, 1870–1970. In J. Schaffarzick & G. Sykes (Eds.), *Value conflicts and curriculum issues*. Berkeley, CA: McCutchan Publishing.

Cuban, L. (1983). Effective schools: A friendly but cautionary note. *Phi Delta Kappan, 64*(10), 695–696.

Cuban, L. (1989). The "at-risk" label and the problem of urban school reform. *Phi Delta Kappan, 70*(10), 780–784, 799–801.

Cubberley, E. P. (1919). *Public education in the United States*. Boston: Houghton Mifflin.

Cunningham, L. L., Hack, W. G., & Nystrand, R. O. (Eds.). (1977). *Educational administration: The developing decades*. Berkeley, CA: McCutchan Publishing.

Dallmayr, F. R., & McCarthy, T. A. (1977). *Understanding and social inquiry*. Notre Dame, IN: University of Notre Dame Press.

Dalton, M. (1959). *Men who manage*. New York: Wiley.

Davis, F. (1963). *Passage through crisis*. Indianapolis: Bobbs-Merrill.

Davis, W. E. (1989). The regular initiative debate: Its promises and problems. *Exceptional Children, 55*(5), 440–446.

Davis, W. E. , & McCaul, E. J. (1988). *New perspectives on education: A review of the issues and implications of the regular education initiative*. Orono, ME: Institute for Research and Policy Analysis on the Education of Students with Learning and Adjustment Problems.

De George, R. T. (1982). *Business ethics*. New York: Macmillan.

Deno, E. (1970). Special education as developmental capital. *Exceptional Children, 37*(3), 229–237.

Derrida, J. (1982a). *Dissemination* (B. Johnson, Trans.). London: Athlone Press. (Original work published 1972)

Derrida, J. (1982b). *Margins of Philosophy* (A. Bass, Trans.). Chicago: University of Chicago Press. (Original work published 1972)

Dertouzos, M. L., Lester, R. K., & Solow, R. M. (1989). *Made in America: Regaining the productive edge*. Cambridge, MA: MIT Press.

Dewey, J. (1897). My pedagogic creed. *School Journal, 54*(3), 77–80.

Dewey, J. (1965). Progressive education and the new science of education. In M. S. Dworkin (Ed.), *Dewey on education* (pp. 113–126). New York: Teachers College Press. (Original work published 1928)

Dewey, J. (1976a). The school and society. In J. A. Boydston (Ed.), *John Dewey: The middle works, 1899–1924* (Vol. 1, pp. 1–109). Carbondale: Southern Illinois University Press. (Original work published 1899)

Dewey, J. (1976b). Studies in logical theory. In J. A. Boydston (Ed.), *John Dewey: The middle works, 1899–1924* (Vol. 2, pp. 293–375). Carbondale: Southern Illinois University Press. (Original work published 1903)

Dewey, J. (1980). Democracy and education. In J. A. Boydston (Ed.), *John Dewey: The middle works, 1899–1924* (Vol. 9, pp. 1–370). Carbondale: Southern Illinois University Press. (Original work published 1916)

Dewey, J. (1982). Reconstruction in philosophy. In J. A. Boydston (Ed.), *John Dewey: The middle works, 1899–1924* (Vol. 12, pp. 77–201). Carbondale: Southern Illinois University Press. (Original work published 1920)

Dewey, J. (1987). The intellectual criterion for truth. In J. A. Boydston (Ed.), *John Dewey: The middle works, 1899–1924* (Vol. 4, pp. 50–75). Carbondale: Southern Illinois University Press. (Original work published 1910)

Dewey, J. (1988a). From absolutism to experimentalism. In J. A. Boydston (Ed.), *John Dewey: The later works, 1925–1953* (Vol. 5, pp. 147–160). Carbondale: Southern Illinois University Press. (Original work published 1930)

Dewey, J. (1988b). Individualism, old and new. In J. A. Boydston (Ed.), *John Dewey: The later works, 1925–1953* (Vol. 5, pp. 41–123). Carbondale: Southern Illinois University Press. (Original work published 1929–1930)

Dewey, J. (1988c). The public and its problems. In J. A. Boydston (Ed.), *John Dewey: The later works, 1925–1953* (Vol. 2, pp. 235–372). Carbondale: Southern Illinois University Press. (Original work published 1927)

Dewey, J. (1988d). The quest for certainty. In J. A. Boydston (Ed.), *John Dewey: The later works, 1925–1953* (Vol. 4, pp. 1–250). Carbondale: Southern Illinois University Press. (Original work published 1929)

Dewey, J. (1989). How we think: A restatement of the relation of reflective thinking to the educative process. In J. A. Boydston (Ed.), *John Dewey: The later works, 1925–1953* (Vol. 8, pp. 105–352). Carbondale: Southern Illinois University Press. (Original work published 1910)

Dewey, J., & Tufts, J. H. (1989). Ethics. In J. A. Boydston (Ed.), *John Dewey: The Later Works, 1925–1953* (Vol. 7, pp. 1–462). Carbondale: Southern Illinois University Press. (Original work published 1932)

Dornbusch, S. M., & Scott, W. R. (1975). *Evaluation and the exercise of authority: A theory of control applied to diverse organizations.* San Francisco: Jossey-Bass.

Dreyfus, H. L., & Rabinow, P. (1983). *Michel Foucault: Beyond structuralism and hermenuetics* (2nd ed.). Chicago: University of Chicago Press.

Drucker, P. F. (1989). *The new realities.* New York: Harper & Row.

Dunn, L. M. (1968). Special education for the mildly retarded—Is much of it justifiable? *Exceptional Children, 35*(1), 5–22.

Dworkin, M. S. (Ed.). (1959). *Dewey on education: A centennial review.* New York: Teachers College Press.

Edel, A., & Flower, E. (1989). Introduction. In J. A. Boydston (Ed.), *John Dewey: The Later Works, 1925–1953* (Vol. 7, pp. vii–xxxv). Carbondale: Southern Illinois University Press.

Edgar, E. (1987). Secondary programs in special education: Are many of them justified? *Exceptional Children, 53*, 555–561.

Edmonds, R. (1979). Some schools work and more can. *Social Policy, 9*(5), 26–31.

Edwards, R. C. (1979). *Contested terrain: The transformation of the workplace in the twentieth century.* New York: Basic Books.

Elliott, J. (1975). *Objectivity, ideology, and teacher participation in educational research.* Norwich, England: Centre for Applied Research in Education, University of East Anglia.

Elmore, R. F. (1987). *Early experiences in restructuring schools: Voices from the field.* Washington, DC: National Governors Association.

Elmore, R. F., & McLaughlin, M. W. (1982). Strategic choice in federal education policy: The compliance-assistance trade-off. In A. Lieberman & M. W. McLaughlin (Eds.), *Policy making in education* (81st yearbook of the National Society for the Study of Education) (pp. 159–194). Chicago: University of Chicago Press.

Elmore, R. F., & McLaughlin, M. W. (1988). *Steady work: Policy, practice, and the reform of American education.* Santa Monica, CA: Rand Corp.

Erickson, D. A. (1977). An overdue paradigm shift in educational administration, or, how can we get that idiot off the freeway? In L. L. Cunningham, W. G. Hack, & R. O. Nystrand (Eds.), *Educational administration: The developing decades* (pp. 129–143). Berkeley, CA: McCutchan Publishing.

Erickson, D. A. (1979). Research on educational administration: The state-of-the-art. *Educational Researcher, 8*(3), 9–14.

Etzioni, A. (1961). *A comparative analysis of complex organizations.* New York: Free Press.

Everhart, R. B. (1990). Descriptive behavior in organizational context. In P. Leone (Ed.), *Understanding troubled and troubling youth: Multidisciplinary perspectives* (pp. 272–289). Beverly Hills, CA: Sage Publications.

Farber, B. (1968). *Mental retardation: Its social context and social consequences.* Boston: Houghton Mifflin.

Fayol, H. (1949). *General and industrial management.* Marshfield, MA; Pitman Publishing. (Original work published 1916)

Feigl, H. (1970). The "orthodox" view of theories: Remarks in defense as well as critique. In M. Radner & S. Winokur (Eds.), *Minnesota studies in the philosophy of science* (Vol. 4). Minneapolis: University of Minnesota Press.

Feinberg, W., & Soltis, J. F. (1985). *School and society.* New York: Teachers College Press.

Ferguson, P. M. (1987). The social construction of mental retardation. *Social Policy, 18*(1), 51–56.

Feyerabend, P. (1975). *Against method.* London: Verso.

Firestone, W. A. (1989). *Accommodation: Toward a paradigm-praxis dialectic.* Paper presented at Alternative Paradigms for Inquiry Conference, Phi Delta Kappa, San Francisco.

Follett, M. P. (1924). *Creative experience.* London: Longmans & Green.

Follett, M. P. (1940). In H. C. Metcalf & L. Urwick (Eds.), *Dynamic administration: The collected papers of Mary Parker Follett.* New York: Harper.

Ford, P. L. (Ed.). (1904). *Thomas Jefferson, works.* New York: Knickerbocker Press.

Forness, S. R., & Kavale, K. A. (1987). Holistic inquiry and the scientific challenge in special education: A reply to Iano. *Remedial & Special Education, 8*(1), 47–51.

Foster, W. (1986). *Paradigms and promises: New approaches to educational administration.* Buffalo, NY: Prometheus Books.

Foucault, M. (1972). *The archaeology of knowledge* (A. M. Sheridan Smith, Trans.). New York: Harper Colophon. (Original work published 1969)

Foucault, M. (1973a). *Madness and civilization: A history of insanity in the age of reason* (R. Howard, Trans.). New York: Vintage/Random House. (Original work published 1961)

Foucault, M. (1973b). *The order of things: An archaeology of the human sciences.* New York: Vintage/Random House. (Original work published 1966)

Foucault, M. (1975). *The birth of the clinic: An archeology of medical perception* (A. M. Sheridan Smith, Trans.). New York: Vintage/Random House. (Original work published 1963)

Foucault, F. (1976). *Mental illness and psychology.* Berkeley, CA: University of California Press. (Original work published 1954)

Foucault, M. (1979). *Discipline and punish: The birth of the prison* (A. M. Sheridan Smith, Trans.). New York: Vintage/Random House. (Original work published 1975)

Foucault, M. (1980a). *Power/knowledge: Selected interviews and other writings, 1972–1977* (C. Gordon, Ed.; C. Gordon, L. Marshall, J. Mepham, & K. Soper, Trans.). New York: Pantheon Books.

Foucault, M. (1980b). Two lectures. In M. Foucault, *Power/Knowlege: Selected interviews and other writings, 1972–1977* (C. Gordon, Ed.; C. Gordon, L. Marshall, J. Mepham, & K. Soper, Trans.) (pp. 78–108). New York: Pantheon Books.

Foucault, M. (1983). The subject and power. In H. L. Dreyfus & P. Rabinow (Eds.), *Michel Foucault: Beyond structuralism and hermeneutics* (pp. 208–226). Chicago: University of Chicago Press.

Foucault M. (1990). Nietzsche, Freud, Marx. In G. L. Ormiston & A. D. Schrift (Eds.), *Transforming the hermeneutic context: From Nietzsche to Nancy* (pp. 59–67). Albany: State University of New York. (Original work published 1964)

Freidson, E. (1988). *Professional powers: A study of the institutionalization of formal knowledge.* Chicago: University of Chicago Press.

Freire, P. (1970). *Pedagogy of the oppressed.* New York: Continuum. (Reprinted 1982).

Freire, P. (1973). *Education for critical consciousness.* New York: Continuum.

Freire, P. (1978). *Pedgogy in process: The letters to Guinea-Bissau.* New York: Continuum.

Gadamer, H. G. (1975). *Truth and method* (G. Barden & J. Cumming, Eds. & Trans.). New York: Seabury Press.

Galbraith, J. K. (1967). *The new industrial state.* Boston: Houghton Mifflin.

Gans, H. (1972). The positive functions of poverty. *American Journal of Sociology, 78,* 275–289.

Gartner, A. (1986). Disabling help: Special education at the crossroads. *Exceptional Children, 53*(1), 72–79.

Gartner, A., & Lipsky, D. K. (1987). Beyond special education: Toward a quality system for all students. *Harvard Educational Review, 57*(4), 367–390.

Gartner, A., & Lipsky, D. K. (1989). *The yoke of special education: How to break it.* Rochester, NY: National Center on Education & the Economy.

Geertz, C. (1983). *Local knowledge: Further essays in interpretive anthropology.* New York: Basic Books.

Gehrke, N. J., & Kay, R. S. (1984). The socialization of beginning teachers through mentor-protege relationships. *Journal of Teacher Education, 35,* 21–24.

Gerardi, R. J., Grohe, B., Benedict, G. C., & Coolidge, P. G. (1984). I.E.P.—More paperwork and wasted time. *Contemporary Education, 56*(1), 39–42.

Gerber, M. M. (1987). Application of cognitive-behavioral training methods to teach basic skills to mildly handicapped elementary school students. In M.C. Wang, M. C. Reynolds, & H. J. Walberg (Eds.), *Handbook of special education: Research and practice: Vol 1. Learner characteristics and adaptive education* (pp. 167–186). Oxford, England: Pergamon.

Gerber, M. M. (1988a). Tolerance and technology of instruction: Implications for special education reform. *Exceptional Children, 54,* 309–314.

Gerber, M. M. (1988b, May 4). Weighing the regular education initiative: Recent calls for change lead to "slippery slope." *Education Week, 7*(32), 28, 36.

Gerber, M. M., & Levine-Donnerstein D. (1989). Educating all children: Ten years later. *Exceptional Children, 56*(1), 17–27.

Gerber, M. M., & Semmel, M. I. (1984). Teacher as imperfect test: Reconceptualizing the referral process. *Educational Psychologist, 19,* 137–148.

Gerber, M. M., & Semmel, M. I. (1985). The microeconomics of referral and reintegration: A paradigm for evaluation of special education. *Studies in Educational Evaluation, 11,* 13–29.

Getzels, J. W., & Guba, E. G. (1957). Social behavior and the administrative process. *School Review, 65,* 423–441.

Getzels, J. W., & Jackson, P. W. (1960). Research on the variable "teacher": Some comments. *School Review, 68,* 450–462.

Geuss, R. (1981). *The idea of critical theory: Habermas and the Frankfort School.* Cambridge, England: Cambridge University Press.

Gilb, C. L. (1966). *Hidden hierarchies: The professions and government.* New York: Harper & Row.

Gilhool, T. K. (1976). Changing public policies: Roots and forces. In M. C. Reynolds (Ed.), *Mainstreaming: Origins and implications* (pp. 8–13). Reston, VA: Council for Exceptional Children.

Gilhool, T. K. (1989). The right to an effective education: From *Brown* to P.L. 94–142 and beyond. In D. K. Lipsky & A. Gartner (Eds.), *Beyond separate education: Quality education for all* (pp. 243–253). Baltimore: Paul H. Brookes.

Giroux, H. A. (1981). *Ideology, culture, and the process of schooling.* Philadelphia: Temple University Press.

Giroux, H. A. (1983a). Theories of reproduction and resistance in the New Sociology of Education: A critical analysis. *Harvard Educational Review, 58*(3), 257, 293.

Giroux, H. A. (1983b). *Theory and resistance in education.* Boston: Bergin & Garvey Publishers.

Giroux, H. A. (1988). *Schooling and the struggle for public life: Critical pedagogy in the modern age.* Minneapolis: University of Minnesota Press.

Glazer, N. (1974). The schools of the minor professions. *Minerva, 12*(3), 346–364.

Goffman, E. (1961). *Asylums: Essays on the social situation of mental patients and other inmates.* Garden City, NY: Doubleday/Anchor Books.

Golding, D. (1980). Establishing blissful clarity in organizational life: Managers. *Sociological Review, 28,* 763–782.

Goodlad, J. I. (1975). *The dynamics of educational change.* New York: McGraw-Hill.

Goodlad, J. I. (1984). *A place called school: Prospects for the future.* New York: McGraw-Hill.

Goodman, P. (1968). *People or personnel & Like a conquered providence.* New York: Vintage.

Gould, S. J. (1981). *The mismeasure of man.* New York: W. W. Norton.

Greene, M. (1978). *Landscapes of learning.* New York: Teachers College Press.

Greenwood, E. (1981). Attributes of a profession. In N. Gilbert & H. Specht (Eds.), *The emergence of social work and social welfare* (pp. 241–255). Itasca, IL: F. E. Peacock.

Greer, C. (1972). *The great school legend: A revisionist interpretation of American public education.* New York: Basic Books.

Griffiths, D. E. (1959). *Administrative theory.* New York: Appleton-Century-Crofts.

Griffiths, D. E. (Ed.). (1964). *Behavioral science and educational administration* (63rd yearbook of the National Society for the Study of Education) (Part 2). Chicago: University of Chicago Press.

Griffiths, D. E. (1979). Intellectual turmoil in educational administration. *Educational Administration Quarterly, 15*(3), 43–65.

Griffiths, D. E. (1983). Evolution in research and theory: A study of prominent researchers. *Educational Administration Quarterly, 19*(3), 201–221.

Griffiths, D. E. (1988). Administrative theory. In N. J. Boyan (Ed.), *Handbook of research on educational administration* (pp. 27–51). New York: Longman.

Guba, E. G., & Lincoln Y. S. (1987). The countenances of fourth generation evaluation: Description, judgement, and negotiation. In D. J. Palumbo (Ed.), *The politics of program evaluation* (pp. 202–234). Beverly Hills, CA: Sage Publications.

Gulick, L., & Urwick, L. (Eds.). (1937). *Papers on the science of administration.* New York: Columbia University, Institute of Public Administration.

Haber, S. (1964). *Efficiency and uplift: Scientific management in the Progressive Era, 1890–1920.* Chicago: University of Chicago Press.

Haberman, M. (1983). Research on preservice laboratory and clinical experiences: Implications for teacher education. In K. R. Howey & W. Gardner (Eds.), *The education of teachers: A look ahead* (pp. 98–117). New York: Longman.

Habermas, J. (1970a). On systematically distorted communication. *Inquiry, 13,* 205–218.

Habermas, J. (1970b). *Toward a rational society* (J. J. Shapiro, Trans.). Boston: Beacon Press. (Original work published 1968)

Habermas, J. (1970c). Towards a theory of communicative competence. *Inquiry, 13,* 360–375.

Habermas, J. (1971). *Knowledge and human interests* (J. J. Shapiro, Trans.). Boston: Beacon Press. (Original work published 1968)

Habermas, J. (1973). *Theory and practice* (J. Viertel, Trans.). Boston: Beacon Press. (Original work published 1963)

Habermas, J. (1975). *Legitimation crisis* (T. McCarthy, Trans.). Boston: Beacon Press. (Original work published 1973)

Habermas, J. (1979). *Communication and the evolution of society* (T. McCarthy, Trans.). Boston: Beacon Press. (Original work published 1976)

Hallahan, D. P., & Kauffman, J. M. (1977). Categories, labels, behavioral characteristics: ED, LD, and EMR reconsidered. *Journal of Special Education, 11,* 139–149.

Hallahan, D. P., Kauffman, J. M., Lloyd, J. W., & McKinney, J. D. (1988). Introduction to the series: Questions about the regular education initiative. *Journal of Learning Disabilities, 21*(1), 3–5.

Hallahan, D. P., & Keller, C. E. (1986). *Study of studies for learning disabilities: A research review and synthesis.* Charleston: West Virginia Department of Education.

Hallahan, D. P., Keller, C. E., McKinney, J. D., Lloyd, J. W., & Bryan, T. (1988). Examining the research base of the regular education initiative: Efficacy studies and the adaptive learning environments model. *Journal of Learning Disabilities, 21*(1), 29–35, 55.

Halpin, A. W. (Ed.). (1958). *Administrative theory in education.* Chicago: University of Chicago, Midwest Administration Center.

Halpin, A. W. (1970). Administrative theory: The fumbled torch. In A. M. Kroll (Ed.), *Issues in American education.* New York: Oxford University Press.

Halpin, A. W., & Hayes, A. E. (1977). The broken ikon, or What ever happened to theory? In L. L. Cunningham, W. G. Hack, & R. O. Nystrand (Eds.), *Educational administration: The developing decades* (pp. 261–297). Berkeley, CA: McCutchan Publishing.

Haring, N. G. (1978). *Behavior of exceptional children: An introduction to special education.* Columbus, OH: Charles E. Merrill.

Harre, R. (1981). The positivist-empiricist approach and its alternative. In P. Reason & J. Rowan (Eds.), *Human inquiry: A sourcebook of new paradigm research.* New York: John Wiley.

Haskell, T. L. (1984). *The authority of experts: Studies in history and theory.* Bloomington: Indiana University Press.

Hayes, D., & Pharis, W. (1967). *National conference of professors of educational administration.* Lincoln: University of Nebraska.

Hegel, G. W. F. (1977). *Phenomenology of spirit.* Oxford, England: Clarendon Press. (Original work published 1807)

Held, D. (1980). *Introduction to critical theory.* Berkeley & Los Angeles: University of California Press.

Heller, K., Holtzman, W., & Messick, S. (1982). *Placing children in special education: A strategy for equity.* Washington, DC: National Academy of Sciences Press.

Heller, W. H., & Schilit, J. (1987). The regular education initiative: A concerned response. *Focus on Exceptional Children, 20*(3), 1–6.

Heshusius, L. (1982). At the heart of the advocacy dilemma: A mechanistic world view. *Exceptional Children, 49*(1), 6–13.

Heshusius, L. (1986). Paradigm shifts and special education: A response to Ulman and Rosenberg. *Exceptional Children, 52*(5), 461–465.

Hesse, M. (1980). *Revolutions and reconstructions in the philosophy of science.* Bloomington: Indiana University Press.

Hobbs, N. (1975). *The futures of children: Categories, labels, and their consequences.* San Francisco: Jossey–Bass.

Hobbs, N. (1980). An ecologically oriented service-based system for the classification of handicapped children. In E. Salzinger, J. Antrobus, & J. Glick (Eds.), *The ecosystem of the "risk" child* (pp. 271–290). New York: Academic Press.

Horkheimer, Max. (1974). *Eclipse of reason.* New York: Seabury. (Original work published 1947)

House, E. R. (1974). *The politics of educational innovation.* Berkeley, CA: McCutchan Publishing.

House, E. R. (1979). Technology versus craft: A ten year perspective on innovation. *Journal of Curriculum Studies, 11*(1), 1–15.

Howe, K. R. (1988). Against the quantitative-qualitative incompatibility thesis, or Dogmas die hard. *Educational Researcher, 17*(8), 10–16.

Hoy, D. (1985). Jacques Derrida. In Q. Skinner (Ed.), *The return of grand theory in the human sciences* (pp. 83–100). Cambridge, England: Cambridge University Press.

Hughes, E. C. (1963). Professions. *Daedalus, 92*, 655–668.

Huff, T. E. (1984). *Max Weber and the methodology of the social sciences.* New Brunswick, NJ: Transaction Books.

Iano, R. P. (1986). The study and development of teaching: With implications for the advancement of special education. *Remedial & Special Education, 7*(5), 50–61.

Iano, R. P. (1987). Rebuttal: Neither the absolute certainty of prescriptive law nor a surrender to mysticism. *Remedial & Special Education, 18*(1), 51–56.

Illich, I. (1976). *Medical nemesis.* New York: Random House.

Immegart, G. L. (1977). The study of educational administration, 1954–1974. In L. L. Cunningham, W. G. Hack, & R. O. Nystrand (Eds.), *Educational administration: The developing decades.* Berkeley, CA: McCutchan Publishing.

James, W. (1978a). The function of cognition. In F. Burkhardt, F. Bowers, & I. K. Skrupskelis (Eds.), The Meaning of Truth: *A sequel to* Pragmatism (pp.13–32). Cambridge, MA: Harvard University Press. (Original work published 1909)

James, W. (1978b). Pragmatism. In F. Burkhardt, F. Bowers, & I. K. Skrupskelis (Eds.), *William James:* Pragmatism *and* The Meaning of Truth (pp. 1–166). Cambridge, MA: Harvard University Press. (Original works published 1907 & 1909)

Janesick, V. J. (1988). Our multicultural society. In E. L. Meyen & T. M. Skrtic (Eds.), *Exceptional children and youth: An introduction.* Denver: Love Publishing.

Jay, M. (1973). *The dialectical imagination.* Boston: Little, Brown.

Johnson, G. O. (1962, October). Special education for the mentally handicapped—A paradox. *Exceptional Children, 29*(2), 62–69.

Jones, R. A. (1977). *Self-fulfilling prophecies.* Hillsdale, NJ: Erlbaum.

Jonsson, S. A., & Lundin, R. A. (1977). Myths and wishful thinking as management tools. In P. C. Nystrom & W. H. Starbuck (Eds.), *Prescriptive models of organizations* (pp. 157–170). New York: Elsevier North-Holland.

Kauffman, J. M. (1988). Revolution can also mean returning to the starting point: Will school psychology help special education complete the circuit? *School Psychology Review, 17*, 490–494.

Kauffman, J. M. (1989a). *The regular education initiative as Reagan-Bush education policy: A trickle-down theory of education of the hard-to-teach.* Austin, TX: Pro-Ed.

Kauffman, J. M. (1989b). The regular education initiative as Reagan-Bush education policy: A trickle-down theory of education of the hard-to-teach. *Journal of Special Education, 23*(3), 256–278.

Kauffman, J. M., Gerber, M. M., & Semmel, M. I. (1988). Arguable assumptions underlying the regular education initiative. *Journal of Learning Disabilities, 21*(1), 6–11.

Kavale, K. A., & Forness, S. R. (1987). History, politics, and the general education initiative: Sleeter's reinterpretation of learning disabilities as a case study. *Remedial & Special Education, 8*(5), 6–12.

Kearns, D. T. & Doyle, D. P. (1988). *Winning the brain race: A bold plan to make our schools competitive.* San Francisco: Institute for Contemporary Studies.

Keogh, B. K. (1988). Improving services for problem learners: Rethinking and restructuring. *Journal of Learning Disabilities, 21*(1), 19–22.

Keogh, B. K., & Levitt, M. L. (1976). Special education in the mainstream: A confrontation of limitations? *Focus on Exceptional Children, 8*, 1–11.

Kiel, D. C. (in press). The humanist view of special education and disability: Consciousness, freedom and ideology. In T. M. Skrtic (Ed.), *Exploring the theory/practice link in special education: A critical perspective.* Reston, VA: Council for Exceptional Children.

Kiel, D. C., & Skrtic, T. M. (1988). *Modes of organizational accountability: An ideal type analysis.* Unpublished manuscript, University of Kansas, Lawrence.

Kirk, S. A., & Chalfant, J. D. (1983). *Academic and developmental learning disabilities.* Denver: Love Publishing.

Kliebard, H. M. (1988). The effort to reconstruct the modern American curriculum. In L. E. Beyer & M. W. Apple, (Eds.), *The curriculum: Problems, politics, and possibilities* (pp. 19–31). New York: State University of New York Press.

Kloppenberg, J. T. (1986). *Uncertain victory: Social democracy and progressivism in European and American thought, 1870–1920.* New York: Oxford University Press.

Knorr, K. D., Krohn, R., & Whitley, R. (Eds.). (1981). *The social process of scientific investigation.* Boston: D. Reidel Publishing.

Koehler, V. (1985). Research on preservice teacher education. *Journal of Teacher Education, 36*(1), 23–30.

Kohlberg, L., & Mayer, R. (1972). Development as the aim of education. *Harvard Educational Review, 42*(4), 449–496.

Kojeve, A. (1969). *Introduction to the reading of Hegel* (p. 232). New York: Basic Books.

Kozol, J. (1985). *Illiterate America.* New York: New American Library.

Kuhn, T. S. (1962). *The structure of scientific revolutions.* Chicago: University of Chicago Press.

Kuhn, T. S. (1970). *The structure of scientific revolutions* (2d ed.). Chicago: University of Chicago Press.

Kuhn, T. S. (1977). *The essential tension: Selected studies in scientific tradition and change.* Chicago: University of Chicago Press.

Law, J. (1975). Is epistemology redundant? *Philosophy of the Social Sciences, 5,* 317–337.

Lazerson, M. (1983). The origins of special education. In J. G. Chambers & W. T. Hartman (Eds.), *Special education policies: Their history, implementation, and finance.* Philadelphia: Temple University Press.

Lehming, R., & Kane, M. (1981). *Improving schools: Using what we know.* Beverly Hills, CA: Sage Publications.

Lemert, E. (1967). *Human deviance, social problems, and social control.* Englewood Cliffs, NJ: Prentice-Hall.

Lévi-Strauss, C. (1963). *Totemism.* Boston: Beacon Press.

Lezotte, L. W. (1989). School improvement based on the effective schools research. In D. K. Lipsky & A. Gartner (Eds.), *Beyond separate education: Quality education for all* (pp. 25–37). Baltimore: Paul H. Brookes.

Lieberman, A., & Miller, L. (1984). *Teachers, their world and their work: Implications for school improvement.* Alexandria, VA: Association for Supervision & Curriculum Development.

Lieberman, L. M. (1984). *Preventing special education . . . for those who don't need it.* Newton, MA: GloWorm Publications.

Lieberman, L. M. (1985). Special education and regular education: A merger made in heaven? *Exceptional Children, 51*(6), 513–516.

Lieberman, L. M. (1988). *Preserving special education . . . for those who need it.* Newtonville, MA: GloWorm Publications.

Lilly, M. S. (1986, March). The relationship between general and special education: A new face on an old issue. *Counterpoint,* p. 10.

Lilly, M. S. (1987). Lack of focus on special education in literature on education reform. *Exceptional Children, 53*(4), 325–326.

Lilly, M. S. (1989). Teacher preparation. In D. K. Lipsky & A. Gartner (Eds.), *Beyond separate education: Quality education for all* (pp. 143–157). Baltimore: Paul H. Brookes.

Lilly, M. S. (in press). Divestiture in special education: An alternative model for resource and support services. *Educational Forum.*

Lincoln, Y. S. (1985). *Organizational theory and inquiry: The paradigm revolution.* Beverly Hills, CA: Sage Publications.

Lincoln, Y. S., & Guba, E. G. (1985). *Naturalistic inquiry.* Beverly Hills, CA: Sage Publications.

Lipsky, D. K. (1989). The roles of parents. In D. K. Lipsky & A. Gartner (Eds.), *Beyond separate education: Quality education for all* (pp. 159–179). Baltimore: Paul H. Brookes.

Lipsky, D. K., & Gartner, A. (1987). Capable of achievement and worthy of respect: Education for handicapped students as if they were full- fledged human beings. *Exceptional Children, 54*(1), 69–74.

Lipsky, D. K., & Gartner, A. (Eds.). (1989a). *Beyond separate education: Quality education for all.* Baltimore: Paul H. Brookes.

Lipsky, D. K., & Gartner, A. (1989b). School administration and financial arrangements. In S. Stainback, W. Stainback, & M. Forest (Eds.), *Educating all students in the mainstream of regular education* (pp. 105–120). Baltimore: Paul H. Brookes.

Lloyd, J. W. (1987). The art and science of research on teaching. *Remedial & Special Education, 8*(1), 44–46.

Lloyd, J. W., Crowley, E. P., Kohler, F. W., & Strain, P. S. (1988). Redefining the applied research agenda: Cooperative learning, prereferral, teacher consultation, and peer-mediated interventions. *Journal of Learning Disabilities, 21*, 43–52.

Lortie, D. C. (1975). *Schoolteacher: A sociological study.* Chicago: University of Chicago Press.

Lortie, D. C. (1978). Some reflections on renegotiation. In M. C. Reynolds (Ed.), *Futures of education for exceptional students: Emerging structures* (pp. 235–243). Reston, VA: Council for Exceptional Children.

Lyotard, J. F. (1984). *The postmodern condition: A report on knowledge.* Minneapolis: University of Minnesota Press. (Original work published 1979)

MacMillan, D. L. (1971). Special education for the mildly retarded: Servant or savant? *Focus on Exceptional Children, 2*(9), 1–11.

MacMillan, D. L., & Semmel, M. I. (1977). Evaluation of mainstreaming programs. *Focus on Exceptional Children, 9*(4), 1–14.

March, J. G., & Olsen, J. P. (1976). *Ambiguity and choice in organizations.* Bergen, Norway: Universitetsforlaget.

Marcuse, H. (1964). *One-dimensional man.* Boston: Beacon Press.

Marini, F. (1971). *Towards a new public administration.* Scranton, PA: Chandler.

Martin, E. (1978). Preface. In M. C. Reynolds (Ed.), *Futures of education for exceptional students* (pp. iii–vi). Reston, VA: Council for Exceptional Children.

Masterman, M. (1970). The nature of a paradigm. In I. Lakatos & A. Musgrave (Eds.), *Criticism and the growth of knowledge* (pp. 59–89). Cambridge, England: Cambridge University Press.

Mayo, E. (1933). *The human problems of an industrial civilization.* New York: Macmillan.

McDonnell, L. M., & McLaughlin, M. W. (1982). *Education policy and the role of the states* . Santa Monica, CA: Rand Corp.

McKinney, J. D., & Hocutt, A. M. (1988). The need for policy analysis in evaluating the regular education initiative. *Journal of Learning Disabilities, 4*(1).

McNeil, L. M. (1986). *Contradictions of control: School structure and school knowledge.* New York: Methuen/Routledge & Kegan Paul.

Meier, D. (1984). "Getting tough" in the schools. *Dissent, 31*(1), 61–70.

Mercer, J. (1973). *Labeling the mentally retarded: Clinical and social system perspectives on mental retardation.* Berkeley: University of California Press.

Mesinger, J. F. (1985). Commentary on "A Rationale for the Merger of Special and Regular Education." *Exceptional Children, 51*(6), 510–512.

Meyer, J. W., & Rowan, B. (1977). Institutionalized organizations: Formal structure as myth and ceremony. *American Journal of Sociology, 83,* 340–363.

Meyer, J. W., & Rowan, B. (1978). The structure of educational organizations. In M. W. Meyer (Ed.), *Environments and organizations* (pp. 78–109). San Francisco: Jossey-Bass.

Meyer, J. W., & Scott, W. R. (1983). *Organizational environments: Ritual and rationality.* Beverly Hills, CA: Sage Publications.

Meyer, M. W. (1979). Organizational structure as signaling. *Pacific Sociological Review, 22*(4), 481–500.

Miles, M. B. (1964). *Innovation in education.* New York: Columbia University, Teachers College.

Miller, D., & Mintzberg, H. (1983). The case for configuration. In G. Morgan (Ed.), *Beyond method: Strategies for social research* (pp. 57–73). Beverly Hills, CA: Sage Publications.

Minstrell, J. A. (1989). Teaching science for understanding. In L. Resnick & L. Klopfer (Eds.), *Toward the thinking curriculum: Current cognitive research.* Alexandria, VA: Association for Supervision & Curriculum Development.

Mintzberg, H. (1979). *The structuring of organizations.* Englewood Cliffs, NJ: Prentice-Hall.

Mitroff, I. I., & Pondy, L. R. (1974). On the organization of inquiry: A comparison of some radically different approaches to policy analysis. *Public Administration Review, 34*(5), 471–479.

Mommsen, W. J. (1974). *The age of bureaucracy: Perspectives on the political sociology of Max Weber.* New York: Harper & Row.

Moran, M. (1984). Excellence at the cost of instructional equity? The potential impact of recommended reforms upon low achieving students. *Focus on Exceptional Children, 16,* 1–11.

Morgan, G. (1983). *Beyond method.* Beverly Hills, CA: Sage Publications.

Morgan, G., & Smircich, L. (1980). The case for qualitative research. *Academy of Management Review, 5,* 491–500.

Mort, P. R., & Cornell, F. G. (1941). *American schools in transition: How our schools adapt their practices to changing needs.* New York: Columbia University, Teachers College.

Mulkay, M. J. (1979). *Science and the sociology of knowledge.* London: Allen & Unwin.

Murphy, J. T. (1989). The paradox of decentralizing schools: Lessons from business, government, and the Catholic Church. *Phi Delta Kappan, 70*(10), 808–812.

Naisbitt, J., & Aburdene, P. (1985). *Re-inventing the corporation.* New York: Warner Books.

National Commission on Excellence in Education. (1983). *A nation at risk: The imperative for educational reform.* Washington, DC: U. S. Government Printing Office.

National Policy Board. (1989). *Improving the preparation of school administrators: An agenda for reform.* Charlottesville, VA: National Policy Board for Educational Administration.

Noel, M. M., & Fuller, B. C. (1985). The social policy construction of special education: The impact of state characteristics on identification and integration of handicapped children. *Remedial & Special Education, 6*(3), 27–35.

Oakes, J. (1985). *Keeping track: How schools structure inequality.* New Haven, CT: Yale University Press.

Oakes, J. (1986a). Keeping track: Part 1. The policy and practice of curriculum inequality. *Phi Delta Kappan. 68*(1), 12–17.

Oakes, J. (1986b). Keeping track: Part 2. Curriculum inequality and school reform. *Phi Delta Kappan, 68*(2), 148–154.

Parsons, T. (1939, May). The professions and social structure. *Social Forces. 17*, 457–467.

Parsons, T. (1960). *Structure and process in modern societies.* Glencoe, IL: Free Press.

Patrick, J., & Reschly, D. (1982). Relationship of state educational criteria and demographic variables to school-system prevalence of mental retardation. *American Journal of Mental Retardation, 86*, 351–360.

Patton, M. Q. (1975). *Alternative evaluation research paradigm.* Grand Forks: University of North Dakota Press.

Peirce, C. S. (1931–35). In C. Hartshorne & P. Weiss (Eds.), *Collected papers of Charles Sanders Peirce.* Cambridge, MA: Harvard University Press.

Perrow, C. (1970). *Organizational analysis: A sociological review.* Belmont, CA: Wadsworth.

Perrow, C. (1972). *Complex organizations: A critical essay.* New York: Scott, Foresman.

Pettigrew, A. (1979). On studying organizational cultures. *Administrative Science Quarterly, 24*(4), 570–581.

Pfeffer, J. (1982). *Organizations and organization theory.* Marshfield, MA: Pitman Publishing.

Phillips. D. (1973). Paradigms, falsifications and sociology. *Acta Sociologica,* 16, 13–31.

Philp, M. (1985). Michel Foucault. In Q. Skinner (Ed.), *The return of grand theory in the human sciences* (pp. 65–81). Cambridge, MA: Cambridge University Press.

Phillips, D. C. (1987). *Philosophy, science, and social inquiry: Contemporary methodological controversies in social science and related applied fields of research.* Oxford, England: Pergamon Press.

Piaget, J. (1974). *To understand is to invent: The future of education.* New York: Viking. (Original work published 1948)

Popkewitz, T. S. (1980). Paradigms in educational science: Different meanings and purpose to theory. *Journal of Education, 162*, 28–46.

Poplin, M. S. (1984). Toward an holistic view of persons with learning disabilities. *Learning Disabilities Quarterly, 7*(4), 290–294.

Poplin, M. S. (1987). Self-imposed blindness: The scientific method in education. *Remedial & Special Education, 8*(6), 31–37.

Popper, K. R. (1970). Normal science and its dangers. In I. Lakatos & A. Musgrave (Eds.), *Criticism and the growth of knowledge* (pp. 51–58). Cambridge, England: Cambridge University Press.

Pugach, M. (1987). The national education reports and special education: Implications for teacher preparation. *Exceptional Children, 53*, 308–314.

Pugach, M. (1988). Special education as a constraint on teacher educational reform. *Journal of Teacher Education, 39*(3), 52–59.

Pugach, M., & Lilly, M. S. (1984). Reconceptualizing support services for classroom teachers: Implications for teacher education. *Journal of Teacher Education, 35*(5), 48–55.

Pugach, M., & Sapon-Shevin, M. (1987). New agendas for special education policy: What the regular education reports haven't said. *Exceptional Children, 53,* 295–299.

Pugh, D. S., Hickson, D. J., Hinnings, C. R., MacDonald, K. M., Turner, C., & Lupton, T. (1963). A conceptual scheme for organizational analysis. *Administrative Science Quarterly, 8*(4), 289–315.

Ravetz, J. R. (1971). *Scientific knowledge and its social problems.* Oxford, England: Clarendon Press.

Rawls, J. (1971). *A theory of justice.* Cambridge, MA: Belknap Press.

Reich, R. B. (1983). *The next American frontier.* New York: Penguin Books.

Reich, R. B. (1990). Education and the next economy. In S. B. Bacharach (Ed.), *Education reform: Making sense of it all* (pp. 194–212). Boston: Allyn & Bacon.

Resnick, L. B., & Klopfer, L. E. (1989). *Toward the thinking curriculum: Current cognitive research.* Alexandria, VA: Association for Supervision and Curriculum Development.

Resnick, D., & Resnick, L. (1985). Standards, curriculum, and performance: Historical and comparative perspectives. *Educational Researcher, 14*(4), 5–20.

Reynolds, M. C. (1962). A framework for considering some issues in special education. *Exceptional Children, 28,* 367–370.

Reynolds, M. C. (1976). *New perspectives on the instructional cascade.* Paper presented at conference, "The Least Restrictive Alternatives: A Partnership of General and Special Education," sponsored by Minneapolis Public Schools, Special Education Division, November 22–23.

Reynolds, M. C. (1988). A reaction to the JLD special series on the regular education initiative. *Journal of Learning Disabilities, 21*(6), 352–356.

Reynolds, M. C., & Birch, J. W. (1977). *Teaching exceptional children in all America's schools.* Reston, VA: Council for Exceptional Children.

Reynolds, M. C., & Lakin, K. C. (1987). Noncategorical special education: Models for research and practice. In M. C. Wang, M. C. Reynolds, & H. J. Walberg (Eds.), *Handbook of special education: Research and practice: Vol. 1. Learner characteristics and adaptive education)* (pp. 331–356). Oxford, England: Pergamon.

Reynolds, M. C., & Rosen, S. W. (1976). Special education: Past, present, and future. *Education Forum, 40*(4), 551–562.

Reynolds, M. C., & Wang, M. C. (1981, September). *Restructuring "special" school programs.* Paper presented at National Invitational Conference on Public Policy and the Special Education Task of the 1980s, Racine, WI.

Reynolds, M. C., & Wang, M. C. (1983). Restructuring "special" school programs: A position paper. *Policy Studies Review, 2*(1), 189–212.

Reynolds, M. C., Wang, M. C., & Walberg, H. J. (1987). The necessary restructuring of special and general education. *Exceptional Children, 53,* 391–398.

Rhodes, W. C. (1970). A community participation analysis of emotional disturbance. *Exceptional Children, 36*, 306–314.

Ricoeur, P. (1981). *Paul Ricoeur: Hermeneutics and the human sciences* (J. B. Thompson, Ed. and Trans.). Cambridge, England: Cambridge University Press.

Rist, R. (1973). *The urban school: A factory for failure.* Cambridge, MA: MIT Press.

Rist, R., & Harrell, J. (1982). Labeling and the learning disabled child: The social ecology of educational practice. *American Journal of Orthopsychiatry, 52* (1), 146–160.

Ritzer, G. (1980). *Sociology: A multiple paradigm science.* Boston: Allyn & Bacon.

Ritzer, G. (1983). *Sociological theory.* New York: Alfred A. Knopf.

Roethlisberger, F. J., & Dickson, W. J. (1939). *Management and the worker: An account of a research program conducted by the Western Electric Company, Hawthorne Works, Chicago.* Cambridge, MA: Harvard University Press.

Romzek, B. S., & Dubnick, M. J. (1987). Accountability in the public sector: Lessons from the Challenger tragedy. *Public Administration Review, 47*(3), 227–238.

Rorty, R. (1979). *Philosophy and the mirror of nature.* Princeton, NJ: Princeton University Press.

Rorty, R. (1982). *Consequences of pragmatism.* Minneapolis: University of Minnesota Press.

Rorty, R. (1989). *Contingency, irony, and solidarity.* Cambridge, England: Cambridge University Press.

Ross, A. O. (1980). *Psychological disorders of children* (2d ed.). New York: McGraw-Hill.

Rounds, J. (1979). *Social theory, public policy and social order.* Unpublished doctoral dissertation, University of California, Los Angeles.

Rounds, J. (1981). *Information and ambiguity in organizational change.* Paper presented at the Carnegie-Mellon Symposium on Information Processing in Organizations, Pittsburgh.

Rowan, B. (1980). *Organizational structure and the institutional environment: The case of public schools.* Unpublished manuscript, Texas Christian University, Fort Worth.

Rudduck, J. (1977). Dissemination as encounter of cultures. *Research Intelligence, 3*, 3–5.

Ryan, M. (1982). *Marxism and deconstruction: A critical articulation.* Baltimore: Johns Hopkins University Press.

Sailor, W. (1989). The educational, social, and vocational integration of students with the most severe disabilities. In D. K. Lipsky & A. Gartner (Eds.), *Beyond separate education: Quality education for all* (pp. 53–74). Baltimore: Paul H. Brookes.

Sailor, W., & Guess, D. (1983). *Severely handicapped students: An instructional design.* Boston: Houghton Mifflin.

Sailor, W., Halvorsen, A., Anderson, J., Goetz, L., Gee, K., Doering, K., & Hunt, P. (1986). Community integrative instruction. In R. Horner, L. Meyer, & H. Fredericks (Eds.), *Education of learners with severe handicaps.* Baltimore: Paul H. Brookes.

Salancik, G. R. (1979). Field simulations for organizational behavior research. *Administrative Science Quarterly, 24,* 638–649.

Salvia, J., & Ysseldyke, J. E. (1981). *Assessment in special and remedial education.* Boston: Houghton Mifflin.

Sapon-Shevin, M. (1987). The national education reports and special education: Implications for students. *Exceptional Children, 53,* 300–307.

Sapon-Shevin, M. (1988). Working towards merger together: Seeing beyond distrust and fear. *Teacher Education & Special Education, 11*(3), 103–110.

Sarason, S. B. (1971). *The culture of the school and the probelm of change.* Boston: Allyn & Bacon.

Sarason, S. B. (1982). *The culture of the school and the problem of change* (2d ed.). Boston: Allyn & Bacon.

Sarason, S. B. (1983). *Schooling in America: Scapegoat or salvation.* New York: Free Press.

Sarason, S. B., & Doris, J. (1979). *Educational handicap, public policy, and social history.* New York: Free Press.

Schein, E. H. (1968). Organizational socialization and the profession of management. *Industrial Management Review, 9*(2), 1–16.

Schein, E. H. (1972). *Professional education: Some new directions.* New York: McGraw-Hill.

Schenck, S. J. (1980). The diagnostic/instructional link in individualized education programs. *Journal of Special Education, 14*(3), 337–345.

Schenck, S. J., & Levy, W. K. (1979, April). *IEP's: The state of the art—1978.* Paper presented at annual meeting of American Educational Research Association, San Francisco.

Schön, D. A. (1983). *The reflective practitioner: How professionals think in action.* New York: Basic Books.

Schön, D. A. (1987). *Educating the reflective practitioner: Toward a design for teaching and learning in the professions.* San Francisco: Jossey-Bass.

Schön, D. A. (1988). Coaching reflective practice. In P. Grimmett & G. Erickson (Eds.), *Reflection in teacher education.* New York: Columbia Teachers College Press.

Schön, D. A. (1989). Professional knowledge and reflective practice. In T. Sergiovanni & J. Moore (Eds.), *Schooling for tomorrow: Directing reforms to issues that count.* Boston: Allyn & Bacon.

Schrag, P., & Divorky, D. (1975). *The myth of the hyperactive child.* New York: Pantheon.

Schroyer, T. (1973). *The critique of* Domination (pp. 44–100). Boston: Beacon Press.

Schumaker, J. B., & Deshler, D. D. (1988). Implementing the regular education initiative in secondary schools: A different ball game. *Journal of Learning Disabilities, 21,* 36–42.

Schwab, J. (1983, Fall). The practical 4: Something for curriculum professors to do. *Curriculum Inquiry, 13,* 239–266.

Schwartz, P., & Ogilvy, J. (1979). *The emergent paradigm: Changing patterns of thought and belief* (Analytic Report 7, Values and Lifestyle Program). Menlo Park, CA: SRI International.

Schwartz, P., & Ogilvy, J. (1980, June). *The emergent paradigm: Toward an aesthetics of life.* Paper presented at ESOMAR Conference, Barcelona, Spain.

Scott, R. (1969). *The making of blind men.* New York: Russell Sage Foundation.

Scott, W. R. (1981). *Organizations: Rational, natural, and open systems.* Englewood Cliffs, NJ: Prentice-Hall.

Segal, M. (1974). Organization and environment: A typology of adaptability and structure. *Public Administration Review, 34*(3), 212–220.

Sergiovanni, T. J., & Moore, J. H. (1989). *Schooling for tomorrow.* Boston: Allyn & Bacon.

Shepard, L. A. (1987). The new push for excellence: Widening the schism between regular and special education. *Exceptional Children, 53*(4), 327–329.

Shils, E. (1978). The order of learning in the United States from 1865 to 1920: The ascendancy of the universities. *Minerva, 16*(2), 159–195.

Shimony, A. (1977). Is observation theory-laden? A problem in naturalistic epistemology. In R. G. Colony (Ed.), *Logic, laws and life.* Pittsburgh: University of Pittsburgh Press.

Shor, I., & Freire, P. (1987). *A pedagogy for liberation: Dialogues on transforming education.* South Hadley, MA: Bergin & Garvey.

Sigmon, S. B. (1987). *Radical analysis of special education: Focus on historical development and learning disabilities.* London: Falmer Press.

Simon, H. (1947). *Administrative behavior.* New York: Macmillan.

Simon, H. A. (1977). *The new science of management decision.* Englewood Cliffs, NJ: Prentice-Hall.

Simpson, R. G., & Eaves, R. C. (1985). Do we need more qualitative research or more good research? A reaction to Stainback and Stainback. *Exceptional Children, 51*(4), 325–329.

Singer, J. D., & Butler, J. A. (1987). The Education for All Handicapped Children Act: Schools as agents of social reform. *Harvard Educational Review, 57*, 125–152.

Sirotnik, K. A., & Oakes, J. (1986). Critical inquiry for school renewal: Liberating theory and practice. In K. A. Sirotnik & J. Oakes (Eds.), *Critical perspectives on the organization and improvement of schooling* (pp. 3–93). Boston: Kluwer-Nijhoff Publishing.

Sirotnik, K. A., & Oakes, J. (in press). Evaluation as critical inquiry: School improvement as a case in point. In K. A. Sirotnik & J. Oakes (Eds.), *Evaluation and social justice: Issues in public education.* In *New directions for program evaluation.* San Francisco: Jossey-Bass.

Sizer, T. R. (1984). *Horace's compromise: The dilemma of the American high school.* Boston: Houghton Mifflin.

Skinner, B. F. (1953). *Science and human behavior.* New York: Free Press.

Skinner, Q. (Ed.). (1972). *The return of grand theory in the human sciences* (pp. 83–100). Cambridge, England: Cambridge University Press.

Skrtic, T. M. (1985). Doing naturalistic research into educational organizations. In Y. S. Lincoln (Ed.), *Organizational theory and inquiry: The paradigm revolution* (pp. 185–220). Beverly Hills, CA: Sage Publications.

Skrtic, T. M. (1986). The crisis in special education knowledge: A perspective on perspective. *Focus on Exceptional Children, 18*(7), 1–16.

Skrtic, T. M. (1987a). The national inquiry into the future of education for students with special needs. *Counterpoint, 7*(4), 6.

Skrtic, T. M. (1987b). An organizational analysis of special education reform. *Counterpoint, 8*(2), 15–19.

Skrtic, T. M. (1988a). The crisis in special education knowledge. In E. L. Meyen & T. M. Skrtic (Eds.), *Exceptional children and youth: An introduction* (pp. 415–447). Denver: Love Publishing.

Skrtic, T. M. (1988b). The organizational context of special education. In E. L. Meyen & T. M. Skrtic (Eds.), *Exceptional children and youth: An introduction* (pp. 479–517). Denver: Love Publishing.

Skrtic, T. M. (1989). Is special education for "the mildly handicapped" justifiable? (Review of *Handbook of Special Education: Research and Practice: Vol 1. Learner Characteristics and Adaptive Education), Contemporary Psychology, 34*(7), 660–661.

Skrtic, T. M. (1990a). Counter-hegemony: A radical's attempt to demystify special education ideology (Reveiew of *Radical Analysis of Special Education: Focus on Historical Development and Learning Disabilities,* London: Falmer Press, 1987). *Contemporary Psychology,* 35(1), 54–55.

Skrtic, T. M. (1990b). *School psychology and the revolution in modern knowledge.* Paper presented at American Psychological Association convention. Boston, Aug. 10–14.

Skrtic, T. M. (in press a). *Exploring the theory/practice link in special education: A critical perspective.* Reston, VA: Council for Exceptional Children.

Skrtic, T. M. (in press b). Social accommodation: Toward a dialogical discourse in educational inquiry. In E. G. Guba (Ed.), *The paradigm dialog: Options for inquiry in the social sciences.* Beverly Hills, CA: Sage Publications.

Skrtic, T. M. (in press c). Special education and disability from the functionalist view: The traditional outlook. In T. M. Skrtic (Ed.), *Exploring the theory/practice link in special education: A critical perspective.* Reston, VA: Council for Exceptional Children.

Skrtic, T. M. (in press d). Toward a dialogical theory of school organization and adaptability: Special education and disability as organizational pathologies. In T. M. Skrtic (Ed.), *Exploring the theory/practice link in special education: A critical perspective.* Reston, VA: Council for Exceptional Children.

Skrtic, T. M., Guba, E. G., & Knowlton, H. E. (1985). *Interorganizational special education programming in rural areas: Technical report on the multisite naturalistic field study.* Washington, DC: National Institute of Education.

Skrtic, T. M., & Ware, L. P. (in press). Reflective teaching and the problem of school organization. In E. W. Ross, G. McCutcheon, & J. Cornett (Eds.), *Teacher personal theorizing: Issues, problems, and implications.* New York: Teachers College Press.

Slavin, R. E. (1989). PET and the pendulum: Faddism in education and how to stop it. *Phi Delta Kappan, 70*(10), 752–758.

Sleeter, C. E. (1986). Learning disabilities: The social construction of a special education category. *Exceptional Children, 53,* 46–54.

Smith, J. K., & Heshusius, L. (1986). Closing down the conversation: The end of the quantitative-qualitative debate among educational inquirers. *Educational Researcher, 15*(1), 4–12.

Spring, J. (1980). *Educating the worker-citizen: The social, economic, and political foundations of education.* New York: Longman.

Stainback, S., & Stainback, W. (1984a). Broadening the research perspective in special education. *Exceptional Children, 50,* 400–409.

Stainback, S., & Stainback, W. (1984b). A rationale for the merger of special and regular education. *Exceptional Children, 51,* 102–111.

Stainback, S., & Stainback, W. (1985a). *Integration of students with severe handicaps into regular schools.* Reston, VA: Council for Exceptional Children.

Stainback S., & Stainback, W. (1985b). The merger of special and regular education: Can it be done? A response to Lieberman and Mesinger. *Exceptional Children, 51*(6), 517–521.

Stainback, S., & Stainback, W. (1987a). Facilitating merger through personnel preparation. *Teacher Education & Special Education, 10*(4), 185–190.

Stainback, S., & Stainback, W. (1987b). Integration versus cooperation: A commentary on educating children with learning problems: A shared responsibility. *Exceptional Children, 54*(1), 66–68.

Stainback, S., & Stainback, W. (1989). Integration of students with mild and moderate handicaps. In D. K. Lipsky & A. Gartner (Eds.), *Beyond separate education: Quality education for all* (pp. 41–52). Baltimore: Paul H. Brookes.

Stainback, S., Stainback, W., & Forest M. (1989). *Educating all students in the mainstream of regular education.* Baltimore: Paul H. Brookes.

Stainback, W., Stainback, S., Courtnage, L., & Jaben, T. (1985). Facilitating mainstreaming by modifying the mainstream. *Exceptional Children, 52,* 144–152.

Stake, R. (1967). The countenance of educational evaluation. *Teachers College Record, 68,* 523–540.

Stedman, L. C. (1987). It's time we changed the effective schools formula. *Phi Delta Kappan, 69*(3), 215–224.

Swap, S. (1978). The ecological model of emotional disturbance in children: A status report and proposed synthesis. *Behavioral Disorders, 3*(3), 156–186.

Szasz, T. S. (1961). *The myth of mental illness.* New York: Hoeber-Harper.

Taylor, C. (1977). *Hegel.* Cambridge, England: Cambridge University Press.

Taylor, F. W. (1947). *Scientific management.* New York: Harper & Row. (Original work published 1911)

Teacher Education Division, Council for Exceptional Children. (1986, October). *Message to all TED members concerning The National Inquiry into the Future of Education for Students with Special Needs.* Reston, VA: Author.

Teacher Education Division, Council for Exceptional Children (1987). The regular education initiative: A statement by the Teacher Education Division, Council for Exceptional Children. *Journal of Learning Disabilities, 20*(5), 289–293.

Thompson, J. D. (1967). *Organizations in action.* New York: McGraw-Hill.

Thousand, J. S. (1990). Organizational perspectives on teacher education and school renewal: A conversation with Tom Skrtic. *Teacher Education & Special Education, 13*(1), 30–35.

Thousand, J. S., & Villa, R. A. (1989). Enhancing success in heterogeneous schools. In S. Stainback., W. Stainback, & M. Forest (Eds.), *Educating all students in the mainstream of regular education.* Baltimore: Paul H. Brookes.

Thousand, J. S., Fox, T., Reid, R., Godek, J., & Williams, W. (1986). *The homecoming model: Educating students who present intensive educational challenges within regular education environments* (Monograph No. 7–1). Burlington: University of Vermont, Center for Developmental Disabilities.

Timar, T. B., & Kirp, D. L. (1988). *Managing educational excellence*. New York: Falmer Press.

Timar, T. B., & Kirp, D. L. (1989). Education reforms in the 1980's: Lessons from the states. *Phi Delta Kappan, 70*(7), 504–511.

Toffler, A. (1970). *Future shock*. New York: Bantam Books.

Tomlinson, S. (1982). *A sociology of special education*. Boston: Routledge & Kegan Paul.

Tomlinson, S. (in press). Why Johnny can't read: Critical theory and special education. *European Journal of Special Needs Education*.

Turnbull, H. R. (1986). *Free appropriate public education: The law and children with disabilities*. Denver: Love Publishing.

Tweedie, J. (1983). The politics of legalization in special education reform. In J. G. Chambers & W. T. Hartman (Eds.), *Special education policies: Their history, implementation, and finance* (pp. 48–73). Philadelphia: Temple University Press.

Tye, K. A., & Tye, B. B. (1984). Teacher isolation and school reform. *Phi Delta Kappan, 65*(5), 319–322.

Tyler, R. W. (1949). *Basic principles of curriculum and instruction*. Chicago: Unversity of Chicago Press.

Ulman, J. D., & Rosenberg, M. S. (1986). Science and superstition in special education. *Exceptional Children, 52*(5), 459–460.

U.S. Department of Education (USDE), Office of Special Education and Rehabilitative Services (1988). *Annual report to congress on the implementation of the Education for All Handicapped Children Act*. Washington, DC: Author.

Van de Ven, A. H., & Astley, W. G. (1981). Mapping the field to create a dynamic perspective on organization design and behavior. In A. H. Van de Ven & W. F. Joyce (Eds.), *Perspectives on organizational design and behavior* (pp. 427–468). New York: Wiley-Interscience.

Vergason, G. A., & Anderegg, M. L. (1989). Save the baby! A response to "Integrating the Children of the Second System." *Phi Delta Kappan, 71*(1), 61–63.

Walberg, H. J., & Wang, M. C. (1987). Effective educational practices and provisions for individual differences. In M. C. Wang, M. C. Reynolds, & H. J. Walberg (Eds.), *Handbook of special education: Research and practice: Vol. I. Learner characteristics and adaptive education)* (pp. 113–128). Oxford, England: Pergamon Press.

Walker, L. J. (1987). Procedural rights in the wrong system: Special education is not enough. In A. Gartner & T. Joe (Eds.), *Images of the disabled/disabling images*. New York: Praeger.

Wang, M. C. (1981). Mainstreaming exceptional children: Some instructional design and implementation considerations. *Elementary School Journal, 81*, 195–221.

Wang, M. C. (1988, May 4). A promising approach for reforming special education. *Education Week, 7*(32), 28, 36.

Wang, M. C. (1989a). Accommodating student diversity through adaptive instruction. In S. Stainback, W. Stainback, & M. Forest (Eds.), *Educating all students in the mainstream of regular education* (pp. 183–197). Baltimore: Paul H. Brookes.

Wang, M. C. (1989b). Adaptive instruction: An alternative for accommodating student diversity through the curriculum. In D. K. Lipsky & A. Gartner (Eds.), *Beyond separate education: Quality education for all* (pp. 99–119). Baltimore: Paul H. Brookes.

Wang, M. C., & Peverly, S. T. (1987). The role of the learner: An individual difference variable in school learning and functioning. In M. C. Wang, M. C. Reynolds, & H. J. Walberg (Eds.), *Handbook of special education: Research and practice: Vol. 1. Learner characterstics and adaptive education*) (pp. 59–92. Oxford, England: Pergamon Press.

Wang, M. C., & Reynolds, M. C. (1985). Avoiding the "catch-22" in special education reform. *Exceptional Children, 51*(6), 497–502.

Wang, M. C., & Reynolds, M. C. (1986). "Catch 22 and disabling help": A reply to Alan Gartner. *Exceptional Children, 53*, 77–79.

Wang, M. C., Reynolds, M. C., & Walberg, H. J. (1985). *Rethinking special education.* Paper presented at Wingspread Conference, The Education of Students with Special Needs: Research Findings and Implications for Policy and Practice, Racine, WI, December 5–7.

Wang, M. C., Reynolds, M. C., & Walberg, H. J. (1986). Rethinking special education. *Educational Leadership, 44*(1), 26–31.

Wang, M. C., Reynolds, M. C., & Walberg, H. J. (1987a). *Handbook of special education: Research and practice: Vol. I. Learner characteristics and adaptive education.* Oxford, England: Pergamon Press.

Wang, M.C., Reynolds, M.C., & Walberg, H.J. (1987b). *Repairing the second system for students with special needs.* Paper presented at Wingspread Conference, The Education of Children with Special Needs: Gearing Up to Meet the Challenges of the 1990s, Racine, WI, October, 1–3.

Wang, M. C., Reynolds, M. C., & Walberg, H. J. (1988). Integrating the children of the second system. *Phi Delta Kappan, 70*, 248–251.

Wang, M. C., Reynolds, M. C., & Walberg, H. J. (1989). Who benefits from segregation and murky water? *Phi Delta Kappan, 71*(1), 64–67.

Wang, M. C., & Walberg, H. J. (1988). Four fallacies of segregationism. *Exceptional Children, 55*(2), 128–137.

Weatherley, R. (1979). *Reforming special education: Policy implementation from state level to street level.* Cambridge, MA: MIT Press.

Weber, M. (1946a). Bureaucracy. In H. H. Gerth & C. W. Mills (Eds. & Trans.), *From Max Weber: Essays in sociology* (pp. 196–244). New York: Oxford University Press. (Original work published 1922)

Weber, M. (1946b). Politics as a vocation. In H. H. Gerth & C. W. Mills (Eds. & Trans.), *From Max Weber: Essays in sociology* (pp. 77–128). New York: Oxford University Press. (Original work published 1919)

Weber, M. (1947). *The theory of social and economic organization* (A. H. Henderson & T. Parsons, Eds. & Trans.). Glencoe, IL: Free Press. (Original work published 1924)

Weber, M. (1949). "Objectivity" in social science and social policy. In E. A. Shils & H. A. Finch (Eds. & Trans.), *The methodology of the social sciences (pp. 49–112)*. New York: Free Press. (Original work published 1904)

Weber, M. (1978). *Economy and society* (G. Roth & C. Wittich, Eds.; E. Fischoll, Trans.) (2 vols.). Berkeley: University of California Press. (Original work published 1922)

Weick, K. E. (1976). Educational organizations as loosely coupled systems. *Administrative Science Quarterly, 21*(1),1–19.

Weick, K. E. (1979). Cognitive processes in organization. In B. M. Staw (Ed.), *Research in organizational behavior* (Vol. 1, pp. 41–74). Greenwich, CT: JAI Press.

Weick, K. E. (1982). Administering education in loosely coupled schools. *Phi Delta Kappan, 63*(10), 673–676.

Weick, K. E. (1985). Sources of order in underorganized systems. In Y. S. Lincoln (Ed.), *Organizational theory and inquiry: The paradigm revolution* (pp. 106–136). Beverly Hills, CA: Sage Publications.

Weintraub, F. J. (1977). Editorial comment. *Exceptional Children, 44*(2), 114.

Welter, R. (1962). *Popular education and democratic thought in America.* New York: Columbia University Press.

Wertheimer, M. (1959). *Productive thinking.* New York: Harper & Row. (Original work published 1945)

White, O. R., & Haring, N. G. (1976). *Exceptional teaching: A multimedia training package.* Columbus, OH: Charles E. Merrill.

Wilensky, H. L. (1964). The professionalization of everyone? *American Journal of Sociology, 70*, 137–158.

Will, M. C. (1984). Let us pause and reflect—But not too long. *Exceptional Children, 51*, 11–16.

Will, M. C. (1985). *Educating children with learning problems: A shared responsibility.* Paper presented at Wingspread Conference, The Education of Students with Special Needs: Research Findings and Implications for Policy and Practice, Racine, WI, December 5–7.

Will, M. C. (1986a). Educating children with learning problems: A shared responsibility. *Exceptional Children, 52*(5), 411–416.

Will, M. C. (1986b). *Education children with learning problems: A shared responsibility. A report to the secretary.* Washington, DC: U.S. Department of Education.

Wise, A. E. (1988). The two conflicting trends in school reform: Legislated learning revisited. *Phi Delta Kappan, 69*(5), 328–333.

Wolcott, H. F. (1977). *Teachers versus technocrats: An educational innovation in anthropological perspective.* Eugene, OR: Center for Educational Policy & Management.

Wolf, F. A. (1981). *Taking the quantum leap.* San Francisco: Harper & Row.

Woodward, J. (1965). *Industrial organizations: Theory and practice.* Oxford, England: Oxford University Press.

Worthy, J. C. (1950). Organizational structure and employee morale. *American Sociological Review*, 169–179.

Wright, A. R., Cooperstein, R. A., Reneker, E. G., & Padilla, C. (1982). *Local implementation of P.L. 94–142: Final report of a longitudinal study.* Menlo Park, CA: SRI International.

Wright, J. S. (1967). *Hobson v. Hansen: Opinion by Honorable J. Skelly Wright, Judge, United States Court of Appeals for the District of Columbia.* Washington, DC: West Publishing.

Zeichner, K. M., & Tabachnick, B. R. (1981). Are the effects of university teacher education washed out by school experience? *Journal of Teacher Education, 32,* 7–11.

Zucker, L. G. (1977). The role of institutionalization in cultural persistence. *American Sociological Review, 42,* 726–743.

Zucker, L. G. (1981). Institutional structure and organizational processes: The role of evaluation units in schools. In A. Bank & R. C. Williams (Eds.), *Evaluation and decision making* (CSE Monograph Series, No. 10). Los Angeles: UCLA Center for the Study of Evaluation.

# Name Index

# Subject Index